D1196052

The Psychology
of
Politics

The Psychology of Politics

by

WILLIAM F. STONE

THE FREE PRESS
A Division of Macmillan Publishing Co., Inc.
NEW YORK

Collier Macmillan Publishers
LONDON

The Free Press
A Division of Macmillan Publishing Co., Inc.
866 Third Avenue, New York, N.Y. 10022

Collier–Macmillan Canada Ltd.

Library of Congress Catalog Card Number: 73–17647

Printed in the United States of America

printing number
2 3 4 5 6 7 8 9 10

Library of Congress Cataloging in Publication Data

Stone, William F
    The psychology of politics.

    Bibliography: p.
    1. Political psychology. 2. Political participa-
tion.   I. Title. [DNLM: 1. Politics. 2. Psychology,
Social.   JA74.5 S881p 1974]
JA74.5.S8   329'.0019   73-17647
ISBN 0-02-931690-1
ISBN 0-02-931680-4

Contents

Preface

The impetus for this book was my own involvement in politics, which became intense during the 1968 Presidential campaign. As a minor participant in the dramatic events that preceded the Democratic National Convention in Chicago, I became acquainted with many national and state political figures and with many citizen-politicians like myself.

It occurred to me, in 1970, that I might combine my professional interest in psychology and my amateur involvement in politics. I wanted particularly to try to understand the political activity of the average citizen. There were two problems in putting this plan into action. First, there was the problem of deciding just which psychological principles are applicable to the understanding of political behavior. There is no single accepted psychological theory. Rather, there are a great many theories about many different levels of behavior. Which theories, which concepts, may be most fruitfully applied to the understanding of political behavior? Past explanations have taken two directions: the individual psychology direction and the social psychology direction. The individual approach of psychoanalysis, for example, has been used particularly by political scientists to explain political action. The social psychological approach is exemplified in the study of attitudes. Attitudes seem naturally related to politics because they are thought to be psychological predispositions that spur many kinds of behavior, including the political. A primary example of the attitudinal emphasis is Hans J. Eysenck's *Psychology of Politics*, which was published in 1954.

The second problem was the definition of political behavior itself. While voting and running for office are the most commonly studied forms of political action, it seemed to me that we must try to understand politics as but one of the many concerns in the life of an individual. His concerns about his own identity, his interpersonal relationships, his work and family worries may take precedence over questions about the functioning of his community. Political behavior involves awareness and concern about events outside oneself, together with the desire to express these concerns. Such expression may be limited to complaining, or it may involve the organization of a protest group, carrying a petition, or voting in an election. Even more intense political involvements may follow, such as candidacy and the holding of political office.

Political behavior need not be limited to institutionalized settings, however. To emphasize this point, I begin the book with the description of a commune—not a current venture, but, rather, one of the more successful socialist communities of the nineteenth century. In the history of the Oneida Community can be seen some aspects of political behavior unencumbered by the laws and customs that channel the political impulses of man in a highly organized society.

My presentation of the psychology of politics involved making a selection from among the many topics in personality and social psychology that seemed relevant to the understanding of political behavior. While emphasizing research and theory in social psychology, I try throughout to maintain a focus on the whole individual and his relationship to other people. The theme of self in community, which appears in Chapter 1, owes a great deal to Alfred Adler's emphasis on the importance of *social interest* in human activity. Although social interest is difficult to define, it seems to signify the prepotent need for meaningful relationships with others, which is sometimes lost sight of in discussions of learning, perception, and other psychological part-processes.

I have tried to write for the reader who may have little background in psychology. The book begins with an examination of basic questions and historical approaches to the study of political man. In Part Two, I suggest the psychological characteristics that seem to be important in political behavior and discuss the ways in which these characteristics are acquired. Part Three deals with the self and with motivational processes and with specific behavioral tendencies of particular interest to the student of political behavior. In Part Four, political action, from voting to candidacy to officeholding, is examined.

Throughout the book I try to draw on my own observations of political life in the United States. The topics that are included represent my ideas about the psychological factors that are most important to political behavior, as a beginning attempt at systematizing the relevant psychological knowledge. At the least, I hope that the reader will be stimulated to inquire further into the psychological bases of political activity.

I have received help and encouragement from many sources. The book was started while I was on sabbatical leave from the University of Maine (1970–71). Access to the research facilities of the University of Florida during that year was made possible through a Visiting Professorship in Psychology, which was arranged by my friend and former professor, Marvin E. Shaw. James Cron of The Free Press encouraged me to write the book. Walter Rosenbaum and Robert Ziller made many helpful suggestions about organization, and Rosenbaum made valuable criticisms of an early draft.

William T. Neely read the entire manuscript and made many useful suggestions, both editorial and substantive. My wife, Molly, has made perhaps the greatest contribution to the finished book through encouragement, as well as long hours of typing, proofreading, and indexing. The University of Maine Psychology Department has provided essential financial and secretarial help. I want to thank the Department secretaries for considerable help with early drafts. I am grateful to Joan Slyne, who put in long hours typing the final manuscript.

PART I

Introduction to the Study of Political Behavior

1

Politics and the Search for Community

We are not "Free Lovers" in any sense that makes love less binding or less responsible than it is in marriage.

Oneida Handbook

Whatever their persuasion [communitarian, Marxist, Christian, etc.], all Socialists regarded the opposition of self and society as a false one, reflecting the prevailing ethic of greed and domination. All envisioned an end, really a return to the beginning, in the form either of the perfect community, or the Kingdom of Heaven on earth, or the cooperative commonwealth, each the realization of the promise of America.

ALBERT FRIED, *Socialism in America*, 1970

What would you think of a community in which every man is considered married to every woman in the communal group? Where no traditional marriages exist because they represent "special love"? Where every member of the community must love all other residents? Where sex between consenting adults is permitted, provided that measures are taken to prevent conception?

These customs were actually practiced for some 30 years, not by a hippie commune, but by a religious group called the Perfectionists. From 1848 to 1880 the members of the Oneida Community practiced what they called Bible Communism, which included mutual property ownership, communal living, and mutual industry, as well as the strange doctrine of complex marriage. Claiming Biblical justification for all of these practices, and condemned by some of their neighbors in upstate New

York, the Oneidans nonetheless won respect for their industry and honesty, and their religious devotion (Carden, 1969).

One of several communes established in the United States during the 1800s, the Oneida Community was both socially and economically a success for a considerable period and lasted longer than most other communistic societies. But all of them did fail, and we must ask, "Why?" Considering the pleasant life enjoyed by the Oneidans, who, although they worked hard for the common good, had ample leisure, many pleasurable pastimes, opportunities for education, and equal rights for women, one wonders why they gave it all up. The answers lie in the consideration of the psychology of man, the institutions he devises for realization of common ends, and the culture within which such an experiment in community living must exist. Let me begin by describing the Community and its origins in more detail.

John Humphrey Noyes, founder and leader of the Oneida Community, was the son of a Vermont storekeeper. After graduating from Dartmouth College in 1830, Noyes studied in a law office for a year, then turned to the study of theology at Andover Theological Seminary. His religious quest led Noyes toward the then current innovations in theology, and, in consequence, he transferred to the more liberal Yale Divinity School. While at Yale, he became attracted to Perfectionist theology, preached by revivalists who denied man's depravity and asserted that man, on the contrary, "could attain a state of perfect love between himself and God [Carden, 1969, p. 4]."

With characteristic enthusiasm, Noyes adopted this "doctrine of holiness" in respect to man's relation to God and the accompanying belief that man can be perfect in every way. His excessive zeal led him to declare that he himself had reached this ideal state—he *was* perfect. This conceit was too much for the Yale faculty, which asked him to give up his license to preach. In consequence, the members of the small "free church" in New Haven, which had nourished Noyes's radical ideas, voted to eject him from their fellowship.

Although he was barred from the licensed ministry, Noyes embarked at the age of 23 on an independent career, which led him from preaching perfectionism toward radical ideas regarding man's relation to man, socialism, and the institution of marriage. His heretical doctrines were strong medicine for even the unorthodox Perfectionists. Noyes believed that: "The Second Coming had already occurred; man could be perfect; once having attained salvation man could not fall from grace;

man should not allow his inner convictions to be overruled by church authority [Carden, 1969, p. 6]."

The development of his ideas in the 10 years after Noyes left New Haven (1834–44) is recorded in various periodicals, including the *Perfectionist* and later the *Witness*, both of which he edited. A prolific writer, Noyes recorded the development of Bible Communism in these periodicals and in later books. His beliefs on the biblical justification for communal life and his opposition to conventional marriage are summarized in Noyes's (1870) book, *A History of American Socialisms*, which appeared when he was 59 years old.

With a growing number of adherents to his particular brand of Perfectionism, Noyes, in 1846, was ready to put his beliefs into practice. In that year, he established a community with a small group of followers in Putney, Vermont. Each member donated his holdings to the community and agreed to live communally, sharing not only wealth but each other's love in the practice of "complex marriage." The latter practice, when it became known to the people of Putney, led to severe condemnation of Noyes. He "was accused of promoting wild orgies in his house, of indulging in free love and promiscuity and even incest [Fried, 1970, p. 28]." Severe disapproval by the larger community led Noyes, in 1848, to move with his followers to Oneida, in central New York State.

Thus began the history of one of the most famous utopian communities. Armed with an explicit religious justification and a magnetic leader, the perfectionists soon established a community which was socially (and within a few years, economically) self-sufficient. A capsule view of the life of the Oneida Communitarians is provided by Fried: *

> Within a year of their settlement they had laid the foundation of a "Bible Communist" society at Oneida. They had put up a four story building to house themselves and their children—fifty residents in all—and had cleared the ground for cultivation. There was as yet no definite division of labor, and the women took their places alongside the men, often performing the same work. In doing so, the women assumed simple, unaffected modes of dress and appearance. The outside world would have been as scandalized by their functional clothes (they wore bloomers and slacks) and short hair as by their sexual practices. Though the Perfectionists worked long hours and cut their expenses to the bone, Oneida in its first few years kept losing money. The reason was obvious to Noyes: the

* Excerpts from *Socialism in America* copyright © 1970 by Albert Fried. Reprinted by permission of Doubleday & Company, Inc.

community was too dependent on agriculture; to survive it would have to turn to manufacturing. In fact, Oneida's fortunes did change for the better when it began to produce steel traps of excellent quality. The success of this venture persuaded Noyes to establish other profitable enterprises— *e.g.*, sewing silk, preserved fruit, and above all silver cutlery. Though Oneida's population had increased five-fold by 1855 there was more than enough work for everyone. By then Oneida had taken on the aspect of a prosperous, exceedingly well-managed capitalist corporation [1970, pp. 28–29].

The number of members increased continuously; the original 50 grew to 87 by 1849, and to 180 in 1856. The membership in 1880 was 288 men, women, and children (Carden, 1969, p. 41).

LIFE IN THE ONEIDA COMMUNITY

Three aspects of community life at Oneida seem to me of special significance in trying to understand the success and failure of utopian communities. They are: (1) leadership and governance, (2) ideology and daily life, and (3) relationships to the world outside the community. I discuss these aspects in turn, referring the reader to such excellent accounts as Maren Carden's (1969) *Oneida: Utopian Community to Modern Corporation* for further details.

Leadership and Governance of the Oneida Community

Perfectionism and the experiment in communal living which was Oneida were largely the creation of one man, John Humphrey Noyes. According to Fried (1970), ". . . he conceived it, built it, ran it, and oversaw its dissolution [p. 26]." In large measure, Fried's observation is correct. Noyes's influence *was* apparent in most aspects of community life. His was the overall plan, and the members shared a devotion to him and to his philosophy. However, Oneida's governance was not strictly a one-man rule, since the residents did have a voice in community governance. For instance, the implementation of perfectionism in daily life was supervised by a council consisting of a group of older and more spiritually advanced "central members." That Noyes was not essential in day-to-day operations is also attested by the fact that there were periods when he did not even live at Oneida. In the early 1850s and in the mid 1860s, Noyes lived for a time in New York City; he also stayed at a small branch community in Wallingford, Connecticut, for long periods (Carden, 1969, p. 85). Likewise in contradiction to the idea of strict one-man rule was the practice of daily meetings in which all community members participated.

Each evening at eight o'clock the members gathered informally in the big central hall of the Mansion House (the communal residence). Typically, they would hear an instructive talk by Noyes, or, in his absence, a previous talk was read by one of the central members. His ideas were then discussed by the members, letters from outsiders were read, and so on. Each member was free to speak, the arguments usually being framed in terms of Perfectionist ideals. Women were encouraged to voice their concerns, but in practice they participated relatively little in these discussions. Although no rigid agenda was prescribed, the various committees that operated the community also reported when necessary at these daily meetings. According to Carden (1969): "The evening meetings did more than remind members of their ideals, demonstrate how to practice them, and help to resolve conflicts. When members had participated in discussions, they felt more committed to any decision that was made [pp. 48–9]."

Another practice that also seems to have served as a kind of community control device was "mutual criticism." The community could select a person for criticism, or one could volunteer to undergo the process. Usually the criticism was by a committee of six to twelve persons, though in serious cases it could be by the whole community. A member could be criticized for any perceived failing, especially for attachments betokening "special love" for a particular member of the community. The practice of criticism was a very effective technique for enforcing adherence to community norms because each person was dependent upon his fellow members' approval. There were no formal procedures for disciplining members; on rare occasions members were asked to leave, but as a rule departures from the community were by mutual consent.

Ideology and Daily Life

All property of the Oneida Community was held in common; new members surrendered their assets upon joining the group. The same philosophy that led to the sharing of wealth led also to the sharing of love among the community members, following the Perfectionist article of faith that "there is no intrinsic difference between property in persons and property in things [from Noyes's Bible Communism, quoted in Fried, 1970, p. 55]." Noyes viewed conventional marriage as a kind of monopoly of one person by another. The Perfectionist ideal was to love all other members of the community equally. This idea was applied in sexual relations by the practice of complex marriage.

Dedication to "bible communism," together with the members' relative isolation from the outside world, made complex marriage an important basis for the social order of the community. Actually, the system in practice by no means amounted to free love; it was a carefully regulated alternative to conventional marriage. Each member had his or her own private room. If one felt the desire, he or she could ask for an "interview" (the euphemism for sexual intercourse) with any member of the opposite sex. However, these unions were overseen by the central members, who were ever alert to the possible development of forbidden "special attachments" to a particular person. Although interviews were conducted by mutual consent, female members felt some pressure to consent to requests made by spiritually superior male central members. Likewise, young men found virtue in making requests to female central members.

Birth control was by means of a technique advocated by Noyes— *male continence*, which was his term for sexual intercourse in which the man stops short of orgasm and ejaculation. Occasionally children resulted from "accidents"; yet, in the main, those born were planned with the consent of the central members.

Although the charter members of the Community brought with them many useful skills—farming, craft, and domestic—life was austere in the early years. Agriculture proved insufficient as an economic base, and the wealth contributed by incoming members was needed to keep the community solvent. Only with the establishment of its industries did Oneida become financially self-sufficient. Throughout its history, the work ethic prevailed. There was a certain amount of job rotation, and everyone, including Noyes, did a share of manual labor. Women were predominant in the care of house and children, but they also worked alongside men in fields and factory. When one considers the variety of work available to them, the sexual choice, and the freedom from burdensome childbearing and rearing of children, Oneida women were indeed "liberated" in comparison with other women of their day.

Extracommunity Relationships

Though its sexual customs were beyond the permissible limits of the village and state surrounding it, the Oneida Community was long able to maintain good relationships with its neighbors. In large part the good relations resulted from the employment, beginning in 1862, of workers from the area surrounding the Community. As prosperity increased, more workers were added, until in 1875 some 200 outsiders were employed. Kind treatment of these workers added to the Community's reputation for honest dealing with its other neighbors. The good will thus created helped to foil attempts by an irate clergyman or two to censure the immoral practices of Community members.

Nevertheless, the demise of the Oneida Community *was* speeded by its deviation from the norms of the larger society. As Noyes grew older, his interest in promoting Perfectionism diminished. It followed that the unifying ideology embodied in Perfectionist theology declined also, making the Community more vulnerable to internal dissension. The crucial dispute came in 1879, over the initiation of young women to complex marriage. In the early days, Noyes himself had introduced girls, at the age of 15 or so, to sexual experience. Later on, Noyes appointed one or another of the male central members to act as "first husband." Dissenting central members were joined by other men and women in protesting Noyes's authority. Added to this dispute was a new attack on the immorality of the Perfectionists by a group of clergymen from surrounding communities.

Faced with internal, as well as external, threats of legal action, Noyes, the initiator of complex marriage and thus the most responsible party, fled to Canada. Shortly thereafter, an Administrative Council was appointed to govern Oneida. The twelve council members were unable to agree on methods for regulating complex marriage, however, and they voted to end the practice in August of 1879. Members had to choose between monogamous marriages or celibacy. One year later, in September 1880, the Community was reorganized as a joint stock company, Oneida Community, Limited. Although many members stayed on, for all intents and purposes the utopian experiment was at an end.

THE LESSONS OF ONEIDA

In evaluating the experience of the Oneida Community, I find remarkable both its outstanding success and the ultimate failure of a way of life which held so many rewards for its practitioners. I have reviewed the Community's history in some detail because I believe that it represents, in microcosmic form, many of the problems of group living which beset man. These problems fall into two major categories: (1) The conflict between the necessity of cooperative interaction in family and the community and the individual's personal needs for autonomy and privacy, and (2) the conflict among social groups, from clan to nation, whose interests do not coincide with those of other groups. The case of Oneida represents the delicate balance that obtains between such conflicting interests. Maren Carden's (1969, p. 104) description of the Community as a "fragile utopia" highlights this balance.

Carden's analysis agrees with mine in that we both see the strong leadership of John Humphrey Noyes as a major factor in the success of the Oneida Community, and his gradual withdrawal and ultimate departure from the Community as contributing to its decline. We also agree that the practice of complex marriage and its abandonment influenced the course of the utopian experiment. Carden mentioned four factors, however, which I feel should be reemphasized because of their generalizability to other community settings. These factors are: (1) The importance of ideology, (2) the make-up of the community, (3) the tension between individual desires and group participation, and (4) the role of good management. In the following sections I take up each factor in turn.

The Importance of Ideology

My emphasis on unorthodox living practices tends to make us forget that Oneida was basically a religious community. By and large, all community life was governed by the principles of Perfectionism. Common belief in principles transcending the individual provided a cohesive force which helped the community members to stick together in the face of petty differences. Shared ideology, the belief in something "larger than all of us," is an important determinant of the fate of any community. In the case of Oneida, this principle was demonstrated by the decreasing viability of the Community as member interest in its ideological underpinnings declined.

The Make-Up of the Community

I have already pointed out that the individuals who joined the community were believers in Perfectionism. In addition to the test of faith, it is likely that some more subtle selective factors were operative. Carden (1969) has suggested that people with certain psychological tendencies may have been drawn to the community: "One can certainly speculate," she wrote, "that only a select group of people possessed the psychological make-up that made Oneida Perfectionism truly appealing [p. 107]." Carden has proposed, for example, that people with unresolved guilt feelings would be attracted to the promise of freedom from sin inherent in Perfectionist beliefs. For some members, the figure of Noyes and the idealized community provided ideal love objects. Also to be considered among the psychological attractions of Oneida is the possibility of varied sexual relationships without guilt. Finally, people who had strong dependency needs but who had difficulty in forming warm, close, and trusting relationships with one other person found satisfaction in a society where "special" attachments were prohibited.

Individual Desires and Group Responsibility

Though adult members of the Oneida Community had separate rooms, no aspect of their lives was outside the realm of Community scrutiny. Total involvement and total commitment were demanded. A member was expected to think of the Community first and of his own desires only secondarily. Carden recounted one incident involving a salesman for Oneida products who was reprimanded and given a different job because the Community felt that he spent too much time enjoying himself talking to customers. Even the sexual freedom permitted by the group had costs to the individual: "For the sake of engaging in a range of sexual encounters forbidden in the outside world, they gave up the right to establish emotionally satisfying relationships, to experience the culmination of the sexual act, and to select partners of their own choosing [Carden, 1969, p. 106]."

Community Management

The smooth functioning of the community for such a long period of time attests to the good planning that entered into the arrangements for community management. Rooted in Perfectionist ideals and emphasizing the good of the community above all, these practical details of group living attained a reasonable balance between individual and group interests. All the details of life—work, housekeeping, entertainment, child care, and complex marriage—were organized in the light of these basic ideals. Noyes's genius in working out these arrangements with the Perfectionists allowed for a certain amount of flexibility which made change possible within the established social order. Given that conflicts of interest are bound to arise in any social group, a viable community must establish ways of dealing with these conflicts. The peculiar institutions that the Oneidans developed for this purpose served admirably so long as the ideological foundations were strong.

PRESENT-DAY COMMUNES

Reference to the nineteenth-century communistic societies seems appropriate today because of the revival of interest in communal living; such interest is demonstrated by the founding of communes in many parts of the United States. Groups of young people are once again attempting to establish communities where they may live in love, peace, and mutual cooperation. The Twin Oaks Community in Virginia, organized along the lines suggested by the psychologist B. F. Skinner, is one contemporary example (Kinkaide, 1972). Ron Roberts (1971), in *The New Communes,* has described Twin Oaks and a number of other current experiments. In general, it seems to me, these contemporary communes lack the explicit sense of purpose which guided the religious and socialistic communities of the previous century.

There are many other lessons that present-day communalists could learn from socialistic communities of the past—Brook Farm, the Owenite Communities, and the Shakers, for instance. They all had certain features in common, beginning with a dissatisfaction with existing social and economic arrangements and a commitment to the belief that men can cooperate to provide a better life for all. Accordingly, in most communities, property was held in common. On the other hand, there were important differences among these communities. Some had strong religious orientations, while others had none. There were also many variations in social practice. In contrast to the Oneida Community, for example, the Shakers abstained completely from sexual intercourse.

Just what kind of practices and beliefs are essential for a viable community is problematical. We are left with an apparent contradiction: On the one hand, we have evidence that many people at diverse times and places have had strong impulses toward communal living. On the other hand, nowhere have people been able to live in such close communities over an extended period of time. (The longest lasting, perhaps, are the Shaker Communities, which are now disappearing through the absence of childbearing and a scarcity of new recruits). I can offer no solution to this paradox, except to suggest that the founders of communal experiments, in reacting to the oppressive nature of existing institutions, have overlooked the necessity for new political systems to take their place.

POLITICAL ORGANIZATION AND THE NATURE OF MAN

In theory at least, the social, economic, and political customs of a society are free to vary independently. Two countries with socialist economic systems, for example, may differ dramatically in their political arrangements. One country may be ruled democratically, while the other may exist under an iron dictatorship. Similarly, the customs and laws regulating social interrelationships and family life may vary considerably.

In practice, however, we do not seem to find all possible combinations of political, economic, and social systems. There seem to be some restrictions on independent variation of the three factors. Whether a country has experienced a long reign of absolute monarchy is not unrelated to the strong influence of the church, nor to the practice of "free enterprise." Although such restrictions do exist, we must not leap to the assumption that there must always be close relationships between particular factors. Many anticommunist writers in the United States have overlooked the distinction between the economic systems and the political systems of socialist countries. They assume a one-to-one correspondence between socialism and totalitarianism, an assumption that is shown false by the examples of Sweden and Great Britain, among others.

There *are* reasons for believing that a highly centralized economy necessitates dictatorial rule. These reasons include the importance of *planning* to such an economy (Heilbroner, 1969) and the practical difficulties experienced by developing countries. Looking back for a moment to the Oneida experiment, it could be argued that John Humphrey Noyes was essentially a benevolent dictator. Beloved by community members, he governed not through fiat but through reason, an exceptionally high degree of personal activity, and a fertile mind. In spite of the founder's ingenuity, the community did not long survive the decline in his powers and attention.

These questions regarding which political–economic–social system is best suited to man's nature have been discussed endlessly by political philosophers. Other broad questions of interest to the student of political psychology are: Do all men share the impulse toward harmonious group living, which seems to be the energizing force behind the communes of today, as well as the socialistic experiments in nineteenth-century America? Are individualistic and self-serving motives in basic opposition to social interest and the desire for community? How much control does one need over his own life and living arrangements? Are democratic political institutions particularly suitable to man's nature?

By no means do I offer answers to these major questions. But I share the beliefs of those psychologists (John Dewey, Alfred Adler, and Erich Fromm, for instance) who have a hopeful view of man's capacity for living in harmonious relation to others. We believe that man has the potential for cooperative living and we believe that there is no inherent conflict between man's nature and democratic social organization. Yet the number of negative instances often seem to outweigh the positive possibilities. Though the impulse persists, communal living experiments seem never to have survived for long. Similar paradoxes are manifest in more conventional political practices. The direct democracy inherent in the New England town meeting for example, is being given up in favor of management by experts—a trained town manager advised by elected officials. Side-by-side with such willingness to give up control over local government are numerous manifestations of a frustrating sense of powerlessness and a pervading malaise based on lack of control (cf. Seeman, 1966, 1971).

PSYCHOLOGY AND POLITICS

Undoubtedly, many of man's problems lie in the imperfection of his institutions and in their slowness in adapting to new realities which result from changes in culture, technology, and world politics. Understanding these new realities and planning for social change will require the efforts of all the social science disciplines—economics, sociology, and political science in particular. Each has particularly useful concepts and techniques for the analysis of social institutions and arrangements. At the bottom of it all, however, lies man; and my particular bias as a social psychologist is to focus upon the individual person in his interactions with others and with the institutional structures that are part of his inheritance. The light that the psychologist can shed on man's possibilities, limitations, and strivings will certainly not provide a blueprint for the ideal society, but it may suggest preferable directions for institutional change.

This book, then, is an attempt to explore at some length what we *can* say about the *psychology* of political man, at this moment in history. I do not want to raise false hopes about the conclusiveness of psychological investigation, but I do think that psychology has distinctive ways of looking at the problems and certain interesting findings whose applicability to politics has not been thoroughly explored. As a psychologist, my emphasis on the individual actor contrasts with the approach of the sociologist, as well as with that of the political scientist. Today's political scientist *has* moderated his emphasis on governmental institutions and historical analysis and is more interested in man's behavior as datum. His interest in political behavior, however, tends to be in aggregate action (i.e., how Irish Americans vote, their attitudes, etc.). Even though he now emphasizes the study of attitudes and other psychological dispositions, the political scientist's concepts remain more on a sociological, than on a psychological, level.

My focus, then, is on the individual human being. Thus, to me the *psychology* of politics refers to the individual's concerns, to his conceptions, his reactions, and his responses to his political experience and behavior. I do not think that this individualistic orientation suffices to explain the activity or change of political systems. However, an understanding of the psychological dimensions of politics is crucial to a complete understanding of the functioning of governmental institutions. Since mine is a somewhat deviant approach to the study of politics, let us consider the meaning of "political behavior." The term should not be restricted solely to activity in relation to existing governmental institutions. At its most basic level, political behavior involves the control of other people and being controlled *by* other people. In the case of the Oneida Community, for example, certain authority relationships were established early in its history. These relationships tended to be accepted by each incoming member. Of course, John Humphrey Noyes's power over others was not absolute. Members were free to leave and to register disagreements which sometimes led to policy change. The notion that politics is primarily a question of dominance–submission finds support in authoritative political science textbooks. For example, Irish and Prothro (1971) have written: "In its broadest sense, *politics* may be defined as the pursuit and exercise of power [p. 9]."

The definition of politics in such general terms, however, could lead us to believe that almost all human interaction is basically political. Most person-to-person situations raise questions about who initiates, directs, decides, and so on (i.e., who dominates or has power). Thus, a definition of politics or political behavior solely in terms of power relations seems to include too much. Therefore, many political scientists hasten to restrict the definition:

> The distinctive power relations we have in mind when we generally speak of "politics" are those in which some people fix policies or rules of behavior that others are obligated to follow. This means that politics is indistinguishable from government . . . [political scientists] use *politics* interchangeably with the broad term *political system* [Irish and Prothro, 1971, p. 9].

At this point, I depart from the political scientist, who starts with the notion of power relations and ends up defining political behavior as a response to the existing political system, be it the American Government, the French Government, or any other formally organized governmental entity.

I would now like to attempt a psychological definition of political behavior and support this concept by reference to the Oneida Community, which was discussed so extensively in this chapter. *Political behavior includes all of a person's activity that is directed toward cooperative solution of the problems of daily living.* This definition recognizes that political organization, ideally, arises from individual needs and helps to direct our attention to the processes by which institutions arise to meet these needs. Working in the context of existing governmental institutions, it is all too easy to restrict our attention to the way in which man responds to these institutions. A closer study of day-to-day life in the Oneida Community with this in mind could teach us much about how man behaves politically in the abshence of established institutions.

There was no governmental system at the beginning of the Oneida Community, though one ultimately did emerge. The members began with a common purpose and proceeded to work things out—a process which I consider the most basic kind of political activity. Given that one purpose of the members was to establish an alternative to conventional marriage, procedures had to be worked out to accomplish this purpose. A poor solution to this political problem would have resulted in strife which might very well have broken up the Community even sooner. Granted that much of the design of the emerging set of customs and practices was attributable to Noyes, I will hold to the above definition, observing that even a dictator has to obtain the cooperation of his subjetcs.

My reason for offering this unusually broad definition of political behavior is that, as James (1892) has noted, man's political self coexists with other aspects of his social being. He is concerned with his role as employee, husband, father, and friend. One's political behavior occurs in the context of all these aspects of his life; to confine "political" to behavior vis-à-vis existing governmental institutions is unnecessarily restrictive.

In the following pages, I examine various theories and lines of research that seem to me to be related to political behavior, broadly defined. In so doing I hope to offer the reader a somewhat different perspective from that taken by other social scientists who are interested in the same problem. The following section is a preview of some of the topics to come.

POLITICAL APPLICATIONS OF SOCIAL PSYCHOLOGY: A PREVIEW

One line of research that I discuss has to do with psychological "types" and their distinctive characteristics. A type-theory is one which suggests that people can be placed in certain categories according to their dominant disposition (examples are the introverted–extroverted types of man). In theory, by typing a person, we can predict many aspects of his behavior. Two somewhat different type-theories have been offered in connection with the study of political man. The first type-theory is outlined in *The Authoritarian Personality* (Adorno *et al.*, 1950). The authors of this book have assumed there is a continuum of political types ranging from the strongly democratic individual to the strongly authoritarian individual. An "authoritarian" is conceived as a person who is oriented toward status and power relationships among individuals. He differs markedly from the democratic individual in psychological make-up. The authoritarian is likely to deny his sexual feelings, for instance, and by an adroit maneuver called projection to see other people as being preoccupied with sex (more to come on the authoritarian in Chapter 7).

The second type-theory hypothesizes the existence of a type of person who enjoys manipulating other people. The theory of Machiavellianism as a dispositional trait was propounded by Richard Christie (1970). He described it in a book, written with Florence Geis, called *Studies in Machiavellianism*. Simply stated, the Machiavellian can be described as a person who thinks politically much of the time. That is, he is concerned with influencing others to attain his own ends. He likes to manipulate other people and seems unconcerned about the means he uses to attain his ends. In these respects, he accepts Niccolò Machiavelli's diabolical recommendations to *The Prince* (see Chapter 6 of this volume).

In working to achieve his self-defined goals, the Machiavellian uses planful, rational strategy. Not one to "lose his cool," the Machiavellian differs markedly from people who tend to become emotionally involved with their co-workers or the person they are trying to influence. The Machiavellian keeps in mind what *he* wants to accomplish. He initiates action toward this goal insofar as the structure of the situation allows, and he rationally surveys the means for accomplishing his purposes. Most characteristically, the Machiavellian does not allow the ongoing interaction with others to affect his goal orientation. He does not, for instance, allow his anger with his partner's incompetence to interfere with the task at hand.

Other interesting aspects of the Machiavellian person are reviewed in some detail in Chapter 6. A question of major concern is whether or not distinctive personality types (such as the Authoritarian or the Machiavellian) do emerge from different cultural patterns of child reading and systems of education. It has been asserted, for example, that the people of Germany were particularly susceptible to the appeals of a Hitler, whereas Frenchmen may not have been. In the same vein, I have raised the possibility that certain "types" may be selected or self-selected for the experiments in communal living.

So far, I have been treating the question, "What are people like?" particularly with regard to the nature of political man. A second broad area in the psychology of politics is the area of *interpersonal influence*.

What are the techniques men use to try to influence or control other people? Many tactics have been tried, with varying degrees of success.

One basic variable or dimension along which influence must be studied is the variable of psychological distance. An old friend of one's father who has visited the house several times will have a different access to changing one's opinions than his opponent who is seen only on television. As a matter of fact, face-to-face contacts may be entirely different in kind, as compared with the more impersonal kinds of persuasive message.

The range of influence attempts varies tremendously, even within a particular system of government. Yet I am not able here to consider the extreme coercion often used in totalitarian societies, nor the techniques employed in small, face-to-face societies where no formal government is necessary. Rather, I must restrict the discussion to the kinds of influence and control that are practiced in democratic societies, particularly in the United States.

Even with the range of practices so restricted, however, there is an awesome array of possibilities. The three major categories of influence I consider are:

1. leadership and followership
2. group ties, norms, and face-to-face influence
3. attitude and opinion change through the mass media

In addition to discussing these influence processes from the point of view of the laboratory, field, and survey research, I discuss some notable attempts to influence the electorate of the United States. In this vein, the efforts of various Presidents come to mind. President Wilson's valiant attempt to convince this country of the need for joining the League of Nations is a case in point. Wilson's heartbreaking failure to persuade the United States Senate that our interests would be served by joining the League of Nations was one of the most dramatic attempts by a President to mobilize and influence public opinion. Although he stumped the country from one end to the other, speaking and pleading with the American people to demand that Congress authorize the United States' entry into the international body, Wilson's all-out effort failed. Why? Many observers have noted that Wilson, unlike the Machiavellian, was both highly ideological and very emotionally involved in the campaign. A more detached attitude on his part might have better served his cause. Perhaps Wilson should have been more Machiavellian!

In the chapters to follow, I examine in detail both historical and contemporary views of political man. Although at times the discussion strays from the basic theme set in this chapter, I try to maintain a focus on the individual political actor in his efforts to achieve community with other men. Throughout, the reader should keep in mind that political participation is only one avenue of participation in matters that intimately affect a person. One's work, family, community, and hobbies are at least as important as one's duties as a citizen. Some people find satisfaction in political activity, while others won't even vote. Ultimately, I am concerned with the implications of psychological findings for the future of democracy.

2

Approaches to the Study of Political Psychology

> Long before social psychology became a science, political philoso-
> phers sought an answer to the question, What is the social nature
> of man? They well knew, as Vico (1725) observed, that "govern-
> ments must conform to the nature of the men governed."
>
> G. ALLPORT, in *Handbook of Social Psychology*, 1954

The idea that "governments must conform to the nature of the men governed" has been stated in many different ways through the centuries. But what *is* the nature of man? The psychological questions that I raised in connection with the governance of the Oneida Community (see Chapter 1) were of concern to Plato and Aristotle, as they have been to political theorists ever since. Is man basically selfish, or does he have a genuine concern for his fellows? Does man have a fixed nature by which he is better adapted to some types of social governance than to others? Can man work with others in a rational way to solve common problems? What is the basis for a good society?

This chapter touches on some of the answers that have been offered to these questions about the political nature of man. I begin with the Greeks, whose city-states provide such an important beginning and a vital reference point for the discussion of democratic government today. Then, I review some early modern views of the nature of man, particularly those of the philosophers who have debated man's basic nature. The contribution of psychoanalysis to the understanding of the complexities of human motivation, and to thinking about politics, is treated at some length. The final section deals with a major trend in contemporary thinking about man and politics—the attempt to explain the psychological basis for political attitudes and political behavior, which I am calling the *functional approach*.

MAN IN EARLY POLITICAL THOUGHT

The Polis

The speculations of the early political philosophers were conditioned by their experiences in the Greek city-states. These tiny nations, the most renowned of which were Athens and Sparta, were entirely self-governing. Their forms of government ranged from the highly disciplined autocracy of Sparta to the experiment in democracy by the Athenians. The Greek word for these communities, *polis*, is usually translated into English as "city-state," referring to the city and the outlying agricultural land which it controlled. However, Kagan (1965) has noted that the important difference between the Greek *poleis* and other states of that time is omitted from this definition. Whereas most states were oriented toward their rulers, the culture of the Greek cities incorporated an ideological commitment to a form of government suited to the needs of its citizens. "The central idea of the *polis*," wrote Kagan, "is that life suitable for men must be based on justice [p. 16]."

During the period of the Greek Enlightenment, roughly 750–500 B.C., the search for justice through development of the *polis* reflected the view, expressed by Aristotle, that man is by nature a political animal. By this Aristotle meant that man's nature is such that he can achieve the good life only in community with other men. The Greeks had varying opinions, though, about the way in which such a well-ordered community might best be achieved. Steeped in the aristocratic tradition, Plato believed that a majority of the population has no capacity for political life; philosophers of more democratic persuasion asserted that all men have at least minimal gifts for self-government.

These different opinions about man's political abilities were reflected in the contrast between the autocratic practices of militaristic Sparta and the democratic practices that characterized Athens. Spartan youth were subjected to extremely rigorous military training and were schooled in obedience to the state. Authority in Athens, on the other hand, resided in the citizenry. Under the leadership of Cleisthenes (ca. 490 B.C.), for example, political liberty and equality were touted: "all male citizens could vote in the assembly and serve on juries [Kagan, 1965, p. 75]." Although neither women nor slaves were granted citizenship, freemen were granted equal rights without regard to wealth. The dramatist Euripides had Theseus, the legendary founder of Athenian democracy, speak to this point:

> This city is free, and ruled by no one man.
> The people reign in annual succession.
> They do not yield the power to the rich.
> The poor man has an equal share in it.

The Suppliant Women, pp. 405–8
of the Crawley translation.

The history of Greek political thought is a fascinating study. It would be worthwhile to try to understand how the idea of democracy (from *demos*, the people, and *kratein*, to rule) developed. For present purposes, however, I would like to focus on what Kagan termed "the great dialogue" between the aristocratic and democratic thinkers and their contrasting views of human nature and human capabilities. The democratic tradition, as I noted briefly, emphasized equality in ability for political participation. Aristocratic thought, which was always present, emphasized the inherent superiority of certain kinds and classes of men. The idea that some men are fitted to be rulers, while others are suited only to be craftsmen or soldiers, was elaborated in Plato's *Republic*. This book described a utopian society based on the aristocratic notion that always "there will be a large majority of the population with no capacity for political life [Kagan, 1965, p. 172]."

Plato's Republic

In the *Republic*, society was to be sharply divided into three classes based on the need for a division of labor and on the presumption of marked differences in capability among men. Three orders of men, the rulers, the guardians, and the craftsmen, were to participate in the life of the ideal state. These classes paralleled Plato's tripartite division of the human soul, whose divisions have been colorfully referred to as "the head soul, the heart soul, and the belly soul [Brown, 1936, p. 311]." That is, the highest element of the soul, *the rational faculty*, is predominant in the ruling class—the philosopher-kings and their auxiliaries. Courage, will, and a strong sense of honor are characteristics of *the spirited ele-*

ment appropriate to the guardians—the soldiers and defenders of the state. *The appetitive element* of the soul is predominant in the working class—the craftsmen, farmers, and laborers.

It is of interest to note that while Plato believed, in general, that children born into the three classes would be likely to succeed their parents, talent could emerge in the lower classes and should be recognized. His belief in the possibility of environmentally developed capacities is evident in the *Myth of the Metals*, which was intended to justify to the people his ideal division of labor. In Book III of the *Republic*, Socrates in a dialogue with Glaucon,[1] discussed ways of making people into loyal citizens, who would accept their station in life and regard their fellow citizens as brothers. He suggested the myth as a convenient fiction to persuade citizens of all classes to accept the social order:

> "You are all brothers in this state," we shall say in our fable; "but the god who fashioned you mixed gold in the creation of those of you who are fit to rule, so that they are the most precious; and in the guardians, silver; and iron and bronze in the farmers and craftsmen. Now since you are all akin, though your children will generally be like yourselves, sometimes a golden father may have a silver son or a silver father may have a golden son, and so with the other kinds. So the first and chief command that god lays on the rulers is that over nothing else are they to watch with such care as the mixture of metals in the soul of the children. If a child of their own is born with an alloy of bronze or iron, they shall show him no pity but shall assign to him the status proper to his nature and trust him among the craftsmen or the farmers; likewise, if from the latter classes there is born a son with an alloy of gold or silver, they shall according to his worth promote him to become a guardian or an auxiliary. For there is an oracle, as they say, that the state will be ruined whensoever it shall be guarded by a man of iron or of bronze [MacKendrick and Howe, 1952, p. 332]."

It is important to emphasize that the *Myth of the Metals* was a device to explain to people the importance of allowing the best men to govern. Plato believed that man needed the *polis* to achieve the just society; the way to this ideal was not democracy, but through rule by philosopher-kings. The abilities of these rulers were to be developed through a rigorously prescribed regimen of physical training, education in the arts, music, mathematics, and philosophy. It is interesting to note that Plato felt it would be necessary to establish a mythical basis for the

[1] Plato's writings consist of dialogues in which the writer's ideas are expressed through the speeches of Socrates.

division of society for people to accept it. Acceptance of the myth "would have a good effect," said Plato through Socrates, "in making them care more for their state and for one another [*Ibid.*]."

My purpose in dwelling on Greek political thought is to show that an interest in the psychological foundations of politics was present even in ancient times. Centuries later, the seeds planted by the Greeks came to fruition in the thinking of European philosophers. The Greek ideas of man's nature influenced political philosophers as diverse as Machiavelli, Hobbes, Locke, and Rousseau. In turn, these writers' views on man reflect contrasting psychological emphases, which can yet be discerned in political thought.

Rational Man versus Emotional Man

Two distinct views of man were apparent in philosophical thought between the Renaissance and the Industrial Revolution. The first view, represented by Machiavelli and Hobbes, saw man as driven by selfish and irrational urges. In *The Prince* (1513), Machiavelli (1469–1527) argued that the ruler must impose his will through fear and ruthlessness. Such treatment is justified since the people are driven not by high ideals, but by devious, cowardly, and selfish motives. Machiavelli's cynical view of man has its contemporary counterparts, as we see in Chapter 6 of this volume.

Thomas Hobbes (1588–1679) saw man as an egoistic being whose basic goal is power. Man strives for power in order to attain the pleasures of life, to enhance his own status and self-esteem. In the *Leviathan*, Hobbes (1904) likened the state to a great being, a social organism created out of necessity to restrain the selfish egoism inherent in man's nature. The power seeking which results from these natural urges must be restrained if life in society is to be at all possible. Thus, men yield in their own interest to the "common power" of the state. The emphasis on power and ego enhancement is also present today, as is apparent in the discussion of self-esteem, power, and competence in Chapter 5.

A more optimistic view of man is found in the writings of Locke and Rousseau. Their optimism, however, was based on somewhat different views regarding man's nature and the perfectibility of society. John Locke (1632–1704) viewed man as a relatively rational being. A follower of Hobbes in the empirical school of English psychology, Locke nonetheless developed independent ideas on man's nature and governance. He thought that the child begins life with no innate ideas. As the child matures, his rational faculties are developed through experience (education, sensory stimulation, etc.). Locke's (1689) ideas on government followed his belief in the possibility of developing man's rational powers. Unlike Hobbes, Locke saw in the "social contract" an expression of man's rational response to necessity. Man is reasonable and decent, he thought, and thus is able to build a moderate and just society, utilizing the advances of science, technology, and industry to further common ends.

Jean Jacques Rousseau's optimism about man, on the other hand, derived from his belief in man's innate goodness. Rousseau (1712–1778) emphasized the beauty of the "natural" state of man in *The Social Contract* (1762), placing blame on society for the corruption of man's natural innocence. He wrote at length on "the noble savage," whose praise brings to mind the contemporary back-to-nature movement. "Man is born free but is everywhere in chains," Rousseau asserted. The chains, of course, are the unnatural confines of social organization.

From Plato, who thought that men have differing allotments of reason, will, and appetite; through Machiavelli, who focused on man's selfishness; Hobbes, on his urge to power; Locke, on his reason; to the sentimentalism of Rousseau; I have covered with broad strokes the span of ideas on the political nature of man before the twentieth century. With this brief summary of a long historical prologue, let us turn now to the twentieth century and to Sigmund Freud, whose psychology in many ways connects this earlier thought to contemporary psychological perspectives of political man.

THE PSYCHOANALYTIC VIEW OF MAN

Psychoanalysis has undoubtedly had more influence on the psychology of politics than any other psychological theory. Although other thinkers had anticipated the theme of unconscious motivation in human behavior, it took the genius of Sigmund Freud to develop a coherent theory of personality which encompassed these unconscious determinants. Two of Freud's books that have explicit reference to politics are discussed in this section, but it is his theory of the nature of man, rather than his discussion of politics per se, which is of major importance.

Central to Freud's theory is his observation that many of our actions are the result of motives of which we are not aware. He inferred these unconscious motives from such things as slips of the tongue, the forgetting of names, and other supposedly accidental or inadvertent actions. In actuality, Freud believed, none of these are truly accidents. Rather, they result from unconscious feelings.

The adult personality, then, is a composite of conscious, unconscious, and partly conscious desires and beliefs. Freud attempted to make sense of these observations by positing three major components of personality structure. These components are the *id*, the *ego*, and the *superego*. It should be kept in mind that these components are not real objects; rather, they should be looked at as a description of the three central personality processes. It is helpful in conceptualizing these processes to use a diagram such as that shown in Figure 2–1.

The newborn child's psychic constitution can be thought of as unitary or undifferentiated. This unity consists of undirected physiological wants, as well as the sexual and aggressive instincts. These basic strivings constitute the *id*, which in the newborn is the only structure. It operates by the *pleasure principle;* that is, the id seeks satisfaction of these primitive urges. The baby's wants are not always immediately satisfied, however, so the id is inevitably subjected to frustration of its desires. Gradually, the infant develops ways of dealing with his parents and the external world to accomplish at least some of his aims. Through this interaction with the world, a new agent, the *ego*, is formed. The ego operates according to the *reality principle*. When hungry, for example,

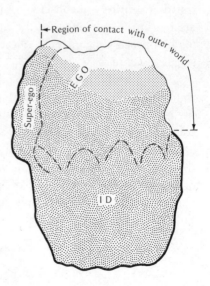

Figure 2–1 Sketch illustrating the theoretical relationship among id, ego, and superego, and the levels of consciousness in psychoanalytic theory: Heavy shading indicates the unconscious areas, no shading the conscious areas, and light shading the preconscious areas of the personality (Adapted from *The Structure and Meaning of Psychoanalysis*, by William Healy, Augusta Bronner, and Anna Mae Bowers. Copyright 1930 and renewed 1958 by Alfred A. Knopf, Inc. Reprinted by permission of the publisher.)

the child learns that he cannot put just anything into his mouth; he must learn to recognize food. Hall (1954) noted that:

> In the well-adjusted person the ego is the executive of the personality, controlling and governing the id and the superego and maintaining commerce with the external world in the interest of the total personality and its far-flung needs [p. 28].

The third component of personality also develops as a consequence of the child's interaction with his parents. Described as "the moral or judicial branch of personality [Hall, 1954, p. 31]," the *superego* incorporates the parents' ideas of what is good (ego ideal) and what is bad (conscience). Through the process of identification, the superego gradually takes the place of the parents. In extreme cases, the superego is so punitive that the ego has great difficulty in mediating between the demands of the id and the restrictions of the superego. In such cases, neurosis is likely to occur.

As I have mentioned, an important tenet of psychoanalysis is the idea of unconscious causes of behavior. Memories or wishes may exist in the unconscious mind and, although the person is unaware of them, they often affect his behavior. Such everyday phenomena as mispronunciation of a person's name or other slips of the tongue may result from unconscious hostility, for example. The preconscious refers to memories that can easily become conscious, although in actuality there are all degrees of consciousness. As suggested in the diagram (Figure 2–1), the wishes of the id are entirely unconscious; that is, the desires emerging from the id are not in the awareness of the individual. The person is most aware of his ego processes, but even these are partly beyond the reach of conscious awareness.

The competing demands of the person's desires and his feelings of right and wrong produce inevitable conflicts within the personality which the ego attempts to reconcile. Often, the ego attempts to resolve inner conflict by the use of *defense mechanisms*, which operate as follows. The ego, faced with the impossible job of harmonizing the demands of the id, the superego, and the external world, often finds itself in trouble. In order to function in the face of guilt or anxiety, the ego defends itself and the person by mechanisms such as *repression* (which means that a threatening memory, idea, or perception is forced out of consciousness).[2]

---

[2] Other important defense mechanisms are rationalization, projection, reaction formation, and regression.

The operation of repression is shown by an incident in the life of a properly brought-up Victorian girl, 15 years old, who visited the beach with her parents. She briefly met a young man there who was so handsome that the thought occurred to her: "I would like to have him make love to me." This wish so conflicted with her strict upbringing that the next day when her mother mentioned "that handsome young man at the beach," the girl had no recollection of him whatsoever. That is, she had *repressed* the memory of the boy.

PSYCHOANALYSIS AND SOCIETY

The implications of psychoanalytic theory for the study of political life are extensive. More than 30 years after Freud's death, political scientists are deliberating the implications of his formulations for their discipline (cf. Roazen, 1968). In addition, many revisionist psychoanalysts, particularly those who emphasize the social, rather than the sexual, side of man's nature, have made contributions to political psychology. Included among these "neo-Freudians" are Alfred Adler and Erich Fromm, who both appear later in this book. At this point, I want to concentrate on Freud's own speculations about the origin of political impulses and then discuss his influence on Harold Lasswell, a prominent authority on political personality.

Freud's ideas about the origin of society were set forth in *Totem and Taboo* (1913). These ideas were suggested to him by Charles Darwin's conjecture "that the primitive form of human society was that of a horde ruled over despotically by a powerful male [Freud, 1930, p. 90]." Although not well-versed in anthropology, Freud was attracted by the myth and its possible relationship to theoretical ideas he had been developing. Hall and Lindzey (1954) summarized the tale:

> In the dawn of human society, man lived in small hordes under the domination of a strong male. This strong male was the father of the whole horde. He had unlimited power which he used sadistically against his sons. Since all of the females of the horde were his property, the father could and did force the sons into sexual abstinence. If they excited his jealousy, they were killed or castrated or driven out of the tribe. Consequently, the sons were forced to steal their wives from other tribes, and this led to intertribal warfare, which further strengthened group ties within the horde. One of the sons, often the favored younger son, was chosen by the father to be his successor.

The sons who were driven out of the tribe organized and overcame the father. After killing the father, the sons ate him in order to produce identification with the father by incorporating a part of him.

Following this patricide, the sons began to quarrel with one another for power. Upon discovering that fraternal aggression was dangerous they formed the first social contract which was based upon a renunciation of instinctual gratification. To ensure group solidarity they established the taboo against incest and the law of exogamy. Thus the first form of society developed out of the family [p. 167].

The idea that the experiences of the horde left a residue in humankind, which exists to the present day, has met a storm of criticism. Not the least of the objections has been the absence of any scientific evidence for the existence of such hordes. Nevertheless, although he admitted that his account of the origin of community life in the transformation of the horde was only a hypothesis, a "Just-So Story," Freud continued to use it in a book written 10 years later. In *Group Psychology and the Analysis of the Ego* (1922), Freud discussed the mechanisms by which individual psychological tendencies produce the emotional ties that are the foundation of all social groups.

Freud began the latter book by considering the then current writings on group psychology. He was particularly intrigued with LeBon's (1895) theory of the *group mind*, noting with approval accounts of crowd behavior in which men seemed to become more primitive in their thought and action. Freud saw this group phenomenon—"the dwindling of the conscious individual personality, the focusing of thoughts and feelings into a common direction, the predominance of the emotions and of the unconscious mental life, the tendency to the immediate carrying out of intentions as they emerge [p. 91]"—as an example of mental regression. The term *regression* refers to a return of a developmentally earlier, less sophisticated mode of psychological functioning; in Freud's words, "a regression of mental activity to an earlier stage such as we find among savages or children [p. 82]." Such primitivization, Freud believed, is regularly found in crowds and other more-or-less temporary groups. In organized groups this tendency can be checked.

Group psychology was very broadly defined by Freud—it focused on the "individual man as a member of a race, or a nation, of a caste, of a profession, of an institution, or as a component part of a crowd of people . . . [p. 3]." In all sorts of groups, the cohesive force is to be found in libidinal ties among men. Such ties, of course, have their origin in the individual libidos, *libido* being "the energy . . . of those instincts which have to do with all that may be comprised under the word love . . . [p. 37]." Freud's examples are two "artificial" (highly organized, with more or less compulsory membership) groups: the Catholic Church and the army. It is relatively easy to think of the church as being held together by love, but it seems strange to speak of an army in this fashion. Therefore, I will discuss the army example, since it is less obvious and since the principles apply to all groups.

The organization of an army is hierarchical. At the top is the commander-in-chief, at the next level are the generals who have overall responsibility for large sections, and so on. The ties of men to their commanders, Freud asserted, are the same ties that bound the sons of the primal horde to the memory of their father. "The Commander-in-Chief is the father who loves all his soldiers equally, and for that reason they are comrades among themselves. . . . Every captain is as it were the Commander-in-Chief and the father of his company, and so is every non-commissioned officer of his section [1922, p. 43]." This assertion may seem strange to the present-day reader, but let me pursue the matter further. There are, Freud admitted, other than libidinal ties that hold an army together. These include love of country, ideas of natural glory, and the like. Nevertheless, the important force in the army, as well as in other groups, is the affectional ties of the members to their leaders.

In the army, as in the family, which is the model for all other groups, the basically sexual instincts are not directly felt or expressed. Rather, they are *aim inhibited*. Love for the leader is perceived as justified respect, and the leader is often regarded as an ideal person. Furthermore, the tendency of a person to lose some of his identity in a group is often the result of the replacement of parents by the leader as the individual's *ego ideal*.

Their mutual relationship to the leader ultimately leads group members to affectionate feelings toward one another. In Freud's (1922) terminology, the members come to *identify* with one another. Identification is seen as "the earliest expression of an emotional tie with another person [p. 60]." The little boy, for example, shows a special interest in his father: "he would like to grow like him and be like him, and take his place everywhere [*Ibid.*]." Although the development of such feelings is complex, the essence of group solidarity is to be found in the common identification of members with one another, as a consequence of their common idealization of the leader.

Freud recognized that day-to-day relationships among people are not altogether characterized by tender feelings; such relationships also involve resentment and hostility. He (1922) touched on these negative feelings in *Group Psychology*, noting that "every intimate emotional relation between two people which lasts for some time . . . leaves a sediment of feelings of aversion and hostility [p. 54]." Freud later came to give even more emphasis to negative feelings in trying to analyze the problems of civilized societies. In *Civilization and Its Discontents* (1930), he gave independent status to man's aggressive instincts.

Simply stated, psychoanalysis in its final form postulated dual sources of man's striving in the life (Eros) and death (Thanatos) instincts. Love, constructiveness, and growth are the tendencies included under the life instincts. Freud adopted the Greek term *Eros* from Plato to signify the libido or love force of psychoanalysis. Destructiveness, aggression, and hostility, on the other hand, are seen as manifestations of the death instincts. Since man could not survive if these instinctual strivings went unregulated, the task of civilization is to repress, redirect, and regulate man's sexual and aggressive urges.

In a way, the growth of social controls parallels the growth of individual controls. Just as the superego comes to assume a regulatory and prohibitive role in the economy of the individual, so society develops norms, laws, and taboos to regulate the interactions of individuals in relation to one another. Sexual expression is permitted only in certain circumstances and with certain persons. Aggression is likewise channeled. Murder is severely prohibited, but killing of outgroup members is encouraged in wartime. Child beating is discouraged, as is assault by one person on another, *except* in the boxing ring, and so on.

This repression of the instinctual urges is necessary for the progress of civilization, as well as for its protection. As Freud pointed out, most productive and cooperative endeavors come about through the sublimation and redirection of the sexual and aggressive urges which are repressed by society. In the case of Eros, direct sexual aims are converted into a more general affection for others. Freud (1930) believed that thus redirected, Eros is responsible for the growth of civilization. The work of Eros "is to combine single human individuals, and after that families, then races, peoples and nations, into one great unity, the unity of mankind [p. 69]." Thanatos, on the other hand, works in opposition to constructive activity. The aggressiveness arising from the death instinct, "the hostility of each against all and of all against each" opposes the building of civilization. Thus, Freud conceived the story of the evolution of civilization in "the struggle between Eros and Death, between the instinct of life and the instinct of destruction, as it works itself out in the human species. This struggle is what all life essentially consists of, and the evolution of civilization may therefore be simply described as the struggle for life of the human species [*Ibid.*].''

This struggle is not without cost to the individual. Pleasure results from satisfaction of the instincts; sacrificing one's sexuality and aggressiveness thus tends to lower one's overall satisfaction. "Civilized man," said Freud (1930), "has exchanged a portion of his possibilities for happiness for a portion of security [p. 62].'' This denial of instinctual gratification exacts its costs in neurotic symptoms, which arise from libidinal urges, and in the sense of guilt, which originates in repressed aggressive urges. Neurotic anxiety and guilt arise primarily from the psychological tendency to internalize external prohibitions. The superego represents this now internal authority and constantly "rides herd" on the ego. The ensuing psychological discomforts are the price man pays for civilization.

Many writers have noted the profound pessimism of Freud's view of man in society. Freud himself was driven from Vienna by the Nazis and spent his last years in London. This experience, together with his own suffering from cancer, must have led Freud to even greater conviction about the ultimate triumph of death and repression. A somewhat more hopeful interpretation of psychoanalysis was taken by Herbert Marcuse (1955) in *Eros and Civilization*. In this book Marcuse introduced the notion of *surplus repression*—the idea that society, in the interest of political domination, has become more repressive than is necessary to protect man from his own impulses. Thus, to some degree man's unhappy state can be relieved through political measures. The reader interested in finding more hopeful alternatives within the basic framework of Freud's theory should examine Marcuse's work.

On the individual level, psychoanalytic theory has been employed as a means of understanding political activity. One notable example is the attempt by the psychologist Theodore Adorno and his co-workers (1950) to understand authoritarian behavior. Their work, *The Authoritarian Personality*, which dealt with the relation of personality to political ideology, is discussed at some length in Chapter 7. Foremost among the political scientists who were influenced by psychoanalytic theory is Harold D. Lasswell, who has used Freudian concepts to analyze the behavior of politicians. Lasswell's thought is briefly described in the following section.

PSYCHOANALYTIC THEORY AND CONTEMPORARY POLITICS

Lasswell was a serious student of psychoanalysis; he studied Freud thoroughly and even underwent a training analysis. In an early book, *Psychopathology and Politics* (1930), Lasswell made careful use of case studies compiled from interviews with politically active people. Based on his study of political activists, Lasswell formulated the psychodynamics of three main political types: The Agitator, the Administrator, and the Theorist. The prototypes for these three types of political character are first, the Old Testament Prophets (Agitators); second, the President who above all advocated cautious, careful, and reasonable government, Herbert Hoover (Administrator); the third, the author of *Das Kapital*, Karl Marx (Theorist). Although the psychogenesis of these types differs, Lasswell (1930) believed the dynamic underlying political life styles to be either sexual guilt or repressed hatred (allowing also that both might be present). "The dynamic of politics," he said, "is to be sought in the tension level of the individuals in society. . . [p. 185]."

The thesis that "[p]olitical movements derive their vitality from the displacement of private affect upon public objects . . . [p. 183]," is elaborated and illustrated by the use of brief case histories collected by psychoanalysts and by Lasswell himself. The interpretations are in orthodox Freudian terms. As such, the cases invariably deal with sexual and aggressive content. Lasswell noted that there were cases where such content was not forthcoming: these people "wanted to talk about their professional career in politics with minimum disclosure of their intimate histories." Such a subject gave little information about his sexual life and could "not lift the amnesia of pre-Oepidal years [p. 273–74]." Note the analyst's insistence that sexual and aggressive tensions *must* be lurking below the surface. Lasswell assumed that these tensions were being repressed.

The style of Lasswell's case analyses may be illustrated by excerpts from the case of Miss G (one of the subjects who sought aid from a physician). Miss G, a 35-year-old activist in many causes, particularly women's rights, "came to the physician complaining that she was bothered by blushing, stage fright, uncertainty, palpitation of the heart, and weeping spells." Lasswell reviewed her parental relationships, particularly in regard to sexual conflicts and her handling of family disagreements, as well as the symptoms she displayed earlier in adulthood.

Miss G had an enormous masculine complex. She chose masculine goals, and ruled out the female role as far as she could. Her narcissism brought her from obscurity to distinction, though at the cost of several neurotic difficulties in which her repressed drives found crippling expression. She swings between vanity and inferiority feelings. She blushes when praised, she blushes in public because of the dependence of her sex on men, and she is timid in the presence of academic people. She always feels ill at ease with strangers and lives in isolation from society.

In theory and in practice Miss G is for free love, and for the complete equality of the sexes. She sought out politics as a career as a means of expressing the male role of dominance, a drive which was powerfully organized in her early childhood experiences [pp. 123–24].

Although she advocated free love, Miss G found herself sexually frigid in actual intercourse with men. Her hatred of men was so strong that she was unable to accept any subordination to a man; these overwhelming feelings caused her to terminate treatment with her male psychoanalyst.

In a later work, *Power and Personality* (1948), Lasswell pursued the idea that political activity results from the displacement of private motives. Unacceptable hatred or guilt feelings, in other words, are transferred to political causes. Righteous indignation against the policies or tactics of political opponents provide the person with socially acceptable outlets for these unconscious motives.

In particular, Lasswell saw the political type as accentuating the value of power. Those people who do so are motivated by low self-estimates; however, they must also possess the requisite skills and be presented with appropriate political opportunities. The political man, then, according to Lasswell (1948, p. 57):

1. accentuates power
2. demands power (and other values) for the self
3. accentuates expectations concerning power
4. acquires at least a minimum proficiency in the skills of power

Lasswell's key hypothesis is that pursuit of power is a compensation for feelings of deprivation: *"Power is expected to overcome low estimates of the self,* by changing either the traits of the self or the environment [p. 39, italics in original]."

Lasswell's hypothesis concerning the relationship of the self-system of the ego to political striving has been pursued by Alexander George

(1968). Of particular interest is the examination of biographical information on Woodrow Wilson (George and George, 1956), in an attempt to understand the tragic failure that capped the career of this brilliant statesman. I have occasion in Chapter 6 to refer to the Georges' hypothesis that the "fatal flaw" in Wilson's character was low self-esteem stemming from his father's impossibly severe expectations for the boy. Their investigation suggested that Wilson sought power as a compensation for his feelings of weakness. In such persons, the "demand for power may be reaction-formative against the fear of passivity, of weakness, of being dominated [George, 1968, p. 35]." George drew upon Freud's description of the "compulsive" character in listing the kinds of behavior that might evidence such compensatory power seeking (1968, p. 37).

THE FUNCTIONAL APPROACH

"Of What Use to a Man Are His Opinions?"

This question orients us to one of the main streams of contemporary thinking about political man. The answer, in brief, is that opinions help him to get along, to *function* in his world. The functional approach, as I shall call it, recognizes that a person's internal conflicts affect his outlook, his prospects, and his adjustment to his environment. Guilt feelings, hostility, and love in its various forms do directly affect a man's political behavior, but they also shape his opinions. An individual's opinions reflect his total personal style and help him to adjust to his social and political world.

The functional approach represents a kind of scaling down of objectives in thinking about political man. Contemporary social scientists have a particular distrust of the grand schemes that attempt to derive the facts of social organization from a particular view of human nature. The more modest approach of the functionalists is a recognition that grand conceptualization such as Plato's or Freud's cannot be decisively proven or disproven.

This more modest approach to political psychology is an outgrowth of the interest in personality stimulated by Freud and of research in attitudes and opinions. I have pointed out the possible uses of psychoanalytic theory in studying political behavior. The theory's concentration on personality dynamics, however, has posed certain limitations on its potential for understanding political man.

The research on attitudes undertaken by psychologists in the 1920s and 1930s also proved to be limited in its explanatory potential. By 1937, for example, considerable research on the relationship of radicalism–conservatism to personality had been reported in the psychological literature (Murphy, Murphy, and Newcomb, 1937). Extreme radicalism or reactionary tendencies were found more often in only children, liberals were asserted to be more intelligent than conservatives, and so on. The findings were often conflicting, however, and seemed to be getting ever further from the central concerns of older political theorists. The functional approach, which combined the interests of personality and attitude researchers, proved more promising than either approach taken alone.

I date the functional approach from Newcomb's (1943) study of changes in political attitudes at Bennington College during the 1930s. His subjects were women from predominantly conservative, upper-middle-class homes, who were exposed to new political ideas when they entered college. Politically, the 1930s was an exciting time in the United States. The Depression still created great economic distress, and President Roosevelt's New Deal was the subject of strong debate in all quarters. The faculty of Bennington College who introduced the women to this debate was young, vigorous, and predominantly liberal.

The liberalizing effect of the Bennington environment on the students was dramatic. In the 1936 election, for example, 84% of juniors and seniors preferred either Roosevelt or one of the more radical candidates. Freshmen women, on the other hand, did not deviate from their parents' preferences—only 38% indicated preferences for the liberal-to-radical candidates. The most important aspect of Newcomb's study for our purposes was the emphasis he put on the personal meanings of a woman's political opinions. These meanings are particularly evident in his recounting the differences between students who changed in the direction of the liberal majority and those who did not.

Liberal attitudes seemed to serve two functions for those women who adopted them; they demonstrated independence from conservative parents, and they helped the woman to gain status in the college community. Newcomb (1943) cited the following statement, made by one of the liberal students at the time, that demonstrates these two functions:

I came to college to get away from my family, who never had any respect
for my mind. Becoming radical meant thinking for myself and, figura-
tively, thumbing my nose at my family. *It also meant intellectual identification with the faculty and students that I most wanted to be like* [p. 131,
italics added].

The students who did *not* change in the majority direction seemed to
be isolates in the college community; they tended to maintain dependent
relationships with their parents. A conservative senior commented:

I wanted to disagree with all the noisy liberals, but I was afraid and I
couldn't. *So I built up a wall inside me against what they said. I found I
couldn't compete, so I decided to stick to my father's ideas. For the last
two years I've been insulated against all college influences* [p. 119, italics
added].

From interviews with twenty-four liberal and nineteen conservative
seniors, Newcomb concluded that changing attitudes (or not changing
them) reflected the woman's adjustment to the conflicting demands of
the college community and her relationship to her parents. Of course, the
situation would be quite different in a conservative college. Also, attitudes
were influenced by the new information about economic and political
issues which the women received at college. This new knowledge forced
them to think in terms of the problems facing "a depression-torn America and a war-threatened world [Krech, *et. al.*, 1962, p. 253]." In the
words of Brewster Smith and his co-workers (1956), an opinion was
found to be "a resultant or compromise between reality demands, social
demands, and inner psychological demands [p. 275]."

Smith, Bruner, and White (1956) have most clearly enunciated the
functional approach foreshadowed by Newcomb's (1943) Bennington
study. The term *functionalism*, which implies adaptation or purposeful
striving, signifies that one's opinions serve particular functions. Moreover, the functional approach, to these authors, pertains to all of man's
behavior:

The human being, according to this approach, is not governed by a rational calculus, nor is he a blank slate on which experience traces its in-
exorable mark. Nor yet is man an ingenious machine translating physical
stimuli into bodily response. Like all animals, he is an organism, a system
of life processes that somehow maintains its identity in active interplay
with its environment. An organism is never passive, but survives and
grows through constant striving, responding selectively to relevant aspects

of its environment, and reaching out to incorporate, modify, fend off, or attain. Final passivity is death; in life there is always striving to maintain the delicate adaptation of the needs of the organism to its environment [p. 30].

The assistance given by one's opinions to this "delicate adaptation" is the subject of *Opinions and Personality* (Smith *et al.*, 1956). The authors conducted extensive interviews and administered test batteries to ten adult men of differing occupations and social backgrounds, at the Harvard psychological clinic. Their objective was to relate this personal information to the men's opinions and attitudes toward Russia.

The attitudes held by the ten men were seen as habitual ways of reacting to social objects or classes of objects (Smith *et al.*, 1956, p. 33). The term *attitude* implies an integrated pattern of reaction, stable and predictable for that individual: first, to *experience* the object in certain ways, with predictable affect or feelings; second, to be *motivated*, or at least desirous of doing something toward or against the object; and finally, to actually *act* with reference to the object in some characteristic fashion (hit it, kiss it, ignore it, avoid it, petition against it). According to Smith and his co-workers, "In brief, an attitude is a predisposition to experience, to be motivated by, and to act toward, a class of objects in a predictable manner [p. 33]."

The authors argued that a person's attitudes are "his major equipment for dealing with reality." The three ways in which attitudes help the person in these dealings are described as the three functions of attitudes: *object appraisal, social adjustment,* and *externalization*. Descriptions of these three functions follow:

OBJECT APPRAISAL. Attitudes have an important role in aiding the person to find his way about in the world. This "reality testing" function may be quite important to the person in choosing which of the multitudinous daily stimuli and situations he will stop and consider. If a speaker or point of view is immediately classified as "radical," many people will not give the event further consideration. "Love of country" or "patriotism" involve a complex of attitudes that for many people preclude consideration of any criticism of national policy. This is particularly true with reference to international affairs. The tendency to appraise social situations in terms of existing attitudes frustrated for years the minority in the United States who opposed the Vietnam war.

SOCIAL ADJUSTMENT. The social adjustment function of attitudes refers to the role attitudes play in relating the person to the various reference groups within his life space. Long-haired youth, at the present time, serve as a strong positive reference group for young people who characterize themselves "freaks." The same long-haired group is referred to disparagingly by another segment of the American society as "hippies."

In addition to self-definition in terms of positive and negative reference groups, Smith *et al.*, noted two other kinds of social adjustment functions that are served by the holding of certain attitudes or opinions. One function is the seeking of autonomy, which is served by developing opinions that the person has worked out independently. Although the holding of opinions at odds with prevailing sentiment may reflect the person's autonomy needs, such opinions may also be an expression of hostility toward others.

Finally, it is noted (Smith *et al.*, 1956) that, "[t]he very act of holding an opinion whatever its nature, may serve the social adjustment of the individual. . . . Given identification with certain groups—let us take the reference group called 'intellectuals'—the individual feels that he *must* have opinions on certain issues to maintain his sense of identification [p. 43]." One of the most widespread examples of political opinion serving adjustmental functions is the tendency of the growing individual to adopt the political attitudes prevailing in the family. Political "rebellion" is much less common than supposed, as is shown by the proportion (70–80%) of people who adhere to their parents' choice of political party.[3] Even student activists seem most often to be pursuing, in somewhat intensified form, their parents' political values (Keniston, 1967, p. 119).

EXTERNALIZATION. Externalization refers to the expression of internal psychological dynamics by adopting certain attitudes and taking particular positions regarding external events. In other words:

> Externalization occurs when an individual, often responding unconsciously, senses an analogy between a perceived environmental event and some unresolved inner problem. He adopts an attitude toward the event in question which is a transformed version of his way of dealing with his inner difficulty. By doing so, he may succeed in reducing some of the anxiety which his own difficulty has been producing [Smith, *et. al.*, 1956, p. 43].

Take, for example, a person whose sexual needs have been severely repressed by his parents. Although his sexual longings persist, they are

[3] As reported by Campbell, Gurin, and Miller (1954, p. 99) for respondents whose parents were both Democrats or both Republicans.

denied expression by a harsh, punitive superego. If this person develops strong puritanical attitudes toward sexual relationships, pornography, and short skirts, it seems likely that such attitudes are externalizations of his inner conflict.

A similar approach to the study of attitudes was taken about the same time by Katz and his co-workers (1956). In an article on the functional approach to the study of attitudes written in 1960, Katz discussed the three functions which had been mentioned by Smith *et al.* (albeit with somewhat different terminology) and added a fourth, the *value-expressive* function.

VALUE-EXPRESSIVE ATTITUDES. The addition of this function calls attention to the observation that many attitudes serve primarily to express deeply held personal values that are central to the person's conception of himself. Katz (1960) has written: "A man may consider himself an enlightened conservative or an internationalist or a liberal, and will hold attitudes which are the appropriate indication of his central values [p. 173]." This ties in very closely with the observation by others of the importance, particularly to the adolescent, of establishing and asserting his identity. Erikson (1963), in reflecting on the "American Identity," pointed to the legend of John Henry, a man who evidences the central values of strength, courage, and endurance in his resistance to the inroads of modern technology:

> "And befo' I'd let that steam drill beat me down I'd die with this hammer in my hand, Lawd, Lawd, I'd die with the hammer in my hand."

In political science, two lines of research seem very compatible with the functional approach I have been discussing. They combine the emphasis on the functional utility of attitudes with a more detailed analysis of the complexities of American political institutions and processes. The first of these research efforts is the work of Lane, who employed extensive, in-depth interviews. The second effort is the study of *The American Voter* (1964) by Campbell and his colleagues at the Survey Research Center.

Lane's Political Man

One of the most prolific writers on politics and psychology is the political scientist Robert E. Lane. The recent book, *Political Man* (1972), is an interesting introduction to his work; in it Lane discussed aspects of two interview studies that were reported at length in earlier books (1962, 1969). The first was an interview study with fifteen men who were residents of a middle-income housing project in an Eastern industrial city.

Lane (1962) interviewed each of these fifteen men for some 10–15 hours, over the course of several interview sessions. His purposes for doing so are given in the title of his book: *Political Ideology: Why the American Common Man Believes What He Does.* The topics discussed during the interviews included: current social questions; political parties; political leaders; social groups; discussion of "democracy" and associated values; personal philosophies; personality interviews and tests; and life histories.

The major differences between this study and that of Smith *et al.* (1956) are first that interviews were conducted in each man's home; second, an attempt was made to survey each man's entire life situation; and third, rather than focusing on one attitudinal object, reponses to a wide range of political issues were explored. Furthermore, the information gained was interpreted within the framework of Lane's impressively broad knowledge of political systems. An example is his interpretation of the meaning of freedom to his subjects. He pointed out that the free mind as understood by members of the affluent middle class does not have the same meaning for his working-class subjects. To a man concerned with health problems, possible loss of work, or inadequate income, many questions of concern to the middle class have little significance. This man's life choices—of a career, of a political party to represent his philosophy, of congenial friends, or of interesting reading matter—are made "within a framework of worry and occasional desperation."

> In this sense one might say that the foundation of freedom is far less a matter of laws than of the health of a people—and for Costa, Woodside, and others, the First Amendment offers less freedom (that is, opens fewer options for choices important to them) than would a good public-health measure. And this is Eastport, not Karadi, Stanleyville, or Port-au-Prince [p. 38].

The ideas that Lane expressed in the foregoing passage have been stated somewhat differently by the psychologist Abraham Maslow (1954). Maslow believed quite strongly that until man's basic needs for food, shelter, and a measure of security are fulfilled, he is not free to exercise the choices expected of a democratic citizen. Knutson (1972) has made an ambitious study of the applicability of Maslow's ideas to political man.

Economic worries do not seem to lead the common man toward acceptance of radical ideologies. Lane discussed the recession that had hit Eastport (his fictitious name for the city) at the time of the interviews and the worry that this economic decline occasioned in his subjects. He pointed out that the problems and anxieties the men faced would, in another time or place, lead them to consider alternatives for political change. But the idea of socialism, for example, seemed to be excluded from their range of alternatives. This exclusion is not because they have escaped hardship under the American system, but because of their philosophical acceptance of the doctrine of individual responsibility and self-help. Lane (1962) proposed that "these men, not proletarians but rather individual climbers from the lower-status tenements of their fathers, need to believe in the power of the individual to survive and achieve [p. 378]."

This brief discussion of Lane's work [4] will serve to indicate the kind of insight that typifies his writing. The observations he is able to make from his wealth of political knowledge highlight the relative ignorance of the psychologist in this area. The need for collaboration between psychology and political science in studying the psychology of politics is hereby made apparent.

The American Voter

Studies of voting behavior done by the Survey Research Center at the University of Michigan have consistently tried to examine psychological factors that could be considered to underly electoral choice. Campbell and his co-workers (1964), in *The American Voter*, used data from political surveys conducted by the Center from 1948 through 1958 in an attempt to examine the psychosocial context of voting behavior.

The level of psychological analysis that can be made from survey studies is necessarily superficial as compared with the individual case studies I have mentioned. Nevertheless, survey research can describe regularities in the behavior of the electorate as a whole and highlight deviant patterns in subgroups of the population. An example of such

---

[4] Lane's (1969) book, *Political Thinking and Consciousness*, discussed the results of his study of the political belief of college students, using a similar case-history approach. Space forbids discussion of it here, but the book will appeal especially to college students who are "thinking things through [Lane, 1962, p. 378]."

findings is the documentation of the relationship between feelings of political efficacy and voting behavior, which is discussed at length in later chapters.

The behavior of the American voter is examined in some depth in Part IV. It would be well for the reader to have certain general findings in mind, however. Let me mention them briefly. First, Americans have a very low emotional involvement in politics. This low involvement is reflected by voting turnout—only about 60% of the voting-age population voted in the 1952 and 1956 Presidential elections. Second, Campbell and his co-workers found the voter to have a rather limited knowledge of public affairs, both in the foreign and domestic realm. Third, few people think in terms of structured ideology. The terms "liberal" and "conservative" mean little to voters, and even party membership is largely unrelated to political ideology. Finally, in spite of all this lack of interest, most Americans have a pervasive attachment to one or the other of the two major political parties.

CONCLUSION

In concluding this whirlwind tour of political psychology through the ages, let me try to summarize the trends that are apparent. First, there has been a pervasive concern with the nature of man. The emphasis on a relatively fixed nature has gradually waned, until today the conception of man as a creature determined by his environment holds sway.

A second pervasive theme has been a concern with equality. In Plato, at least, the inequalities were seen as the result of man's fixed nature. However, other philosophers—Hobbes and Machiavelli—believed inequality to be a necessary condition of existence. If some men were not in a position to rule, all would fall victim to individual self-seeking.

The third thread that can be discerned is the issue of freedom. Freedom of choice is most explicitly raised by Lane, but it is discernible in the previous writers, as well. How free is the man posited by psychoanalysis, for instance? Is he not the prisoner of his own nature? I shall not try to answer these questions, but I hope that the reader will find clues toward his own answers in the chapters that follow and in his own experience.

PART II

Political Socialization

3

Focus on the Individual:
A Conceptual Framework

*Man's impulses and thoughts and acts result from the relation be-
tween his nature and the environment into which he is born.*

WALLAS, *Human Nature in Politics*, 1908

Man's political acts are determined by his impulses and thoughts and
by the situation in which he finds himself. Of necessity, the psychologist
always takes into account the setting in which behavior occurs. My
present objective, however, is to deal with the question: What are the
important psychological characteristics that must be considered in analyzing man's social and political behavior?

My purpose in this chapter is to submit, for the reader's consideration, a model of human character structure in the form of an outline
of the most important psychological factors. Because such a discussion
can become abstract, I shall introduce a concrete individual who I am
calling Joan Pirelli. By keeping her in mind, it will be easier to understand
the relation of character structure to political behavior.

Joan Pirelli is an attractive 31-year-old housewife. She is 5'7" tall,
weighs 140 pounds, has light brown hair and green eyes. The mother of
three small children, Joan has been married for 10 years. She met her husband in college and quit school at the end of her sophomore year when
they were married. Joan worked in a nursery school for a year until her
husband graduated and then worked in an insurance office for another
year and a half. Her husband makes an adequate income as a real estate
salesman, so Joan hasn't worked since her first child was born.

Although Joan's family had a rather small income (her father was a
machine operator in a Providence, Rhode Island, textile factory) and

there were two younger children at home, she was able to attend the University of Rhode Island with the help of a scholarship and part-time work as a waitress. Her family was disappointed that she did not continue in college, but with 2 years of post-secondary education, Joan had exceeded her family's educational attainments (her mother completed high school; her father did not go beyond the eighth grade).

Of more concern to Joan's Protestant parents than her plan to break off her education were her plans to marry a Catholic of Italian descent. Their objections were overcome, however, as they got to know Tony, Joan's fiancé. Tony was charming and attentive to the family and exhibited an engagingly casual manner toward his religious affiliation. Then, too, his father was a fairly well-to-do businessman, so the prospects for financial security were good

As of today, Joan's interest in politics is slight. Her political interest quickens only in Presidential election years, a pattern typical of middle-class housewives in the small Massachusetts town where she now lives. Forsaking the Republican Party of her parents, she joined her husband's party, although politics had never been an issue between them. Strongly affected by the antiwar feeling that they shared with their friends, the Pirellis both enthusiastically supported George McGovern, the 1972 Democratic Presidential candidate. The following February, however, in the election for town officials, neither Joan nor her husband voted. Asked by a neighbor on election day if she would like a ride to the polls, Joan declined with the reply that she didn't even know who was running.

Many other aspects of Joan Pirelli's life and her personality are necessary to the understanding of her political behavior. This brief sketch should suffice as an introduction to Joan, however, since I use illustrations from her case in presenting my model of character structure.

THE PERSON IN SOCIETY

In the quote that began this chapter, Graham Wallas referred to a person's "nature" and the environment into which he is born. In the psychological language of 1908, Wallas was discussing the causes of a person's political actions. He spoke first of impulse and instinct, then of "political entities" in the environment to which the person responds.

Although our terminology has changed considerably since the beginning of the century, psychologists are still inclined to look for the causes of behavior either in the person himself or in his environment. In other words, either the person or the environment can be seen as the *locus,* or place of origin, of the forces that cause the person to behave in a certain way. First, we look at the person herself. In Joan Pirelli's case, you may wonder what she is like as a person. What does she look like? Is she intelligent? What are her interests, what does she like to talk about? Does she speak clearly, without hesitation? The list is endless unless we have in mind certain factors as being most important to political behavior.

The second source of causes is generally referred to collectively as the environment. Specifically, I am referring to the forces in Joan's environment that affect her behavior. These external factors include her husband, children, political issues, the house and the town she lives in, the weather—everything in what I call her *life space.* Included in Joan's life space are moment-to-moment or temporary factors (a proposal to bus her oldest child a considerable distance to school might have aroused her interest in the last town election), as well as more permanent forces (such as her husband's political philosophy).

Of course, personal and environmental forces may jointly influence behavior. Joan voted for McGovern because of her own attitudes *and* because of her husband's enthusiasm for the Democratic candidate. It is easier to understand the joint effects of the multiple influences on the individual if we think of her or him as behaving in a field of forces referred to as the individual's life space.

This way of thinking about man's behavior is called *field theory.* The field view of behavior was proposed by the psychologist Kurt Lewin (1951), who is famous for his contributions to the understanding of individual and group behavior. He used the term *life space* to refer to the totality of forces acting on the person at a given moment in time. In actuality, the life space includes both the person and his psychological environment. Lewin used a schematic diagram, an egg-shaped Jordan Curve, to represent the forces in the life space:

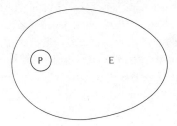

The life space is the region bounded by the curved line; conceptually, it includes all of the factors or forces affecting the individual at a given moment. It consists of the person (P), with all of his unique attributes, and the environment (E). The diagram is intended to represent things as they are at the present time for the person as he is right now in a particular situation.

This emphasis on the present is an important tenet of Lewin's field theory. It is called the "principle of contemporaneity," which is to say that at the time a person acts, his behavior is the product of forces acting at that moment in time. In the voting booth, for example, Joan Pirelli is confronted by two rows of names listed by twos, or occasionally by threes, under the titles of various political offices (the immediate situation). She pulls down all the levers in the top row, thereby voting straight Democratic (political behavior). The reasons why Joan pulled the top row levers as opposed to the bottom or some of each must be sought in her life space at the time she acted. A diagram of her life space would include the voting booth with its rows of levers as Joan perceives it, contemporary forces in her psychological environment (what she knows about the candidates, her feelings about the parties, and her husband's preferences, among other things), and her own personal make-up.

Note that the only factors immediately present other than Joan herself are the physical surroundings of the voting booth, which is the same for every voter. The forces that make her behave differently from a Republican voter, for example, are incorporated within her as the person who entered the booth. Her behavior, then, is determined by the traces left on her by her previous experiences. Among these inner determinants are memory, attitudes, personality dispositions, state of the organism (fatigued, hungry, tired, etc.), emotional state (angry, afraid), knowledge of the candidates and issues, and so forth.

Complete representation of the psychological situation requires depiction of goal areas in the life space. A person's goals can vary greatly in nature. They range from concrete, specific goals such as going to the supermarket to more abstract goals such as attaining the "good life." They can also vary along a time dimension from transient goals (food to the hungry person) to more permanent goals (such as financial security). Further elaboration of the life space can be made by showing the barriers to attainment of a person's goal. For example, Joan may not be able to go to the supermarket because her car has a flat tire, or her prospects for financial security may be marred because she must contribute to the support of her widowed mother.

This discussion of the life space should serve, for the time being, to point out to the reader that I do not hold a one-sidedly personalistic view of political behavior. The individual is part of a larger social and political system: he must adapt to institutions and to the behavior of other people. He is shaped by these external forces; in turn, he influences them. Later in the chapter I return to the complexities of the system within which political behavior occurs. Right now, I want to discuss the characteristics of the person.

PERSONAL CHARACTER: STABILITY AND CHANGE

Let me begin the discussion of character with an example from the psychology of racial prejudice. Psychologists often speak of prejudice as being either *normative* or *character-conditioned*. In the former category of prejudiced individuals are those whose behavior simply follows local customs (norms) with regard to dealing with members of another race. A white person reared in the South, for example, may avoid inviting black people to his home, not out of personal animosity toward blacks, but because "it simply isn't done" in his community. Character-conditioned prejudice, on the other hand, is applied to the person whose hatred of blacks stems from his own personal conflicts or deficiencies; this person would be likely to hate members of any minority group, regardless of community custom. By the same reasoning, we can think of a person's political proclivities as being either character-conditioned or normative.

In general, then, we can think broadly of culture and personality as two major determinants of political tendencies. Note that I say "tendencies," because we must always take into account the specific situation in which the political actor is operating. The discussion that follows, however, concentrates on personality, assuming for purposes of simplification that we can ignore the particular situation.

At the outset, let me distinguish between temporary states of the person and the more permanent dispositions that constitute *personality*. As an example of the former, consider that we are looking in on Joan Pirelli one Sunday morning. It is ten o'clock, and Joan, having fed the children, is sleeping on the couch in her robe, without make-up, her hair disheveled. How shall we explain her behavior? Does she have a "tired personality?" A housewife *can* suffer from chronic fatigue, but in the case at hand the explanation recognizes the temporary nature of the subject's tiredness: "Joan is fagged from being up partying until 3 A.M." Likewise, anger, hunger, and fear are temporary states of the person; as such, they affect one's behavior only temporarily. None of these things is generally thought of as a personality characteristic, though each affects behavior at the time.

In this chapter, I refer to the more enduring characteristics of the person as *character*. Following Yinger (1965), the term, character, refers to "the individual's organization of predispositions to behavior." One reason for choosing *character*, rather than the term *personality*, is that the latter term is often used both to describe behavior and to refer to predispositions of the person. A second reason for preferring character to personality is the rather broad set of personal attributes that we wish to include under the heading. Character is also a more neutral term, not possessing the multitude of connotations with which various personality theorists have imbued the term "personality."

Stability and Change

Although the distinction between temporary and permanent characteristics of a person seems arbitrary, it is useful for scientific inquiry. It would be more exact to speak of rapidly changing or slowly changing characteristics, since change is typical of life processes. No matter how permanent social institutions or, for that matter, the physical environment may seem, change can be discerned over a period of time. Change also occurs in the comparatively permanent aspects of personal character.

For example, Joan Pirelli can be described as an alert person of average intelligence, with comparatively little knowledge of political institutions or personages. Shy in social situations, Joan defers to her husband's opinions, rather than asserting her own. She tends to hold liberal views on civil rights and has expressed dovish opinions on the Vietnam war. These observations are by no means an exhaustive character description, but they do serve to indicate that Joan does have certain fairly permanent dispositions.

Now let us look into the future—a few years hence when Joan's children are more independent—Joan has begun taking some college courses and through a friend's urging has become active in the League of Women Voters. The changes in her character structure are apparent. She appears more confident, is well-informed on many subjects, and is assertive in her opinions. On occasion, fortified by a cocktail or two, she even ventures to challenge her husband's political views in social gatherings.

The reader will grant that such personal change is not unheard of; everyone changes somewhat over the course of his life. I recognize the problem of accounting for change as well as stability in individual character, although in talking about structure I may seem to be neglecting the possibility of change. When I discuss the components of character structure, I shall mention some of the processes of learning and habit formation that help to account for the formation and change of such structures.

AN OUTLINE OF CHARACTER STRUCTURE

It seems to me that we can usefully think of a person's character in terms of three factors. These three factors, identity, cognitive and emotional, are shown in Table 3–1. One's *identity* is the person's awareness of self as object and as active agent. Knowing and thinking are the basic *cognitive* processes. Under *emotion* are included one's feelings and desires. Before discussing this scheme in detail, I shall explain, by way of orientation, the assumptions underlying the choice of these particular characteristics.

In proposing this particular outline, I have accepted the general structure of personality outlined by Freud (id, ego, superego) as a working framework. I make no attempt, however, to adhere to the specific meanings that a psychoanalyst might assign to the terms. In my usage, the *id* is seen as the locus of the life force underlying the individual's strivings. It is the repository of universal human biological urges. As these urges become socialized, a coherent, largely conscious self (*ego*) emerges. The ego attempts to deal with the demands of the id in a rational way; that is, within the limits set by the real world and other people. Certain prohibitions (don'ts) and compulsions (shoulds and oughts) are learned in the process of development, and these guide the ego in the

Table 3–1 Three-factor scheme for character analysis

A. Identity factors (ego)

Self-concept
Self-esteem
Complexity
Social orientation

Competence striving
Direction
Intensity
Area

B. Cognitive factors (ego)

Style
Intelligence
Cognitive complexity
Field orientation
Openness

Content and organization
Beliefs, attitudes, and values
Motivations and aspirations
Dominant attitude establishments; e.g., Authoritarianism and Machia-
vellianism
Belief subsystems
Interconnections among subsystems

C. Emotional factors (id, superego)

Basic trust
Defensiveness
Anxiety
Prejudices, aversions
Likes, desires
Sexual orientations

---

process of want fulfillment. These restraints and compulsions are sys-
tematized in the *superego*. The two functions of the superego are embodied in its parts, the *conscience* (restraints) and the *ego ideal* (compulsions—this is what one should be like).

This tripartite division of character is a convenience rather than a
reality. I could analyze character structure in many other ways, but the
Freudian scheme has the virtue of being well-known, colorful, and
adaptable to the facts of personality organization. Thus, I take Freud's
basic structure as a useful model for analytical purposes, while warning

the reader not to believe that ids, egos, and superegos actually exist as entities.

A. Identity Factors

The ego functions are particularly important to the psychology of politics, especially that aspect of the ego which concerns one's definition of self, one's *identity*. The growth of a child's sense of self is a gradual process. He learns first to distinguish himself from all things that are not-self. As time goes on, the experiences of his own body, the sound of his name, and the reactions of others contribute to his sense of personal identity. Of particular importance are the identifications that the child forms with his parents and other models. One's ego identity is formed, bit by bit, throughout childhood, with continuous reevaluation and change. At puberty, however, a "particularly large reworking" occurs (White, 1964, p. 148). The identity crisis in adolescence occurs largely because the individual, on the verge of adulthood, must prepare himself for love and work in the adult world. Erik Erikson (1963), a psychoanalyst who has studied identity problems extensively, emphasized the importance of one's meaning for others, as well as for oneself.

> The sense of ego identity, then, is the accrued confidence that the inner sameness and continuity prepared in the past are matched by the sameness and continuity of one's meaning for others, as evidenced in the tangible promise of a "career" [pp. 261–62].

Essential to one's identity, then, are the ideas about *who* one is and *what* one can do. The first of these ideas refers to the individual's *self-concept*, the second to his feelings of *competence* in dealing with different aspects of his world. My discussion of these factors is purposefully brief, in anticipation of their extended treatment in Chapter 5.

I have selected three aspects of self-concept for special mention: *self-esteem, complexity,* and *social orientation.* Self-esteem can be thought of as positive self-feeling. An individual may have either a large or a small amount of self-esteem. Negative concepts of self may also exist, although they are not necessarily the opposite of self-esteem; that is, an individual may have little self-esteem, but this need not imply *negative* self-evaluation.

The second aspect of an individual's self-concept is the *complexity* of his self-picture. Ziller (1970) measures complexity by means of an adjective checklist. The intricacy of the person's self-image is indicated by the number of adjectives—positive and negative traits—which he uses to describe himself. Finally, one's social orientation refers to the degree to which the individual has developed self-direction and a sense of autonomy, as opposed to being continually dependent upon other people for self-definition.

Competence striving refers to the degree to which the person strives for competence, or adequacy, in dealing with his world. White (1959) has pointed out that such striving is a universal tendency of higher organisms. In man, a sense of personal effectiveness is essential to a mature identity. I have already referred to the importance of finding one's life work—one of the most important competencies in life. The direction of a person's competence striving will depend upon his previous successes, his identifications with other people, and his abilities. The areas that the individual particularly emphasizes (intellectual, mechanical, social, and so on) and the intensity with which he pursues excellence in these areas depend on his differential abilities, the successes he experiences, and also on the general level of his ego defensiveness.

B. Cognitive Factors

One's mental apparatus can be thought of in terms of its functioning, which is referred to here as cognitive *style*, and in terms of one's accumulated knowledge, or cognitive *content*.

Of utmost importance for personality functioning is the inborn quality of adaptability. I refer thereby to individual differences in ability to learn and to adapt to the environment. Our best indication of this characteristic is *intelligence*, which, as everyone knows, is greatly affected by the individual's experiences in life, as well as by genetic inheritance. Affecting his self-concept, as well as the style and content of his cognitive system, the individual's intelligence also markedly affects the kinds of ego defense mechanisms he employs.

Intelligence acts to shape the person's self-concept chiefly through its impact on his feelings of effectiveness. Of course, intelligence is not an entirely general trait. It has been found necessary to assess a whole cluster of "intelligences"—such as numerical, spatial, vocabulary, verbal reasoning, and so forth—in order to measure the general capacity for adaptation which is called "intelligence."

Other attributes of the cognitive system that affect personal style are *cognitive complexity* and *field orientation*. Complexity is an acquired attribute; the origins of field orientation are less clear. Put simply, complexity refers to the amount and variety of intellectual resources that one can bring to bear in solving a problem or thinking through an issue. The opposite of a complex cognitive system is a simplex system. Given a particular issue, such as tariff protection for domestic shoe producers, the approach and conclusions of a man with simplex cognitive structure would vary greatly from those of a man with complex cognitive structure. The former might focus on the plight of the domestic shoe worker and conclude that his job must be protected. The complex individual, however, would consider the domestic industry, but would also take into account the economic, social, and political ramifications of the issue. These two individuals may come to the same conclusion, but whether they agree or not, the processes by which each arrives at a decision will differ considerably.

Complexity does relate to the amount of acquired knowledge, but is not simply the amount of knowledge acquired. For example, an extremely defensive person may reject much information about his world. A second man may acquire a great deal of knowledge regarding electrical generators or some other kind of specialized knowledge. Neither has a very complex cognitive system. Cognitive complexity is relatively independent of intelligence, but it is an important determinant of response to new situations (cf. Krech, Crutchfield, and Ballachey, 1962).

Field orientation, more familiarly referred to as field dependence or field independence, has been extensively related to perception. In fact, the term *perceptual style* is often used to denote this dimension of cognitive functioning, though it does have extensive personality implications beyond the purely perceptual (Witkin *et al.,* 1954). For present purposes, we are simply interested in field orientation as an important dimension of cognitive functioning. The term *field dependence* denotes the extent to which a person is influenced by the content, background, or the existing situation in assessing a stimulus. One of the tests used, for instance, requires the individual to judge the tilt or verticality of a luminous rod in a dark room. When the rod is tilted, and the luminous frame is also tilted at the same or different angle, the field-independent person can more easily report the true position of the rod. The field-dependent person depends more on the frame or background in making his judgment; in life, he finds analysis of a particular situation more difficult than does the field-independent person.

COGNITIVE CONTENT. The specific *contents* of the cognitive system—the beliefs and attitudes held by the individual—and the organization of these cognitions are both very important aspects of the personality of the individual. Of course, the individual's basic emotional orientation is also an important determinant of the beliefs, attitudes, and values that he will acquire. Child–parent relationships determine the pattern of identifications and thereby the extent to which parental beliefs are accepted by the child. Chapter 4 is devoted to the study of the acquisition of the beliefs and attitudes which are the contents of the cognitive system.

In politics, we often think in terms of a basic left–right continuum along which most attitudes and opinions can be ranged. Legislative bodies recognize this tendency in their seating patterns. In either chamber of the United States Congress, the Democrats sit on the left and the Republicans on the right. In countries having a greater party spectrum—the centrist parties are indeed seated toward the center of the assembly hall. Whether such left–right orientations are basic to ideology and personality, as Tomkins (1963) has asserted, or whether there are perils in trying to force all people and political opinions onto the left–right axis (see Shils in Christie and Jahoda, 1954), are issues that are further discussed in Chapter 8. I do believe that there are great individual differences in the amount of change that individuals are willing to tolerate. These differences in attitude toward change are deeply rooted in the individual's character structure; indeed, these attitudes toward change involve both cognitive and emotional factors.

C. Emotional Factors

Many psychological observers have noted that even in infancy, individual differences in emotional responsivity are apparent. One child, lying quietly in its crib, can be described as placid or even apathetic; another smiles and gurgles at an interesting object, be it a sunbeam or a human face; a third is fussy and irritable, quick to cry, and wakens at the slightest sound. Such differences, presumably related to physiological structure or prenatal and very early postnatal influences, form the basis for later emotional development.

The basic learning process thought to underlie emotional development is *classical conditioning*, a phenomenon discovered by Pavlov.

Changes in emotional response to objects in the environment are effected through conditioning of the underlying visceral, glandular, and vascular responses. John B. Watson (1925), for example, demonstrated in a famous experiment that an infant's friendly approaches to a white rabbit could be turned into fear of this animal through conditioning. By associating the sound of a loud gong with the rabbit, Watson showed that the emotion of fear could become attached to the previously positive stimulus object, as well as to other furry objects.

Eysenck (1954) has claimed that an important personality orientation, introversion–extraversion, is related to innate differences in conditionability. He believes that the introverted child forms conditioned responses easily, while extraverts condition only with great difficulty. These initial differences are magnified as children grow because they differ in the extent to which emotional responses can be established or modified through learning.

The idea that characteristic patterns of reactivity are to be found in infants is expressed by many authors. Erik Erikson (1963), in *Childhood and Society*, suggested that as the child goes through stages of his psychosexual development, basic emotional orientations are established. In the first year of life, for example, basic trust or mistrust of others is established through the infant's social experiences. Upon basic trust, the child builds other emotional orientations in the succeeding crises of childhood and adolescence. [Expectancies and interpersonal trust in older people are being investigated by Rotter (1971).] The emotional tendencies established throughout these developmental periods will color the individual's interactions and reactions to situations and issues throughout his life.

These basic emotional predispositions, then, will manifest themselves in various emotional traits that appear in later childhood and adulthood. Persons who do not establish trusting orientations will exhibit various degrees of suspicion up to the extreme of paranoia. In later stages of development, one must resolve conflicts centering around questions of autonomy and initiative. Failure to do so may lead to emotional dependency, which is often accompanied by resentment and hostility toward the object of attachment. Successful resolution of the emotional conflicts generated in these and later life stages will result in self-assurance, emotional security, and confidence; failure will result in feelings of insecurity and defensive orientations.

LEARNING, INDIVIDUAL CHARACTER, AND POLITICAL SOCIALIZATION

Existing treatments of political socialization (see Dawson and Prewitt, 1969) have tended to emphasize the acquisition of cognitive content with regard to political institutions and persons. The respected political scientist Gabriel Almond (1960) has defined political socialization as:

> . . . the process of induction into the political culture. Its end product is a set of attitudes, cognitions, value standards, and feelings—toward the political system, its various roles, and role incumbents [pp. 27–28].

In contrast, I think we must consider the whole person who is being socialized. Even when acting in a formal political context, he brings to the setting his whole set of character dispositions. In other words, the understanding of fundamental political orientations in the broadest sense depends upon an understanding of individual character. This approach finds some sympathy among political scientists. Fred Greenstein (1968), for instance, has defined political socialization as:

> . . . all political learning, formal and informal, deliberate and unplanned, at every stage of the life cycle, including not only explicitly political learning that affects political behavior but also nominally non-political learning that affects political behavior, such as learning of politically relevant social attitudes and the acquisition of politically relevant personality characteristics [p. 551].

The focus of this chapter has been on the "politically relevant personality characteristics" mentioned by Greenstein. So far, I have discussed the important dimensions of character in terms of the list presented in Table 3–1. In the following section, I try to show how character traits develop. Explicitly political learning, the acquisition of attitudes about political objects, is treated in Chapter 4.

Learning in Human Development

In citing the case of Joan Pirelli, I am attempting to help the reader to think in psychological terms about a concrete person. As Joan exists at this moment, sitting in a suburban Massachusetts home, she can be described by the various positions she holds in her social setting. She belongs to a certain age group, is a dutiful daughter, a wife, a mother, and a resident of her community. She is also a citizen of her town, her state, and the United States of America. Much of Joan's behavior can be explained in terms of what others expect of her in these various positions. In other words, a *role* (a set of expected behaviors) is associated with each of these positions. These expectations are important features of her psychological environment: "A good mother sees that her children are clean and well fed." "A good citizen should vote in every election."

While the obligations of her social positions are indeed important, Joan's behavior is not determined by these environmental forces alone. Referring back to the diagram representing her life space, Joan's behavior (B) is determined by both the environment (E) and the person (P). Lewin (1951) used a simple formula to state this proposition:

$$B = f(P,E)$$

Stated in words, this formula states that *behavior is a function of the person and his psychological environment.* Joan is not a passive creature in her environment. She may rebel against her parents', her husband's, or her neighbor's definition of the "good mother" role. Even if she does not resist, Joan's role performance in any of her positions can vary within certain limits as a function of her own character. We are interested, then, in how Joan became the person she is—a person who is somewhat introverted, who has certain talents, who is resentful of her husband's dominance, and so on. It is to this question that we now turn.

Heredity and Environment

The nature–nurture controversy, which flares up every so often, concerns the relative degree to which learned versus constitutional factors affect behavior. The extreme behavioristic position asserts the supremacy of learning in the formation of the behavioral repertoire of the adult individual. John B. Watson (1925), the psychologist whose book *Behaviorism* influenced American psychology so profoundly, wrote:

> Give me a dozen healthy infants, well-formed, and my own specified world to bring them up in and I'll guarantee to take any one at random and train him to become any type of specialist I might select—doctor, lawyer, artist, merchant-chief and, yes, beggar-man and thief, regardless of his talents, penchants, tendencies, abilities, vocations, and race of his ancestors [p. 85].

Watson's position has attracted psychologists since it disposes of factors that are difficult to observe and that are also difficult to control or change.

Even though I am also emphasizing the learned nature of personality, I do want to call attention to some of the evidence for the importance of inherited factors. It requires no great scientific sophistication to observe the interaction between inherited physical traits and behavior. Take athletic involvement, for instance: The exceptional case of a superb, 135-pound quarterback does not belie the generalization that such a lightweight is more suited to track-and-field events than to football. There is also evidence of some inherited psychological dispositions. Hall (1941), for example, selectively bred together those rats in his colony who showed the greatest timidity. The rats who showed the most aggressive behavior were also mated. Within a few generations he had produced two distinct strains of rats, one of which was markedly more timid than the other. I have previously commented on another line of evidence for genetically produced differences—the marked individual differences in the reactivity of newborn infants. Finally, I remind you of Eysenck's work with Extraversion–Introversion, which he claims is related to innate differences in conditionability.

Basic Learning Processes

Having noted that constitutional factors are important, I shall nevertheless concentrate on learning as the basis for most of the important variations in personality. The three learning processes on which there is fairly broad agreement are conditioning, operant learning, and imitation. I think that all three are important in character development.

Conditioning follows the classical-conditioning paradigm of Pavlov (see Kimble, 1961). Certain stimuli have the innate (unconditioned) capacity to elicit certain autonomic nervous system (emotional) responses. A loud noise produces startle, a warm breast, relaxation and pleasurable responses in the newborn infant. The noise or the breast are examples of *unconditioned stimuli*. The pairing of either of these unconditioned stimuli with a novel stimulus soon "conditions" the individual to respond to the novel stimulus as he did to the unconditioned.[1] That is, new situations, people, or objects come to elicit emotional responses because they have

[1] An example of this process was observed in one of my sons. As a young infant, the boy was regularly nursed in a particular chair in the living room. On the wall beside the chair was a large watercolor painting with a colorful border. After a few weeks, he was observed to smile when held in front of the painting. In this instance the painting served as the novel stimulus.

been previously associated with fear- or pleasure-producing stimuli. Prejudices, aversions, and phobias all have a large conditioned component. Much of the so-called unconscious background of behavior is the welling up of these conditioned emotional responses.

Operant learning is what most people refer to when they use the term "learning." Operant learning is most often associated with the psychologist B. F. Skinner (1953). We speak of using "the carrot and the stick" to refer to the use of rewards and punishments by people in authority. While teachers, parents, and other authority figures employ reward and punishment daily, their understanding of reinforcement principles is often poor. (Skinner uses the term *positive reinforcement* in place of *reward*). The cardinal principle may be stated as the *law of effect:* A response is more likely to be repeated when followed by a reward. Similarly, a response followed by punishment is less likely to recur. Reward and punishment have been shown experimentally to be most effective when delivered immediately following a response. While a more thorough discussion would go into the question of the relative effectiveness of reward and punishment, it is sufficient here to say that current research findings strongly attest to the greater efficacy of reward.

Perhaps the most generally effective reward is approval from other people. Through operant learning, we acquire motor skills, cognitive styles, basic attitudes toward the self, and even some cognitive content. The reinforcement for these learnings is often difficult to identify. Most commonly, the reward is social approval, though what some people have called self-reinforcement also occurs. By self-reinforcement I mean that the person's behavior is rewarded simply by the accomplishment of a desired end.

Imitation is the third basic learning process. The child learns a great deal through imitation of parents and other children. He will mimic an act or repeat a phrase spoken by an adult, for example. The child is even more likely to repeat a catchy phrase uttered by an admired adult. That is, he will repeat the phrase because it "sounds good" to himself (self-reinforcement) and also because he likes, admires, and wants to be similar to (identifies with) a particular adult actor.

There is continuing controversy over the exact status of imitative behavior. Some researchers (e.g., Miller and Dollard, 1941) assign imitation the status of a complex chain of responses acquired through operant learning. Other authors place more emphasis on the mechanism of identification. Simply explained, identification with another person is a strong liking and wanting to be like that person. Thus, if Joan *identifies* with her mother, it follows that doing and saying things that her mother does and says (imitation) will be rewarding.

The way in which these learning processes summate can be illustrated by reference to Joan's shyness. Her tendency to be quiet and reserved is partly in imitation of her mother, who is not a great talker. What is more, Joan was not given much attention when she did talk at family gatherings, particularly after her younger brothers came along. (Expression of her opinions and feelings was not rewarded.) Finally, the prospect of speaking in any group larger than three or four people arouses conditioned fears, which interfere with her ability to speak effectively.

Political Socialization and Political Behavior

The context within which a person votes, campaigns, discusses, or performs any political act is even more complicated than we have so far indicated. An attempt to describe the complex system within which the individual is enmeshed has been made by M. Brewster Smith (1968). A liberally translated version of his "Map for the analysis of personality and politics" is shown in Figure 3–1, with some illustrative factors from the life of Joan Pirelli. Smith takes into account: (1) the individual's larger social milieu; (2) his immediate social contacts—family, neighborhood, school; (3) his "personality processes and dispositions"; and, finally, (4) the immediate situation, as determinants of political behavior.

Smith's map of the political system within which Joan exists depicts these major components in the five panels indicated by roman numerals I–V. The causal relations are indicated by arrows, with the final behavioral outcome in panel V, the political behavior. Of course, some political behavior has effects on other parts of the system, hence the dotted "feedback loops" on the map. The feedback from panel V to III, for example, might indicate that voting for a successful candidate has actually changed the voter—for example, it may have produced a greater commitment to the political process.

CONCLUSION

By referring to the case of Joan Pirelli I have tried to provide the reader with a conceptual framework for understanding the role of personal character in the determination of behavior. The relationship of these

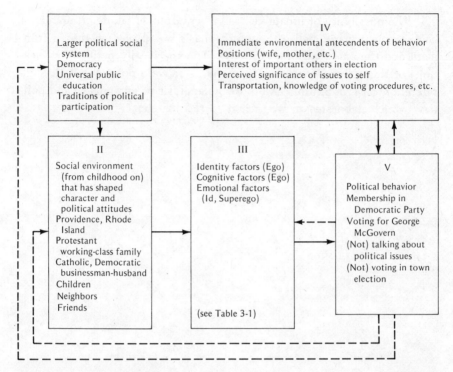

Figure 3–1 Map for the analysis of social and psychological factors affecting political behaviors (Adapted from M. B. Smith, "A map for the analysis of personality and politics," *The Journal of Social Issues,* 1968, 24, 15–28. Copyright © 1968 by The Society for the Psychological Study of Social Issues. Used by permission of the Society and M. B. Smith.)

personal factors to the external demands placed upon the individual was explained through the use of a field-theoretical model. The formula $B = f(P,E)$ summarizes this model (behavior is a function of the person in his psychological environment). Together, the person and his environment constitute the individual's *life space,* the total context in which he lives and behaves.

The aspects of the person that seem important to the understanding of political behavior were referred to as his *character.* The three basic factors in personal character structure, the *identity, cognitive,* and *emotional* components, were described in some detail. I suggested that these three factors relate to psychoanalytic theory in that the identity and cognitive factors parallel the ego functions, and the emotional factor is closely related to the demands of the id and the superego.

The possibility of innate, as well as environmental, determinants of character was mentioned, although emphasis was placed on the environment and the basic learning processes. The specifically political implications of this scheme for analysis of character were pointed out through reference to M. B. Smith's "Map for the analysis of personality and politics," which elaborates on my basic $B = f(P,E)$ model.

4
Learning
Political Attitudes

One of the intriguing aspects of my first real involvement in party politics was the realization of what strange bedfellows are to be found within each of the two major political parties in the United States. Of course, I was aware of the differences within the Democratic Party, which sheltered Southern segregationists like George Wallace along with the egalitarian Kennedys. But it was experiences of working with my own neighbors within the party that brought my personal realization of the wide discrepancies of belief.

The Democratic Party activists in my city have for years been largely men and women of Irish descent. Their influence lay in the large number of the Irish Catholic voters, descendants of immigrants who arrived before the turn of the century, who have without question been Democrats ever since. Over the years, however, as this subcultural group's economic situation has improved, its members have tended to become more conservative. This dominance of the liberal party by a relatively conservative ethnic group has occasioned a certain amount of conflict in my city and in others.

To be Irish is not always to be united against the world, however. The recent conflicts within Northern Ireland attest to that. The conflict within Ireland remains on the same basis it has for many years—conflict over religious differences. (There are, of course, related social and economic issues.) Differences in belief often result in serious antagonisms. Indeed, it often happens that individuals prefer a member of an opposite political party or another race who holds similar beliefs to a fellow group member who holds divergent beliefs (Rokeach, 1968).

Of course, there is a strong tendency to see people who hold common group membership with ourselves as holding similar beliefs. In the

Southern United States, race has long been the important grouping upon which common beliefs have hinged.

POLITICAL ATTITUDES IN DAYVILLE

To illustrate the importance of racial considerations in the thinking of Southerners, let me recount some observations made in the small Florida fishing village where I spent 9 months with my family a few years ago. Dayville, as I will call it, is a town of less than 1,000 people. The community numbered perhaps 5,000 inhabitants in the 1920s, but with decline in the fisheries, people gradually left to find work elsewhere.

The black population of Dayville numbers only a few families. They are mostly old people, the younger blacks having gone elsewhere in search of jobs. The relations between the races have always been harmonious, within the memory of my respondents. There is no ghetto; black families live side-by-side with whites. Registering to vote has never been a problem for blacks either. One elderly black lady told me, for instance, that she'd been voting "ever since they'd let us." Upon inquiry, I found that she meant ever since passage of the Nineteenth Amendment to the Constitution in 1920.

In spite of the surface harmony that pervades race relations in Dayville, there are signs that race figures prominently in the political thinking of its citizens. In the 1968 election, for example, 64% of the town's voters chose George Wallace over Hubert Humphrey (19%) or the victorious Republican candidate, Richard Nixon (17%). Of course, Wallace's vote in part reflected regional pride rather than racism, and many of the town's voters (91% Democratic) felt that Wallace was really a Democrat, but my interviews [1] left little doubt in my mind that Wallace votes were racially inspired: Eight out of the nineteen voters I talked with, for example, spontaneously brought up racial considerations. One of my black informants, when asked the reason why so many voted for Wallace, re-

[1] Interviews were conducted with a panel of those voters who were available from a random sample of twenty-nine taken from the Dayville voter registration list. Two of the twenty-nine were out of town; the other twenty-seven were interviewed from one to three times over a 5-month period. Of these, only nineteen talked enough to be useful to this discussion. Three of the others refused to talk with me about politics, and five either indicated disinterest or lack of knowledge: "I always voted with my husband when he was alive," one elderly white lady told me, "he just had two votes, that's all."

plied without hesitation that it was "against us." This response was rather surprising, in the light of her previous protestations of liking for white people. She continued with some candor to berate particular white Wal lace supporters who had benefited economically from cordial relations and assistance by blacks in their businesses.

The interrelation of racial views, political preferences, and other opinions and attitudes are best shown as they exist in the mind of a particular individual. Therefore, I would like to discuss the views expressed by two of my interviewees. One of them is the black woman mentioned in the previous paragraph, whom I shall call Alice Johnson. My reason for selecting the second case, that of "Harry McCormick," is the interesting inconsistencies in his ideas. Another reason for the choice of these two cases is that both are older people, with vivid memories of the Depression in the 1930s; both stated their admiration for President Franklin D. Roosevelt, who did so much to help the victims of that troubled era.

Alice Johnson

Mrs. Johnson, as I have said, is black. At 77 years old, she is alert, vigorous, and interested in politics. She was one of the few interviewees, for example, who, when shown a photograph of Senator Muskie, showed instant recognition of the man and who recalled his name without hesitation.

On my first visit, Mrs. Johnson was very guarded and was hesitant to express her views. She would not say for whom she planned to vote in the upcoming (1970) U.S. Senate election, but when asked her party preference, she said she was a Democrat. "I voted for F.D.R., I will say that," she told me. Later, during my second and third interviews, she warmed up considerably. With increasing rapport between us, Mrs. Johnson more openly expressed the ambivalence she felt toward white people, as expressed in her reaction to the question about why people voted for Wallace.

Born in Dayville, Alice Johnson displayed an obvious sense of pride in the community. She mentioned the white people with whom she had worked in the factory when she was younger and the presence of white neighbors next door. Alice recounted with pleasure how surprised her out-of-town visitors where when white passers-by, seeing her sitting on the front porch of her little house, would stop for a friendly chat. Negative feelings were evident in her recounting of her daughter's 20-mile trip to a segregated school, after the closing of the black school in Dayville. Hostility was also evident when she gleefully took up the joke upon my half-serious suggestion that it seemed to me that the whites were lazy and the young blacks hard-working and industrious, since so many of the latter had left Dayville to find work in other parts of the state.

Mrs. Johnson spoke knowledgeably about problems of the poor. She discussed the problems of a disabled relative and complaints about the administration of the surplus food program. Relatively uneducated, but aware, liberal, and articulate, Alice Johnson showed no evidence of alienation or powerlessness. For example, I asked if she had ever sought help from the County Commissioner regarding the problems she had mentioned. She replied that she had done so and that he had been helpful.

Overall, this woman's beliefs and opinions seem integrated, rational, and in keeping with her social setting. Her liberal political views seem to accord with her social-class interests, and her positive and negative feelings toward the whites in her community both seem to be warranted. Her political preferences (she indicated a preference for Muskie over Nixon at the time, when it seemed likely that Muskie would be the 1972 Democratic Presidential nominee) seem to be in accordance with her own self-interest and with the other opinions she expressed. My second case reveals more contradictions.

Harry McCormick

A white, male fisherman, about 60 years old, Harry McCormick was eager to talk about politics. One of his favorite sources of information is a conservative religious weekly published in New Orleans. I first met him when I called to talk with his wife, who was included in my random sample of Dayville voters. They came to the door together, and I asked for "Mrs. McCormick." When I explained the political purpose of my interviews, however, they both replied that she had voted only once. Mrs. McCormick said there was no doubt but that her husband was the one with whom I should talk. Assenting, I received in short order a summary of *Mr.* McCormick's views.

The following beliefs and opinions came out in this first interview with Harry McCormick, with little prompting on my part. He believes that:

1. What the country needs is a stronger belief and faith in God. Unfortunately, people are losing both today.
2. Politicians are dishonest and are mostly "out for themselves."
3. He is concerned about welfare chiseling and also about the unfairness he sees in the administration of the Social Security system.
4. The Jews control the money, in Russia as well as the United States.
5. Although we (white people) are responsible for bringing Negroes to this country, and although integration is good, the politicians are trying to move them (the blacks) too fast. "Negroes are just too close to the jungle," he said. He mentioned in particular a former Florida Governor whom he disliked for pushing integration too fast.
6. He has no doubt about his ability to affect those things relating to his own life, but he is "just discouraged about doing it."

I asked McCormick if he admired any politicians, if there was any politician whom he felt was reasonably honest. To my surprise, he mentioned Franklin Roosevelt, whom McCormick admired for the measures taken during the Roosevelt administration to stem the Depression. The cynicism and conservative ideas he had previously expressed were not consistent with his choice of a liberal President as an object of admiration. My impression of inconsistency among his beliefs was strengthened in our second interview, when I asked Harry why so many Dayville voters chose Wallace in the last election.

McCormick's reply to my question about Wallace was that "primitive people" (which I interpreted to mean simple, everyday working people) liked an "honest man." In response, I related some observations on Wallace's political career, mentioning that only after an unsuccessful candidacy in Alabama as a racial "moderate" did Wallace become a die-hard segregationist. "Is that honesty?" I inquired. Without batting an eye, he assented and added that nobody who had made so much money as Wallace had ("he's worth millions") could possibly be honest. He then reiterated his previous assertion that no politician is honest and went on to discuss the shady dealings of some of the local politicians.

In contrast to my first case, Harry McCormick's system of beliefs seems curiously illogical and inconsistent. He admires Roosevelt, yet disagrees with most liberal ideals. He supported Wallace, yet could not defend this support. It seems obvious that Mr. McCormick's religious and racial views enter into his thinking about politics, as does his cynicism about politics and politicians. That these views reflect his character structure would be the likely conclusion from further study of Harry's case.

ATTITUDES AND OPINIONS

To this point I have referred to attitudes, beliefs, and opinions rather haphazardly. Some psychologists do in fact use the terms interchangeably. In discussing *Opinions and Personality*, Smith and his co-workers (1956) asked "of what use to a man are his preferences and opinions?" and shortly thereafter use the term *attitude* as a synonym. Smith *et al.* stated: "We are not fussy about the word used to denote the phenomenon described in our definition. Attitude, opinion, sentiment—all of these terms refer to the kind of predisposition we have in mind [p. 33]." There are good reasons to make distinctions among these terms, however, as I point out.

In Chapter 3, I presented attitudes as important components of personal character. Although they are not visible (we infer them as we do all personal characteristics), attitudes, beliefs, and values are important characteristics of the person. An *opinion* on the other hand, is "a verbal expression of some underlying belief, attitude or value [Rokeach, 1968, p. 125]." The notion that what a person says (his opinion) should be distinguished from his internal tendencies is not especially new. Thurstone and Chave's (1929) classic on *The Measurement of Attitude* reflected the same distinction. They defined opinion as "a verbal expression of attitude. . . . An opinion symbolizes an attitude. . . . We shall use opinions as the means for measuring attitudes [p. 7]."

An illustration of the distinction between opinions and the underlying characteristics of the person's belief system is to be found in the case of Alice Johnson. The answers she was willing to give to the question, For whom do you plan to vote? reflected not only her liberal attitudes and her beliefs about the candidates, but also her beliefs about the white interviewer's intentions, her attitudes toward strangers, and so on. As she got to know me in succeeding interviews, she became more trusting; that is, she came to believe that "that man will not use what I say against me." As her "opinions" became less determined by these extraneous factors, I felt more confident that I could infer her "real" attitudes, that is, the political attitudes in which I was most interested. If she had been completely trusting of me in the first place, and if she had not wanted to make a certain impression on me, then perhaps the distinction between Mrs. Johnson's attitudes and opinions would be unnecessary.

However, this distinction between opinions and the underlying beliefs and attitudes should not be taken to derogate the importance of the study of *opinion*, so important to political analyses. Where would we be without public opinion surveys? How could one discuss political psychology without reference to the *Public Opinion Quarterly*? Undoubtedly, opinions do reflect the person's beliefs and attitudes. Sometimes, however, they reflect these internal structures only indirectly. An opinion is an item of behavior that reflects both these underlying states and behavioral intentions. The answer to: "Do you intend to vote for Nixon or Muskie?" certainly does not directly reflect either a belief or an attitude. The person's answer is a statement of intended behavior, which, if the respondent is not simply lying or concealing his true intentions, certainly is *partly* determined by his political attitudes and beliefs.

Incongruence between stated opinions and attitudes may come about for many reasons. A person's political attitudes (liberal or conservative) may *incline* him to answer in a certain way, but *other* attitudes may impel him to answer in another way. There will almost always be some conflict among different attitudes that a person holds. Then, too, with reference to the question about voting intentions, there are various items of knowledge (single beliefs) about the candidates, impressions mainly of an affective nature, and so forth. Even if the net outcome of all these psychological factors was "Muskie," his response might still be "Nixon" if the respondent is within hearing distance of several co-workers, the large majority of whom are Republicans. The reader can undoubtedly supply many reasons of his own for the imperfect relationship between his attitudes and the *opinion* he states to a friend, boss, co-worker, or public opinion interviewer.

Beliefs, Attitudes, and Values

The case studies of Alice Johnson and Harry McCormick presented a sampling of their political opinions. I have suggested that such opinions are determined in part by the situation and in part by the respondent's group memberships. Also, I have made the case that opinions are surface manifestations of some deeper-lying characteristics of the person. These underlying characteristics are the beliefs, attitudes, and values that form the individual's *cognitive system*. My treatment of these cognitive elements follows the theory that has been worked out by Milton Rokeach (1968).

The smallest element, the basic structural unit in cognitive systems, is the *belief*. According to Rokeach (1968): "A belief is any simple proposition, conscious or unconscious, inferred from what a person says or does, capable of being preceded by the phrase 'I believe that. . . .' [p. 113]." Beliefs may be simply descriptive, as denoted by the statement, "I believe that robins have red breasts." On the other hand, they may be evaluative: "This is a nice day"; or prescriptive: "One should drink six glasses of water a day." Whatever the knowledge and with whatever degree of certainty it is held, there are associated tendencies to *feel* strongly or weakly, pro or con, and to *act* with respect to the belief.

An *attitude*, the term I shall have occasion to use most often, is an organized set of beliefs, persisting over time, which is useful in explaining the individual's response tendencies. Thus, I infer a negative attitude toward politicians from the statements Mr. McCormick made about them. Attitudes always refer to a specific object or situation. That is, we have attitudes toward policemen, toward socialized medicine, or toward blacks. Rokeach's (1968) definition takes this object centeredness into account: "An attitude is a relatively enduring organization of beliefs around an object or situation predisposing one to respond in some preferential manner [p. 112]."

The key ideas in the definition of *attitude*, then, are: (1) It is an organization of beliefs; that is, a complex of beliefs about blacks, the war in Vietnam, or whatever object or situation. (2) It is enduring; that is, an attitude is not just a momentary tendency. While attitudes can be changed, they reflect long-term characteristics of the person—they are an important part of his character. (3) When activated, attitudes impel their holder to act in certain ways toward the objects of the attitudes. Thus, a person with positive attitudes toward retarded children may visit their schools, raise money, and so forth. Usually, according to Rokeach, at least two attitudes must be considered in explaining any social behavior. Thus, the opinions of my Dayville respondents can be seen as the product of a specific political attitude and an attitude toward the interview situation.

A person's *values* are not simply clusters of attitudes or beliefs. Rather, they are very basic personal orientations. Rokeach considers values to be very central beliefs: "abstract ideals . . . not tied to any specific object or situation, representing a person's beliefs about ideal modes of conduct and ideal terminal goals. . . [p. 124]." Values relating to ideal modes of behavior include those prescribing cleanliness, honesty in dealing with others, loyalty, and compassion. Terminal values include desirable end states such as security, equality, justice, happiness, and power. A well-known psychological test, the Allport–Vernon–Lindzey *Study of Values* (1960), enables one to measure the relative importance to the person of six general classes of values: *Theoretical, Social, Political, Religious, Aesthetic,* and *Economic*.

The individual's values are relatively few in number. Rokeach has proposed that: "An adult probably has tens or hundreds of thousands of beliefs, thousands of attitudes, but only dozens of values [p. 124]." While there is a considerable empirical literature on the acquisition of beliefs and attitudes, our knowledge of value acquisition is more speculative. Because of the importance of general orientations such as trust, sincerity, honesty, and the like, it may eventually be found that value acquisition is one of the most important processes for understanding political behavior. A number of studies have shown, for example, that New Left radicals come from predominantly liberal homes. This could mean that although there are strong differences between parent and child in belief (the United States is imperialistic), or in attitude (e.g., toward the government of the United States), there has been a very accurate transfer of basic values (equality, justice, helping others).

The Cognitive System

All of a person's beliefs, attitudes, and values taken together constitute his cognitive system. The basic building blocks, as I have noted, are the beliefs that the individual begins developing, probably even before he has language. Some particularly important beliefs seem to serve as keystones in this system. These keystones, of course, are the person's values. Clusters of beliefs become organized around important social and political ideas and objects; we call these clusters, attitudes. With all these thousands of beliefs and hundreds of attitudes, the cognitive system seems pretty much of a jumble. Fortunately, certain ideas or beliefs seem to attract one another so that the cognitions become organized. That is, various *subsystems* or groups of attitudes are formed. One's attitudes toward other people, toward government, or toward food are possible subsystems.

If space permitted, it would be useful for me to discuss in more detail the organization of cognitive systems. For example, both the number of clusters and the way they are interconnected are important aspects of cognitive organization. Another aspect is the degree to which the system is *closed* and rigid, or *open* to modification by new experiences. The extremes, of course, are typified by the mind of an old person who is extremely set in his ways and a child of 5 years whose mind is constantly growing and changing with the intake of information. In his book on *The Open and Closed Mind* (1960), Rokeach suggested that people of all ages can be ranged along a scale of open- to closed- mindedness. He measures these characteristics by means of the Dogmatism scale. Agreement with the following sample statement from this scale is evidence of closed-mindedness:

> It is only natural that a person would have a much better acquaintance with ideas he believes than with ideas he opposes [p. 74].

> When it comes to differences of opinion in religion we must be careful not to compromise with those who believe differently from the way we do [p. 77].

A *dogmatic*, or closed-minded, person is likely to reject beliefs that do not fit with his existing beliefs and attitudes. Also, he is likely to be rigid and to depend upon external authority. In this sense, Rokeach's dogmatism has been suggested as a kind of general authoritarianism, and I look at dogmatism from this point of view in Chapter 7. Rokeach has suggested that members of extreme political parties are likely to be more dogmatic than members of more moderate political groups. Fascists and Communists, by this reasoning, should prove to be closed-minded. There seems to be little evidence to support Rokeach's hypothesis, however. In fact, DiRenzo's (1967) study of Italian Deputies tended to show the opposite. Members of the two left-wing parties (Communist and Socialist) were most open-minded, whereas the dogmatism scores of members of the six other parties did not differ significantly.

THE FORMATION OF ATTITUDES. The contents of one's cognitive system—one's beliefs, attitudes, and values—develop over time. The newborn infant soon begins to acquire feelings that can be conceived as elementary beliefs about himself and the world with which he comes in contact. Next, the child begins developing beliefs involving "passive language"—his preverbal understanding of some of the things said in his presence. With the advent of active language, the child's acquisition of beliefs proceeds at an ever-increasing rate.

The learning of specific beliefs is important, but most attention of researchers has been paid to the development of attitudes. Therefore, I will focus on the attitude formation, recognizing that attitudes are organizations of beliefs and that the acquisition of new beliefs often will modify or change existing attitudes. The formation of attitudes proceeds apace with the development of the individual's whole character structure. He learns from his parents and from other people according to the general principles of learning that were described in Chapter 3. Later learning is based upon earlier learning; that is, existing attitudes form the basis for the formation of new ones according to the principles of cognitive organization. Also, the attitudes that are formed are *functional;* in other words, they help the developing person to adapt to his world.

ATTITUDE ORGANIZATION AND FUNCTIONS. Attitudes are acquired in accordance with the principles of psychological organization. These principles might be termed: *balance, simplicity,* and *harmony* (many of these ideas on organization are found in Heider, 1958). Take "Attitude Toward the Negro" (Hinckley, 1932) as an example. A positive attitude toward Negroes consists of an organized set of beliefs, such as: "The Negro's intellectual potential is as great as anyone's"; "The Negro is, first of all, a human being, a person"; and "The Negro is deserving of special consideration because of past oppression." Underlying the acquisition of these beliefs, undoubtedly, are some basic values (organizing principles) regarding "equality," "kindness," "the dignity of man," and so forth. These values are not always easy to identify, but the hypothesis of some such tendencies seems worthwhile to account for the selectivity with which some beliefs are accepted and others rejected. So we assert that beliefs, to be accepted, are generally in *harmony* with underlying values.

The principle of *balance* refers to accord within a particular attitude. It is extremely unlikely, for example, that a person with a positive attitude toward Negroes, including the beliefs listed above, would also subscribe to negative beliefs that have had currency in the past: "Negroes smell bad"; or, "Negroes are more sensual than white people," etc. Whenever an attitude does contain both positive and negative beliefs, we speak of imbalance, a condition whose magnitude depends upon the importance of the contradictory beliefs. The notion of balance is very important to current theories of attitude change. We later return to this topic.

The third principle of cognitive organization, *simplicity*, refers to the tendency to try to resolve the ambiguities and complexities of life by making definite categorizations of people and things. A very complex argument for the admission of the people's Republic of China to the United Nations, for example, may be simply rendered and stored: "That Red (the speaker) wants to let the fox (China) into the henhouse (the U.N.)." Gordon Allport and Leo Postman (1947) demonstrated this tendency years ago in their study of rumor. Experimental subjects were shown a slide depicting a scene on an old-fashioned trolley car. The first subject described the scene in intimate detail to another subject who, not having seen the picture, described it to another, and so on. In addition to sometimes dramatic distortions (e.g., a razor in the hand of a white man in painter's garb was transferred to the hand of a well-dressed black man), the outstanding tendency was toward simplification of the information. Thus, a lengthy description became, at the end of the chain: "The picture shows a streetcar with two men standing arguing. One is a Negro. That's about all."

In Chapter 2, I discussed the *functions* that attitudes serve in orienting and adjusting the person to his social world. The four functions, to summarize, were:

1. *Object appraisal.* Also referred to as the knowledge function, this category refers to the attitudes that fulfill the individual's need to find meaning, to understand his universe. The child learns that his parents will feed and care for him, that a radiator is hot, and that he can go out and play when the sun is shining. He doesn't have to keep learning these things over and over again, but instead learns attitudes that serve as short cuts the next time he encounters a similar situation.

2. *Social adjustment.* Close to what Katz (1960) has called instrumental attitudes, attitudes that serve the social adjustment function help to maintain the person's relationships with other people. In particular, the child learns what attitudes are necessary to fit into the important groups with which he identifies. These *reference groups* often require the holding of certain attitudes by their members or those who aspire to membership.

3. *Externalization* refers to the ego defenses by which a person protects himself from unpleasant truths about himself or the external world. A person who harbors strong hostility, for example, may develop attitudes that emphasize the ill will of other people.
4. The *value-expressive* function refers to those attitudes that serve to express the individual's cherished central beliefs. These values are primary to one's self-definition, and thereby certain attitudes develop that serve the purpose of self-expression. One's *identity* includes those attitudes about self and social objects that express his basic values.

With a little imagination, we can trace the development of the attitudes expressed by either of the Dayville respondents discussed at the beginning of this chapter. Harry McCormick's attitudes were shaped by early experiences in his family, which in turn reflected white Southern culture and the particular norms of a small Florida fishing community as it existed around 1915. His parents and other people in the community disapproved when he played with black children, and he often heard the term "nigger" expressed. Although his parents were poor, he always knew that he was better than the children from poor Negro families. These racial attitudes were supported by the minister of the Southern Baptist church he attended with his parents; nobody of importance seemed to disagree.

The basic organization of Harry McCormick's beliefs and attitudes seems inconsistent at face value, but some of this seeming inconsistency can be explained by the observation that I was dealing with expressed opinions and not with the underlying attitudes and beliefs. Not that Harry necessarily lied to me; he may be unaware of some of the attitudes that underlie his behavior. Certainly, his racial beliefs are in balance with his support for George Wallace. A possible explanation for the seeming inconsistency between his attitudes regarding politicians and his attempt to justify support for Wallace on the basis of his "honesty" is that the latter reason is simply a vain attempt to justify this support to the interviewer.

It is easy, too, to see in McCormick's attitudes both simplification (*all* politicians are dishonest) and the knowledge function. His strong religious beliefs help him to *understand* the world he lives in: it is God's purpose, and so on.

THE COURSE OF POLITICAL LEARNING

The attitudes that make up the clusters I have mentioned are extremely varied. They range from relative specific attitudes concerning Communism, Negroes, welfare, socialized medicine, and foreign aid to more general inclinations such as attitudes toward democratic principles, ethnocentrism, and political efficacy. Aside from the hundreds of specific questions the public opinion pollsters have used to infer political attitudes, a great many attitude scales have been developed to measure these attitudes more reliably. A compilation of political attitude scales sponsored by the Survey Research Center (Robinson *et al.*, 1968), for example, includes ninety-five different scales.

Acquisition of these political attitudes, first of all, is based upon the individual's character structure. The identity, cognitive, and emotional aspects of character determine both the receptivity of the individual to beliefs about different aspects of his political world and how he organizes these beliefs. Basic trust, dependency, adaptation to the authority structure of the family, cognitive structure, and conceptions of self in relation to other people are among these characterological dispositions. Upon this personal foundation is built up the structure of beliefs and attitudes that constitutes that person's orientation to his political environment. This structure is formed through experience with the political and the quasi-political system.

I use the term *quasi-political* to indicate that many of the young person's experiences in the school, the family, and in clubs produce beliefs about getting along with one's fellows that are transferable to the political system. Dawson and Prewitt (1969) have referred to these kinds of learning as *indirect* political socialization. This indirect political learning involves "the acquisition of predispositions which are not in themselves political . . . [but which are] later directed toward specifically political objects to form political orientations [p. 63]." These authors have labeled manifestly political experiences as *direct* political socialization. "Whereas indirect political socialization entails the type of two-step process outlined above, this mode involves the direct transmission of political outlooks [p. 64]." The postulation of these two general processes is congruent with the emphasis I have placed on the importance of individual orientations that are not manifestly political, while placing emphasis on the *"specific learning of orientations to politics and of experience with the political system,"* which Almond and Verba (1965) believe to have been "seriously underemphasized [p. 33]."

Indirect Political Socialization

Indirect political socialization, as conceived by Almond (1960), primarily involves the child's early experiences in the family. In this view, political attitudes are seen as projections of the character traits shaped by one's experiences in family and other primary groups. This *psychocultural* interpretation of socialization was proposed by cultural anthropologists influenced by the psychoanalytic emphasis on the critical role of family relationships in the socialization of the child (see, for example, Whiting and Child's 1960 *Child Training and Personality*). This anthropological perspective on political learning was summarized by Almond and Verba (1965):

> The early psychocultural approach to the subject regarded political socialization as a rather simple process. Three assumptions were usually made: (1) The significant socialization experiences that will affect later political behavior take place quite early in life; (2) these experiences are not manifestly political experiences, but they have latent political consequences— that is, they are neither intended to have political effects nor are these effects recognized; and (3) the direction of socialization is a unidirectional one: the more "basic" family experiences have a significant impact upon the secondary structures but are not in turn affected by them" [p. 266].

The individual's character is undoubtedly shaped by his experiences in the family, and this character structure does affect his behavior. There are other kinds of learning, however, in the family, neighborhood, and school, which are not specifically political, but which develop certain attitudinal *orientations*. These orientations involve attitudes toward authority, toward cooperation with others, trust in other people, and so on.

Hess and Torney (1967), for example, have suggested that the child develops attitudes toward authority in early life which *transfer* to political objects:

> By virtue of his experience as a child in the family and as a pupil in school, he has developed multifaceted relationships to figures of authority. In subsequent relationships with figures of authority, he will establish modes of interaction which are similar to those he has experienced with persons in early life. For example, as soon as the President has been identified as an

authority figure, established patterns of interaction with authority will become relevant [p. 20].

Many authors consider the individual's attitudes toward authority to be the most important orientation, in terms of its significance for later political development (see Fromm, 1941). An authoritarian family, headed by a strict disciplinarian father, will lead the child to expect dominance and submission to be part of all group relationships. He will, in other words, either expect to defer to a strong leader *or* to take the initiative himself. In a more democratically oriented family, the child will learn to participate in decision making and to carry expectations about shared authority forward to his later life.

A second type of indirect political learning, *apprenticeship*, is proposed by Dawson and Prewitt (1969). Their suggestion is that many nonpolitical life experiences teach basic attitudes, values, and skills which are directly useful when the child enters political life. "From various nonpolitical experiences the individual acquires skills and insights which he uses to find his way in the political world [p. 69]."

The apprentice-training sites for the child growing up in the United States are many. He often learns to participate in decision making in the school setting. Class projects and other questions may be decided by majority vote. He plays with other children on the playground and the street, learning in games the importance of rules, the delights of competition, and the acceptance of losses. The many voluntary organizations for children, from Little League to the Boy Scouts, also teach the component skills, habits, behaviors, and practices pertinent to political activity. Apprenticeship training is not necessarily restricted to children, however, but occurs throughout life in any setting where the skills and attitudes gained have transferability to the political world.

Generalization refers to the important implications that a person's belief system has in shaping his political outlook. Think of the system of beliefs Mrs. Johnson or Mr. McCormick acquired as they grew up in the black and white world of Dayville, as you read Sidney Verba's (1965) assertion about the importance of these general beliefs to their political concerns:

> Such basic belief dimensions as the view of man's relation to nature, as time perspective, as the view of human nature and of the proper way to orient toward one's fellow man, as well as toward activity and activism in general would be clearly interdependent with specifically political attitudes [pp. 521–22].

One's optimism or cynicism about one's fellow man is likely to generalize to either a friendly interest in things political or a deep distrust of politics and politicians. Likewise, a sense of personal competence will likely lead to belief in one's own political efficacy. In short, many aspects of one's political orientation, in addition to those relating to authority, stem from social encounters that are not obviously political.

Direct Political Socialization

A great deal of attention has been paid to the learning of specifically political knowledge and attitudes. Public opinion polls have documented the kinds of information people have about the operation of government and various issues of the day. In spite of diverse opportunities for political learning, most U. S. citizens fall far short of the democratic ideal of alert, informed, and active participants.

The low level of information of most citizens was documented by Alfred Hero (in Robinson *et al.*, 1968), who summarized the trends in public opinion regarding political issues over a span of 30 years. Hero found that the majority of Americans pay little atttention to either domestic or international issues. Whether questioned about the Marshall Plan, farm policy, or government initiatives in race relations, many Americans have little awareness of the subject. Amount of knowledge about all aspects of government is strongly related to the respondent's level of education.

There is some evidence, Hero found, that increasing educational attainment in the United States is improving the distribution of information. The chronic "know nothings," for example, have declined from 35% of the poll respondents in the late 1930s to 15–20% in the late 1960s. Television seems not to have lived up to its promise as an educationally uplifting medium of communication since, Hero (1968) reported, the "gaps between different educational background groups in knowledge have remained at least as wide in the 1960's as they were in the 1930's and early 1940's [p. 39]." He concluded that the observed increases in public understanding have resulted from a greater proportion of better-educated citizens rather than better-informed members of the grade school educated and high school drop-out groups.

Much of the research in political socialization has been devoted to the study of children's attitudes. Hess and Torney (1967), for example, reported data from interviews with 12,000 school children in grades two through eight in *The Development of Political Attitudes in Children*. It is impossible to discuss their very extensive findings here, but I think their observations regarding the child's beginning political involvement are particularly significant. The child's first involvement, they found, is "a strong positive attachment to the country . . . [it is] essentially an emotional tie [p. 213]." This attachment develops early and persists throughout the elementary school years. Children see the United States as an ideal country, superior to all others.

This initial emotional attachment to country begins a long process of political socialization. Growth of political attitudes, information, and identification is particularly rapid during grade school, but learning and change do occur in the high school years and throughout adult life (Jennings and Niemi, 1968). As the person's roles in life change with age, so do his political attitudes, from twelfth grade right through the life span. Even in the adult years, Jennings and Niemi found "sizeable alterations in political interest and activities, in the conceptualization of political parties and attachment to them, in the differential saliency of political systems, in the relative emphasis on various citizenship norms, and in overall political cynicism and objects of political trust [pp. 159–60]."

There are at least four ways in which direct learning about the political environment occurs (Dawson and Prewitt, 1969). These are: (1) imitation, (2) anticipatory socialization, (3) political education, and (4) political experiences. I have already mentioned *imitation*, whch is based upon copying an adult with whom the child identifies. One example of such imitation is in choice of political party. A number of studies have shown that there is a strong correspondence between parents and children in party preference. However, one critic—Connell—questions whether many other political attitudes are learned through direct imitation of parental models.

Connell (1972) surveyed studies done between 1930 and 1965 of the correspondence between parents' and children's attitudes. While there was a strong similarity between parent and child in political party preference, there was less correspondence on a whole range of social issues. Referring only to those studies that used adequate research methods, Connell found a surprising lack of parent–child correspondence on attitudes toward war and communism, political involvement, prejudice, achievement, and family roles. He concluded that with the exception of party choice, the parents' specific opinions were largely irrelevant to those expressed by their children.

Connell's explanation for his findings was that the child's experiences with groups and institutions, rather than direct transmission from parent to child, shape political attitudes. Thus, by this interpretation at least, direct political learning must be more a function of *anticipatory socialization, education,* and *political experience* than of imitation. These three processes all involve more directly society's indoctrination of the child into the political system. *Anticipatory socialization* refers to the observed tendency of an individual who aspires to a higher social position to adopt the values and attitudes typical of people in that position long before the individual himself reaches the position. Thus, medical students begin to act like doctors in their first year of medical school. A young man from the working class with strong upward mobility aspirations, then, is likely to adopt in advance the more conservative attitudes typical of the middle class. The school child, by like reasoning, is likely to anticipate the attitudes and behavior of a "good citizen," as he imagines them to be.

Political education refers to direct, deliberate attempts to teach political ideas. We think primarily of the schools in this respect, though the family is also a teaching agent, as are political parties, governmental agencies, and other organizations. The American Legion, for example, sponsors an annual *Boys State* in Maine for high school students. The students participate in election of a governor, in a mock legislature, and so on.

One of the commonest forms of political education in the United States is the high school civics course. There is some doubt about the influence of such courses, however. Litt (1963) found that the civics course did have some effect on attitudes toward democratic processes and other political beliefs, but, in the main, only when the teachings were supported by the norms of other agents of political learning in the community. For example, the civics education curriculum had no effect on attitudes toward the political participation of citizens. Litt concluded that attitudes toward participation were formed by contact with community norms, which are much more powerful than the classroom teaching. Another study (Langton and Jennings, 1968) showed that civics courses had different effects on white and black students.

Courses in American government are designed to enhance political information, the individual's sense of political effectiveness, his patriotism, and the student's attitudes toward political participation. What Langton and Jennings found was that the average white high school student already knew most of those things. The civics course had little influence on these students. Blacks, on the other hand, were found to alter their political views after taking such courses. The investigators explained the difference in this manner: to the blacks, learning about government and politics is new, presenting them with issues and ideas not part of their previous experience. To the middle-class white youth, the value of "civics" is marginal because of his broader exposure in terms of family discussion, travel, and reading matter available in the home.

The teacher is thought to be a significant transmitter of political attitudes, although some observers question whether the teacher's influence is entirely beneficial. Sears (1968) for example, has questioned the tendency of many teachers to downgrade political partisanship, in light of the real and important conflicts about policy that are an essential part of political life. Unfortunately, teachers tend to act as conveyors of community consensus, rather than as stimulators of independent political thought. Teachers themselves are likely to be "conservators of traditional values," if not necessarily politically conservative. One study of high school teachers, for example, found 42% of the teachers accepted the following as a statement of *fact* (Ziegler, 1966, cited in Dawson and Prewitt, 1969, p. 161): "The American form of government may not be perfect, but it is the best type of government yet devised by man." Of all the teachers surveyed, including those who considered the statement an "opinion," 97% believed the view was one that could be freely expressed in the classroom. The classroom atmosphere is also an important function of the teacher. He or she may encourage student participation and active learning, or may insist on disciplined submission to a prearranged learning plan.

The final type of direct experience, the actual political experiences of the growing child or young adult, vary tremendously. Some young people do have opportunity for first-hand observation of political processes, others do not. Changes in adults' conceptions of politics are more likely to be influenced by such direct experiences.

Learning and Political Culture

Growing up in Dayville, Florida, or in a village in Mexico, the child acquires orientations toward government which are peculiar to his own community. In the previous section, we were concerned with *how* the child acquires such general orientations and specific knowledge in the

United States. There are considerable differences among communities within this country, and even greater differences among countries in *what* the child learns. I am referring to differences in *political culture*. The following discussion focuses on the differences in political culture among nations, but insofar as there are regional differences within one country, as between North and South in the United States, the same principles apply.

The Civic Culture, by Almond and Verba (1965), is a study of political attitudes in five countries—the United States, Britain, Germany, Italy, and Mexico. Their comparisons of the countries lead Almond and Verba to distinguish three distinctive types of political culture. They use the term *culture* in the sense of the individual's *psychological orientation* toward the political system in which he lives. The political culture of a society is "the political system as internalized in the cognitions, feelings, and evaluations of its population [p. 13]." The three types of culture, then, refer to the beliefs and attitudes held by citizens living under three types of political system. The cultures are termed the *parochial political culture,* the *subject political culture,* and the *participant political culture.* Consideration of these cultures is important for comparing different nations and, more important for our purposes, for distinguishing three ways in which a citizen can relate to his government. It is these distinctive forms of relatedness that I want to emphasize.

None of the three types of political culture which Almond and Verba hypothesize is found in its pure form in any particular country. Rather, the parochial, subject, or participant orientations should be seen as "ideal types," each being a different system of attitudes toward government. In order to discuss variations in these attitude structures, I want to emphasize the *object* in Rokeach's (1968) definition of an attitude as "a relatively enduring organization of beliefs around an object. . . [p. 112]." Just what are the objects around which political attitudes are focused? Almond and Verba (1965) have suggested four aspects of government, four "political objects" if you will, which provide a basis for comparison from country to country.

The first object is the *political system of one's nation as a general object.* What knowledge does the citizen have about his country, its history, its place in the world, and so on? Is he proud of his country? What other evaluations, feelings, and opinions does he express about his country?

The second object of a citizen's attitudes concerns his view of *who does what* to get things done. Who are the people who have "input," what kinds of channels or structures exist, how are laws made and policies stated that will ultimately affect the individual and his family? These are referred to as *input objects.*

As you might expect, the third class of objects to be considered is termed *output objects.* The output of a governmental system involves the implementation of laws, policies, and other decisions. The individual's treatment by courts, the police, and by government officials are outputs from the citizen's perspective. He may view governmental activity as helpful or harmful to himself, or he may have very little awareness of these outputs.

Finally, the fourth object, *the self as a participant in governmental affairs* is an object about which attitudes may vary. How does the citizen see himself in relation to the local and national system? Can he influence government? Does he believe that he has rights, duties, or obligations? Does he feel that his participation is necessary, or expected, or does he see himself as a passive spectator?

Each of the political cultures, as a pure type, involves a particular pattern of reactions to these four political objects. Table 4–1 represents the typical reactions of persons socialized in the parochial, subject, or participant cultures, as presented by Almond and Verba. Refer carefully to the two-way matrix shown in the table as you read my description of the three cultures. You will see that it is a simple, ingenious way of think-

Table 4–1 Patterns of orientation to four political objects in the different types of political culture

| TYPE OF POLITICAL CULTURE | OBJECTS | | | |
	(1) The System as a General Object	(2) "Inputs"	(3) "Outputs"	(4) Self as Participant
Parochial	0	0	0	0
Subject	1	0	1	0
Participant	1	1	1	1

Source: Adapted from *The Civic Culture: Political Attitudes and Democracy in Five Nations,* by Gabriel A. Almond and Sidney Verba (copyright © 1963 by Princeton University Press), published for the Center of International Studies, Princeton University: Table 2, p. 17. (Table I.2, p. 17, in the Little, Brown paperback edition, 1965.)

ing about different ways a citizen can relate to his government. I shall begin with the parochial culture.

A *parochial* culture can be conceived as the most primitive orientation to government. Note that the entries in the parochial row of Table 4–1 are all zeros. The political "system" in parochial cultures is so simple and unobtrusive that the individual doesn't think twice about whether it exists: "In these societies there are no specialized political roles: headmanship, chieftainship, 'shamanship' are diffuse political-economic-religious roles, and for members of these societies the political orientations to these roles are not separated from their religious and social orientations [p. 17]." A parochial does not expect anything of his political "system" because he is unaware, or in more differentiated societies only dimly aware on a feeling level, of the existence of a political regime. Comparatively speaking, the Mexican villager who feels hostility rather than loyalty to the national government and whose only sense of obligation is to his own village and its customs, is closest to the parochial culture among the five nations studied. (Although some similar tendencies to folk culture are said to be found in the south of Italy as well.) In any event, the zero entries for parochial cultures require little further explanation: How can one have attitudes toward objects that do not exist?

The second, or the next higher, type of political culture, is the *subject culture*. The term conveys its meaning adequately: One is *subject* to the crown, the emphasis being on loyalty, dedication to the ruler, and the rewards appropriate to loyal service. Thus, clear attitudes toward the governmental system are present, as represented by a "1" in that column, and toward one's treatment under that system as represented by the "1" in the output column. But the typical subject does not think of himself as being able to change, or make any input into, the system, nor does he think of himself as an active participant. As Almond and Verba have aptly noted: "it is essentially a passive relationship [pp. 17–18]." Insofar as it has retained the monarchy and all of its institutional trappings, Great Britain has a subject culture. Of course, the British political culture as it exists today contains lively participant traditions, as well.

The *participant culture* "is one in which the members of the society tend to be explicitly oriented to the system as a whole and to both the political and administrative structures and processes [p. 18]." The activist traditions of the United States perhaps best exemplify the participant culture. Of course, any society represents a "mix" of these different orientations, which both pertain to individual differences among citizens and the heterogeneity of the political structures of the various countries.

A political structure may be maladaptive for the society. For example, a model parliamentary democracy could be set up in a small African country whose political culture is mixed parochial and subject. Difficulties are to be anticipated in such a situation since the attitudes of the citizenry do not correspond to the demands for active participation imposed by the structure of the system. "In general," Almond and Verba pointed out, "a parochial, subject, or participant culture would be most congruent with, respectively, a traditional political structure, a centralized authoritarian structure, and a democratic political structure [p. 20]."

CONCLUSION

Politics is not a central concern for most people. Because of their concern with the subject, writers on political socialization tend to leave the impression that political concerns are more salient (that is, important in relation to the individual's other preoccupations) than they actually are. When interviewed about their political beliefs, people do try hard to please the interviewer, but their answers leave doubt as to the amount of consideration they have given to the topic. Family, recreational pursuits, peer relations, and self-interest in terms of personal goals all tend to overshadow political thinking, even in a "democratic" society such as that of the United States.

This lack of centrality of political concerns is shown at all age levels. Hess and Torney's (1967) extensive investigation of political socialization in the child showed gradually increasing accuracy of perceptions of the governmental system. Such studies do not, however, tell us much about the importance of such knowledge to the child. Young people certainly do try hard to answer the questions put to them, as indicated by the response of a second-grade boy when asked whether he would rather be an Englishman or an American:

> Well, I wouldn't like to be an Englishman because I wouldn't like to talk their way, and I'd rather be an American because they have better toys, because they have better things, better stores, and better beds and blankets, and they have better play guns, and better boots, and mittens and coats, and better schools and teachers [Hess and Torney, 1967, p. 27].

In another excerpt, an 11-year-old boy talks about the President:

> [What does the President do?]
> Well, he has to sign the laws, and they go through, You know . . .
> bills. If he doesn't sign it, why then it doesn't become a law. And, well,
> he's just like the President of a company; he does good things for the
> country and shows what he thinks would be best for it. I think he's O.K.

> [How do you think the President is different from most other men?]

> Well, I know he's a brave man and he has to be nice so the people like
> him and will vote for him; he's a higher class man so he's President, and
> I think any man could run for President but maybe all of them couldn't
> do as good a job as he could [pp. 4–5].

Hess and Torney have suggested that their observations of children illustrate a great emotional involvement of children with their country, its political system, and its leaders. Their suggestion of strong emotional involvements between a citizen and his country's political processes is a bit overstated, at the least. Observations of the primitive ideological orientations of adults in the United States support my assertion.

McCloskey (1964), for instance, found that the basic values and beliefs that undergird American democracy and the Constitution are supported mainly by a small minority of politically informed and active citizens. This conclusion was based on a comparison of the beliefs of delegates and alternates to the Democratic and Republican conventions in 1956 with the beliefs of a random sample of voters. Both the "influentials" (party workers) and the adults from the general public were interviewed by Gallup poll interviewers. The influentials were found to be markedly more "committed to liberal democracy and aware of the rights and obligations which attend that commitment," than was the average voter. Members of the general electorate tended to be more apathetic (62% agree that "Nothing I ever do seems to have any effect on what happens in politics," compared with 8% of the influentials) and to hold confused and contradictory beliefs about the meaning of democratic ideals.

McCloskey's observations on the incompleteness of socialization of the democratic public are supported by Sears's (1969) review of the public's political sophistication. Sears (1969, p. 337) concluded first that only the most important political personages and events are recognized by the general public. Many voters, for example, cannot recall even their Congressman's name. Second, few people seem to apply any ideological principles in their political deliberations. Half of the voting public, for example, has little or no comprehension of the terms "liberal" and "conservative." Furthermore, only about 10–15% of the public describes party differences in terms of liberal–conservative ideology, although 50% can correctly apply the labels to Democrats and Republicans when asked. Third, Sears reported that when asked about concrete policy issues—taxation, trade, or defense—most voters have shallow and unstated preferences. Attitudes on these issues are not systematically related in the minds of the average voter. Fourth, loyalty might be termed the most consistent characteristic of Mr. Average Voter's attitudes. Loyalty to his membership groups, and particularly his political party, is the most stable and meaningful aspect of the individual's belief system. The content of these group-selected attitudes does not focus on issues of policy, although a minority of voters does recognize the policy implications of these party commitments.

The point at issue is that politics plays a minor role for citizens of most countries. Apathy and ignorance is not confined to the United States. "It is difficult," McCloskey (1964) noted, "to imagine any circumstance, short of war or revolutionary crisis, in which the mass of men will evince more interest in the community's affairs than in their own concerns [p. 374]." He goes on to note that this lack of general interest is not necessarily selfishness but, rather, results from the remoteness of most political issues from a person's daily life. One could hardly expect the intense concern about abstract and intangible public affairs that the ordinary person displays in reacting to the immediate and compelling issues of everyday life. "Since many voters lack education, opportunity, or even tangible and compelling reasons for busying themselves with political ideas, they respond to political stimuli (if they respond at all) without much reflection or consistency [McCloskey, 1964, p. 374]."

PART III

Personality and Motivational Factors

5

Self-Esteem, Power, and Competence

> The ego consists of many attitudes which from infancy on are related to the delimited, differentiated and accumulating "I," "me," "mine" experiences.
>
> SHERIF and CANTRIL, *The Psychology of Ego-Involvements*, 1947

> Men like power so long as they believe in their own competence to handle the business in question, but when they know themselves incompetent they prefer to follow a leader.
>
> BERTRAND RUSSELL, *Power: A New Social Analysis*, 1938

Self, or ego, refers to the sense of selfhood that forms the core of personality. I shall use these terms interchangeably to refer to the central attitudes that constitute a person's identity. The self is a major point of reference in any person's cognitive system. I write as I do because I am a psychologist, a professor, a father, and husband, and a sometime political activist. Many of my beliefs and opinions are *ego involved*. That is, they are closely related to my sense of self. This is not to draw any special attention to myself, but to emphasize that any actor in any situation is, with rare exceptions, behaving in accordance with his own self-conception. The responses of a politician, a voter, a student, or a factory worker depend upon who he is and how he compares himself to others with whom he is interacting.

One's sense of selfhood is not inborn. Nor does it necessarily await the development of language. At birth, the infant probably does not distinguish self from not self. Gradually, through experience with his own inner sensations, as well as the sights, sounds, and feelings coming from outside himself, the infant acquires a primitive identity. This process of differentiation of the sense of "I," "me," "mine," was aptly described by Murphy, Murphy, and Newcomb (1937). Their description is as appropriate now as when it was written many years ago:

> The thing known as the self is a selection and organization of experiences involving the visceral tensions, muscular strains, the sound of one's name, one's mirror image, and so on; and the thing which knows this pattern is simply the organism as a whole. . . . As the primitive, vague, ill-defined experience of personal identity gives place to a more well-defined experience, as the individual learns where his own existence stops and the rest of the world begins, the self in the accepted narrow sense is born and becomes an *empirical object* toward which the attitudes of the organism are built up, just as attitudes are built up toward anything else. The self is lovable; it is also hateful; it is something to guard and protect against injury; it is also something to be disparaged, condemned and punished [pp. 209–11].

The self is a product of interaction with the social world, as well as with the physical world. In addition to the simple perception of oneself as an object, the self reflects evaluations and comparisons with other people. One's self-conception is strongly rooted in group membership, as shown by Kuhn and McPartland's (1954) study. They asked college students to write twenty answers to the question: "Who am I?" The students tended to describe themselves first in terms of group and social-class membership, e.g., man, student, Catholic, son, or husband. Later items were couched in more evaluative terms such as good student, happy, pretty, not very handsome, and so on. The way in which other people regard us is central to our self-pictures. The extreme statement of this point was Cooley's assertion that the most important determinant of a person's self-concept is how he thinks other people think of him. Cooley (1902) said: "A social self of this sort might be called the reflected or looking-glass self":

> Each to each a looking glass
> Reflects the other that doth pass.

To Cooley, one's *self-esteem* was largely "founded upon the opinions of others." My own position is that self-esteem is based on objective indications of one's worth; that is, on one's achievements and competence, as well as on "reflections" from other people. Everyone strives to maintain a positive image of himself; or, in other words, to maintain high *self-esteem*. One's self-esteem is based partially upon the regard in which one is held by others, but it also is dependent upon one's subjective feelings of *competence*. William James (1961) suggested that one's self-esteem could be expressed as a ratio of our accomplishments to the things that we think we can do:

$$\text{Self-Esteem} = \frac{\text{Success}}{\text{Pretensions}}$$

". . . our self-feeling in this world depends entirely on what we *back* ourselves to be and do [p. 54]," James observed. Thus, one can, to some extent, raise his self-esteem by lowering his aspirations (pretensions), as well as by succeeding at more difficult tasks.

The relationship between self-esteem and political behavior was first stated clearly by Harold Lasswell (1948), as I noted in Chapter 2. The *political personality*, Lasswell thought, chooses to accentuate power over other possible values. The underlying reason for this emphasis on power is compensation for feelings of inferiority. "Power," Lasswell (1948) wrote, "*is expected to overcome low estimates of the self*, by changing either the traits of the self or the environment in which it functions [p. 39; italics in original]."

The chain of causality that seems to be implied in Lasswell's writing begins with low self-esteem, which in turn leads to the striving for power. Then follows the seeking of positions of influence, the assessment of social situations with regard to their potential for fulfilling this desire for influence, and the acquisition of the necessary knowledge and skills to achieve political goals. Although there is some doubt whether they occur in this exact sequence, there is considerable evidence linking the elements of Lasswell's model to political activism. These elements—self-esteem, motivation, competence, expectancies, and opportunity—are examined in the pages that follow. I begin the discussion by examining the relationship between self-esteem and political behavior.

SELF-ESTEEM AND POLITICAL PERSONALITY

Many current writers present evidence in contradiction to Lasswell's hypothesis that low self-esteem leads to power seeking and thence to political activity. Barber (1965), for example, has suggested that high

Personality and Motivational Factors

self-esteem leads to political activity: "The more healthy, efficacious and confident a person is, the more he participates in politics [p. 217]."

There is considerable evidence for Barber's assertion. Campbell *et al.* (1960), for example, found that the citizens most likely to vote are those highest in personal efficacy, which they thought related to positive self-evaluation. Other researchers have found that people with high self-esteem are more likely to be politically active (Milbrath and Klein, 1962) and more interested in public affairs (Rosenberg, 1962).

On the other hand, Lasswell's case studies and the assessment of President Wilson's biographical data by George and George (1963) tend to support the Lasswell hypothesis. Ziller's findings, which are described shortly, also suggest that *low* self-esteem may often be found in success-ful political activists. Barber (1965) has suggested a resolution of these contradictory findings regarding self-esteem and politics in terms of the *participation hypothesis.*

The participation hypothesis emphasizes variation in the *nature,* as well as the *quantity,* of political participation. In Barber's (1965) words, there is

> . . . a marked discontinuity between minor forms of political participa-tion, on the one hand, and running for or holding public office, on the other. The former represent a collection of relatively widesperad, general activities, while the latter are restricted to a small, specialized segment of the population. There are reasons for believing that at the level of citizen politics, self-esteem and participation are strongly related, while at the official level the picture is mixed [p. 219].

Barber's observation of state legislators suggested that some of them did seem to be trying to compensate for low self-estimates, while others were secure and self-confident. The selection of such different types is related to the change in life style entailed in entry into the legislator's role.

Most legislators are people who have worked in various careers, usually business, law, or another profession. Entering political office, Barber suggested, is often a significant departure from the person's pre-vious occupation: "Insofar as such a step depends upon deeper motives, it is likely to be taken by two kinds of people: those who have such *high* self-esteem that they can manage relatively easily the threats and strains and anxieties involved in this change; and those who have such *low* self-esteem that they are ready to do this extraordinary thing to raise it [pp. 223–24]."

Insofar as it proposes multiple determinants of political activity, Barber's participation hypothesis seems plausible to the contemporary psychologist. However, Barber's observations, as were Lasswell's, were based upon interviews. The psychologist is reluctant to place all his trust in clinical inferences about self-esteem or any other character disposition. We are more comfortable with objective *measurements* of such traits. Ziller's (1973) theory of self–other orientation is based on such *operational* definitions of self-esteem and other variables. Since some evidence is available regarding the relation of these self-variables to political activity, I shall discuss the theory at some length.

Self–Other Orientation

Ziller's (1973) theory of self–other orientation takes as a starting point the individual's perceived relationship to others. In particular, the theory emphasizes definition of the self with reference to the individual's social context. Ziller has developed some rather ingenious ways of measuring these self-perceptions and of demonstrating their psychological importance.

MEASURING SELF-ESTEEM. The measurement of self–other orientation utilizes diagrams that represent the ways in which people think about themselves in relation to others. The basic approach owes much to Kurt Lewin's (1935) notion that psychological situations can be represented by means of diagrams on a two-dimensional surface. Lewin spoke of these as *topological* diagrams; I have previously referred to his diagram of the life space (see Chapter 3). There is considerable evidence that responses to simple diagrams or the placement of figures on a background does give evidence of one's social "schemata."

DeSoto *et al.* (1965), for example, found that people tend to order stimuli according to decreasing value either in left–right or vertical arrays. Also, Keuthe (1964) has shown that people use "social schemata" in ordering their perceptions of their social world. Based on these findings, Ziller began exploring the use of diagrams to represent the person's concept of himself in relation to his social environment. [In addition to self-esteem, "social interest" and "self-centrality" have been explored through the use of geometric representations (see Ziller, 1973).] Self-esteem, for example, is measured by the person's response to items like those shown in Figure 5–1. The person is asked to place a letter representing himself in one of the six circles in the horizontal array, along with letters repre-

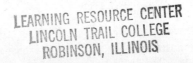

The circles below stand for people. Mark each circle with the letter standing for one of the people in the list. Do this in any way you like, but use each person only once and do not omit anyone.

F — someone who is flunking   S — yourself
H — the happiest person you know Su — someone you know who is
K — someone you know who is kind   successful
                                 St — the strongest person you know

Figure 5–1   Item for measurement of self-esteem (Adaptation of Fig. 1 from Robert C. Ziller *et al.*, "Self-esteem: A self–social construct." *Journal of Consulting and Clinical Psychology*, 1969, *33*, 85. Copyright © 1968 by The American Psychological Association. Used by permission of publisher and author.)

senting five other significant people. Several such items are typically used, each containing a different set of "others." Another item, for example, includes: "doctor, father, friend, mother, yourself, teacher."

Ziller's research has established that positions to the left of the array of circles are associated with higher esteem. A person's self-esteem score for a particular item is the position he uses for *self*, counted from the right. For example, if he puts the letter "S" in the third circle from the left, he would receive a score of four for that item. Scores are summed over six such items to yield the subject's total self-esteem (SE) score. People tend to be rather consistent in their self-placements, that is the self-esteem score is reliable. There also seems to be evidence that self-esteem measured in this way is meaningful. For example, popular individuals (sociometric "stars" in the classroom) have higher SE than do their less socially desired classmates (Ziller *et al.*, 1964).

The importance of this scheme for political psychology is easily explained. Although there are a great many measures of self-esteem (Wylie, 1961), the measures are generally based on self-report. That is, the person is asked to describe himself in terms of trait adjectives (e.g., humorous, stingy, fair, reasonable) or in terms of descriptive statements ("Although I am shy, I am compelled to speak out when I see someone wronged"). Even if the person tries to answer honestly, self-reports are likely to be biased by tendencies to self-delusion, as well as by the natural tendency to put oneself in as good a social light as possible. Given the extra pressures operating on political figures, some type of indirect measure seems necessary to study the role of self-esteem in the politician's behavior.

Ziller's topographical technique overcomes many of the difficulties posed by self-report. It is in some respects a *projective* technique. That is, the ordinary person is not aware of the significance attributed to his self-placements. Thus, not only is a person less defensive in filling out the questionnaire, he is more likely to agree to fill it out in the first place.[1]

PERSONALITY AND POLITICAL SUCCESS. The first study of political candidates using the topographical measure of self-esteem was conducted in Oregon. Ziller (1969) was able to secure the cooperation of ninety-one candidates for election to the Oregon State Legislature. The candidates filled out questionnaires both before and after the election, so that changes in self-concept of winning and losing candidates could be studied. As might be expected, there were changes from before to after the election. Fifteen of the twenty-three winners showed increased self-esteem, with only four showing a decrease. Eleven of the twenty-one losers, however, decreased in self-esteem. These significant results were encouraging with regard to the validity of the construct of social self-esteem. The central question, however, concerned the relation of self-esteem to winning or losing the election.

There was a tendency for candidates with low self-esteem to be elected more often (twenty-eight out of forty-one) as opposed to twenty-seven out of fifty high self-esteem candidates). The findings were not statistically significant, however. It was necessary to consider another aspect of the individual's self–other orientation in the prediction of a candidate's success. This aspect of the self-concept, *complexity*, had also been assessed in the questionnaires filled out by the legislative candidates.

Complexity of the self-concept is defined as the number of different facets of self perceived by the person. It is measured by the number of adjectives, from a list of 110, which the person checks as being characteristic of himself. Theoretically, the individual who perceives himself as complex has more possible ways of relating to other people. Ziller and his co-workers have shown (1970) that complex individuals report more identification with other people and with groups. They also see themselves as more similar to others and enjoy greater popularity.

The joint effects of self-esteem and complexity were significantly related to the election or nonelection of the Oregon candidates. The results, which hold even with incumbency controlled, are reported in

---

[1] In a study I am currently conducting, forty-five of the forty-nine state legislators who were approached agreed to fill in a self–other inventory.

Table 5–1 Percentage of candidates elected to Oregon Legislature as a function of self-esteem and self-complexity *

		SELF-ESTEEM	
		High	Low
COMPLEXITY OF SELF-CONCEPT	High	28% (18)	88% (16)
	Low	69% (32)	56% (25)

* Total N's for each cell shown in parentheses.
Source: Adapted from data reported by Robert Ziller *et al.,* "The Political Personality," unpublished manuscript, University of Oregon, 1969.

Table 5–1. Fifty-five of the ninety-one candidates included in the sample won election; that is, 60% of those who had filled out the questionnaire were successful. Neither the thirty-two candidates who were high in self-esteem and low in complexity, nor the twenty-five who had low scores on both variables deviated significantly from 60%. The interesting deviations from the average success rate were found in the two categories of politicians who were *high* on complexity.

Low self-esteem when paired with high complexity resulted in significantly greater success: 88% of the candidates with this personality pattern were elected. Because such a person seems to be particularly successful, Ziller suggested that low self-esteem coupled with high complexity characterizes the *political personality.* Only 28% of the candidates high in self-esteem and high in complexity won their elections, indicating *lack* of voter appeal. Thus, Ziller suggested the term *apolitical* for the latter personality pattern.

RESPONSIVENESS AND THE POLITICAL PERSONALITY. The *political personality,* defined by those traits which lead to election (or good probability of election) in a state legislative race, is low in self-esteem and has a complex self-concept. The apolitical personality, in Ziller's terminology, is the person who is unsuccessful, but not politically uninvolved. This personality type is characterized by high self-esteem and high complexity. What accounts for these findings?

Ziller suggested that the "political" person is more *responsive* than his apolitical counterpart. Responsivity is a joint function of the *desire* to relate to other people and the *ability* to relate to others. These two characteristics stem from low self-esteem and high complexity.

A person with low self-esteem is thought to have a less stable basis for self-evaluation. Thus, he is more likely to try to adapt to other people, to change his self-presentation according to the group in which he finds himself. As contrasted with the high self-esteem individual, who could be considered stubborn or inflexible, the person with low self-regard is like a reed in the wind. Taken by itself, however, self-esteem does not predict political success; the crucial factor seems to be added by self-complexity.

The more complex person, according to Ziller (1973), is more able to find points of similarity with other people. Thus, the political personality, according to the theory of self–other orientation and the supporting findings, is successful because of his responsivity. He is responsive because of his tendency to conform to social pressures and to adapt to different social situations by modification of his self-presentation, his ability to perceive similarities between himself and others, and his tendency to emphasize these similarities.

It is interesting that this picture of the "responsive" politician is so close to the popular stereotype. Two reservations should be emphasized. First, it may be genuine points of similarity that are emphasized by the politician. Second, this is but one study with some uncontrolled factors. Therefore, the findings must be considered tentative. It is also quite likely, as I have previously noted, that there are important differences among candidates for local, state, and national offices.

That Ziller's findings cannot be dismissed as a fluke stemming from conditions in one election, however, is shown by his data on school personnel. Using the same two self-concept variables, Ziller (1969) tested Oregon school teachers, principals, and superintendents. His hypothesis was that the personalities of incumbent superintendents would be similar to those of successful politicians, reasoning that the role demands of school superintendency involve the same kind of responsivity. That is, the superintendents must walk a tightrope, trying to satisfy at one and the same time the demands of teachers, school boards, taxpayers, and parents (Gross *et al.*, 1958). The numbers in each category having the nonpolitical personality (high SE, high complexity) were: teachers, 27%; principals, 27%; and superintendents, 9%. The "political personality pattern" was present in 20%, 19%, and 25% of the teachers, principals, and superintendents, respectively.

These results with regard to school personnel suggest that the apolitical person is more distinctive than the "political." That is, very few superintendents (four in forty-four, or 9%) are of the high SE–high complexity pattern. The person having this personality type, according to Ziller, is the least responsive of all.

The example of Ziller's research shows the promise that study of the self-concept holds for future understanding of political candidates. While his research deals with electoral success, self-esteem and other self-social variables may also be related to political participation and to the motivation to become a candidate. We return to the participation question in Chapter 9; the relationship of self-conception to motivation is discussed in the section that follows.

SOCIAL MOTIVATION: THE SEARCH FOR COMPETENCE

Many possible psychological mechanisms can be invoked as explanations for variations in behavior. The oldest and most pervasive explanatory concepts are motives, drives, and urges. What these terms have in common is the idea of an internal force that pushes the individual to behave in certain ways. Thus, a motive is thought to be *activating* and to *direct* the individual toward certain goals. An example of the activating and directing functions of motives is the case of the hungry man who begins fidgeting and then stirs himself toward the refrigerator.

The specific motives that have been suggested over the years range in character from Freud's libido, the sexual instinct which he thought provided the driving force for all behavior, to Abraham Maslow's concept of the need for self-actualization. In spite of all of the effort expended in the century since psychology became an experimental science, the term *motive* remains ambiguous. Some psychologists avoid the use of the concept altogether (Skinner, 1953).

If we avoid past theoretical controversies, however, it is possible to elaborate a theory of motivation that is in agreement with the known facts and that promises to be useful in understanding political behavior. In discussing what I call *effectance theory*, I shall concentrate on the *competence motives*, including achievement, affiliation, and power, all of which are based on the effectance need.

The use of the term "motive" seems warranted for a number of reasons. McClelland (1965) has defined motive as an affectively charged associative network. That is, it involves a whole network or system of ideas, beliefs, and wants of the individual. When a person has a strong, driving concern in life whether it be for power, achievement, or affiliation, this dominant motive serves to organize and integrate almost everything he does. Thus, such motives integrate the part-processes of character that were discussed in Chapter 3. A strong power motive will affect not only the person's self-concept (identity), but also his beliefs and ways of thinking (cognitive) and his emotional orientation.

The power motive is one of a whole series of competence motives, which also includes the achievement and affiliation motives. A complete listing is unnecessary since the specific motives learned reflect the concerns of the social groups to which the individual belongs. My view of human motivation, which follows McClelland's (1955, 1965) theory of motivation to a considerable degree, is that *all motives are learned.* This proposition, of course, must be clarified since I have already spoken of unlearned tendencies determined by the structure and function of the human organism. While I do not minimize the effects of basic biological (tissue) needs, such as needs for food and water, the manifestations of these needs in social behavior are greatly modified by learning. Thus, the statement "all motives are learned" applies to hunger and sex, as well as to more distinctively social motives. As an illustration of this point, let me call the reader's attention to the rather direct satisfaction of sex and hunger needs in the dog, cat, or even the chimpanzee. Compare this direct satisfaction with the elaborate customs and rituals surrounding eating and dating behavior that are found in the human species. The implications of this view of motivation will become clearer as I discuss the competence and power motives.

Competence and the Effectance Motive

In a very influential paper, Robert White (1959) reviewed evidence from several sources ranging from animal psychology to the psychoanalytic writers in support of his belief that a very basic and universal human tendency is the striving for competence.

> Repeatedly we find reference to the familiar series of learned skills which starts with sucking, grasping, and visual exploration and continues with crawling and walking, acts of focal attention and perception, memory, language and thinking, anticipation, the exploring of novel places and

objects, effecting stimulus changes in the environment, manipulating and exploiting the surroundings, and achieving higher levels of motor and mental coordination [p. 317].

White (1959) proposed that these varied activities of the growing child could all be classed under the heading of *competence*. These behaviors, reflective of the need for effective interaction with the environment, are "directed, selective, and persistent [p. 318]" and thereby fit the criteria for motivated behavior.

COMPETENCE AND INFERIORITY. Freud spoke at times of a need for *mastery*, a term that also conveys the idea of effective interaction with one's environment. It was a one-time colleague of Freud, however, who made the person's feelings of effectiveness vis-à-vis other people the cornerstone of his psychological theory. Alfred Adler's clinical observations led him increasingly away from Freud's emphasis on the instinctual bases of human interaction. More and more, Adler (1938) saw in his cases a social basis for psychological problems. In his psychoanalytic practice, Adler encountered many patients who expressed wishes to control, win over, and similarly dominate other people. In these wishes, he saw an overall tendency to strive for social superiority. In particular, Adler found a recurring pattern, which he termed the *inferiority complex*.

The child's feelings of inferiority are grounded in his infant experience of weakness and dependence, but are also affected by his own special abilities or weaknesses. Adler spoke of various *organ inferiorities* (i.e., physical deficiencies) which may contribute to the child's sense of helplessness. All persons experience infant dependence and various physical weaknesses, but the way in which the child learns to cope with these experiences determines his later adaptation. A seemingly able child, for example, may incorrectly estimate his abilities because of parental criticism or competition with older siblings. The consequent inferiority complex, a pattern of persistent self-doubt and low self-estimation, will have serious and far-reaching consequences for this person's future development. The exact nature of such consequences depends upon the mechanisms adopted by the child to offset his feelings of inferiority.

One way of dealing with one's personal inadequacies is by *compensation*. A child who is physically puny, for example, may compensate by excelling in his school work. Often, however, intense feelings of inferiority lead the child to go beyond mere compensation; the child *overcompensates* for his inferiority. Overcompensation, according to Adler, often involves both fantasies and actual attempts to dominate other people. In some individuals, such overcompensation results in striving for power and dominance that may reach remarkable extremes, as in the cases of Napoleon Bonaparte and Theodore Roosevelt. Napoleon, you may remember, was a pint-sized man whose dreams of domination led him to tremendous feats of military conquest. Roosevelt, a weak and sickly child, subjected himself to such discipline that he became a "Rough Rider," a big-game hunter, and an aggressive President.

Unfavorable comparisons of self with others certainly may result in feelings of inferiority. These feelings in turn may lead to overcompensation in the form of thinking and working for power over other people. It seems simpler to me, and more in accordance with contemporary research, to think of power striving in terms of competence. While power motivation may to some extent result from attempts to compensate for inferiority, I shall try to explain it as a direct outgrowth of the competence motive.

COMPETENCE AND EFFECTANCE. Heretofore, I have been using the terms *competence* and *effectance* indiscriminately. It is time to be more precise, so let me note the distinction White (1959) drew between the two terms. *Competence* is the capacity that a person attains for dealing with the physical and social environment. It is simply illustrated by reference to physical skills. The woodsman who can fell a tree within a foot or two of his chosen spot possesses a certain kind of acquired competence. The same woodsman may be incompetent when asked to write a letter or to mix a martini. All of us have competencies in some areas of life and difficulties in other areas. Some of us were muscular enough to hold our own in childhood games and competition, others excelled in school work, and still others found success in crafts. Whatever one's skills and shortcomings, everyone has a need to deal effectively with the environment. It seems useful to distinguish this basic need from the attained competencies; White has suggested we call it the need for *effectance*.

The effectance need is universally found in human beings; it grows out of an intrinsic need to deal effectively with the environment, a need man shares with other animals. The effectance need is first manifested in the playful acts of children. The infant, waving his arms aimlessly, chances to hit a rattle dangling over his crib. In a few minutes, he hits it again. The action may be repeated over and over again, in a way reminiscent of the "circular reflex" described by Allport (1924). That is, the *effect* the child has on his environment seems to reward the behavior that

Personality and Motivational Factors

preceded this effect. Playful behavior seems to have a function in developing the child's competence for dealing with the social environment, as well as the inanimate world. Various behaviors such as curiosity, exploration, and stimulation seeking are also attributable to the basic effectance need. It seems likely that stimulation of the organism's neural structure, along with the pleasurable effects of certain patterns of stimulation and the perceived sequences of stimulation–movement–consequence, are the rewards that lead from the diffuse effectance need to the attainment of competence.

Effectance as the Basis for Motives

Further argument for the existence of effectance needs and supporting evidence are to be found in White's (1959) paper. The primary points I want to make are that *effectance is a basic, unlearned tendency of organisms;* and *what we generally think of as "human" motives are learned elaborations from this base.* The differences observed among people, in preferences for interaction with, and control over, people or things and differences in the intensity of these preferences are learned. It is but a simple extension of David McClelland's (1965) theory of motivation to suggest that the underlying basis for achievement, power, affiliation, and other learned motives is the need for effectance.

These motives, which can be collectively referred to as the *competence* motives, are especially important to the understanding of political behavior.

Taking some liberties with McClelland's theory, I define a motive as a closely interrelated set of ideas, beliefs, and feelings oriented toward some goal, with strong emotional components. A motive is usually defined in terms of its aim: The achievement motive, the affiliation motive, and the power motive are commonly named because their goals seem to be pursued quite regularly by Western man. The basic postulates of the *effectance theory* of motivation are quite straightforward. First, *all motives are learned;* even such basic needs as hunger are expressed in learned motives produced by cultural and familial conditioning. Second, the motive tends to be aroused by certain *environmental cues.* Third, these cues tend to arouse *affect* (emotion). Finally, these environmental cues also arouse a particular set of *ideas and beliefs.* The role of learned motives in the expression of biological needs is evident in Stanley Schachter's (1971) recent work on obesity. Schachter's studies show that eating among fat people, much more than among people of normal weight, is governed by environmental cues. Seeing a refrigerator, looking at the clock, or observing other people eating arouses hunger in the obese. These cues have much less effect on people with more normal eating habits.

THE ACHIEVEMENT MOTIVE. The example of learned hunger motivation and the chain of motive arousal (cue → arousal of affect → associations → goal-directed activity) is also apparent in the motive most discussed by McClelland: the achievement motive. A person with high need for achievement (*n*Ach) responds to certain kinds of challenges (cues) in the environment. Since the cues most often discussed in connection with the achievement motive are those associated with business dealings, I shall use a business example:

> A businessman, operator of a small hotel in a town of 50,000 people, is approached with an offer to participate in a venture which holds the possibility of a large financial return. The venture involves construction and operation of a motel just outside a large city. The offer itself is not enough to arouse the achievement motivation of a person characteristically achievement oriented. Other cues must be present: (1) a moderate degree of risk (neither a sure thing nor a long-shot will engage our high *n*Ach businessman); (2) the opportunity to exercise his own skills, training, and judgment toward success of the venture; and (3) tangible signs of success or failure (making or losing money).

According to McClelland, the person high in achievement motivation values money, not so much for itself, but as a concrete indication of his accomplishment. When risk, opportunity, and tangible evidence of success are present, the achievement motive will be engaged. I think of the achievement motive, or any other sort of motive, as a sort of obsession. It consists of a network of ideas about achievement or power, along with strong ego involvements. The person who has a strong motive is not constantly spurred on by it. The motive exists in latent form at all times, but is operative only when the proper set of environmental cues are present. The businessman from the example above might express such ideas as:

> I am a capable person.
> I can manage a hotel so as to make it a going concern.
> My judgment is good.
> I would like to see if I can make a go of this.

Of course, realistic appraisals of probabilities such as knowledge of growth of the city in question, its traffic patterns, and so on, will enter into the businessman's assessment of risk and profit.

In his book *The Achieving Society*, McClelland (1961) has presented considerable evidence that the rise and fall of nations depends upon the overall level of achievement present among the country's people. If changes in achievement motivation can have such profound effects, it seems probable that power motivation is equally important in determining the fate of civilizations. Unfortunately, much less is known about the constellation of ideas that bound the power motive. It may be that power and its manifestations are much more idiosyncratic than is the achievement motive. I am proceeding, however, on the basis of the assumption that the power motive is similarly learned. Because of its centrality in the psychology of politics, I devote the following section to the power motive.

THE POWER MOTIVE

Many observers of political man have suggested that he is primarily motivated by power seeking. From the standpoint of political philosophy, Bertrand Russell (1938) argued that power is "the fundamental concept in social science . . . in the same sense in which Energy is the fundamental concept in physics [p. 10]." Russell defined power as "the production of intended effects" and suggested that while personal power could be sought as a means toward desirable ends, some men seek power as an end in itself.

The importance of power as a concept in political science was emphasized by Charles Merriam's (1934) survey of *Political Power*. Merriam anticipated the notion of high power motivation when he spoke of "power hungry personalities." Closer perhaps to modern psychological views is the approach taken by the political scientist Harold Lasswell. I have already discussed the centrality of power striving to Lasswell's (1948) conception of the political personality.

Psychologists have been concerned with the study of power for many years. As I have mentioned, Alfred Adler's conception of power motivation agreed with Lasswell's. Adler saw power seeking as a compensation for inferiority. In the universities of the United States, the study of power seems to have followed three major trends. The first of these is the study of *dominance–submission*. Empirical and theoretical work in this area has ranged from studies of dominance hierarchies in animal colonies (Maslow, 1936) to the investigation of ascendance–submission as personality traits (Allport, 1928). A second line of research involved the study of *power usage*, particularly in the small-group context. The group dynamics literature contains many examples; the article by French and Raven (1959) dealing with the bases of social power is one of the best. These authors made explicit the different ways in which one person gains power over another person or over a group. The power to deliver rewards (reward power) and the possession of information essential to a group (expert power) are two examples. Finally, there have been, in recent years, a number of attempts to subject *power motivation* to scientific scrutiny. Current research efforts in this area seem to be following the line of work begun by Joseph Veroff (1957).

Power in Fantasy

Veroff's approach to the study of power motivation is similar to that used by McClelland in the study of achievement motivation. That is, the power motive is inferred from the ideas expressed in imaginative stories written by the subjects under investigation. Veroff's study (1957) compared two groups of college students, one of which was selected because the members' desires for power and leadership were aroused. This group consisted of thirty-four candidates for student government positions at a large university, who were tested while waiting for the election ballots to be counted. The comparison group consisted of thirty-four men in an undergraduate psychology course. The students in each of the two groups were shown a series of five pictures of people in various settings and were asked to write imaginative stories based on each of the pictures.

After reading the stories written by both groups, Veroff developed a scoring system by means of which the degree of power motivation present in a person's stories could be quantified. The first thing to be identified in a story was *power imagery;* that is, a reference indicating that one of the characters is "concerned with the control of the means of influencing a person." If such imagery is present, additional points are added to the subject's score for that story for such things as expression of a need or of activity directed toward control of someone else. There may be isolated references to such power-related concerns, or the whole theme of the story may be power. Veroff (1958) gave an example of a story whose theme is power:

> Here are a number of workers for the Republican party. They have gathered together to outline the campaign. Each of them has been nominated for a post in the City Elections. Since they want to win the election, they have come together to plan the campaign. They are thinking of their chances for election and would like to win very much. To celebrate they throw a party [p. 233].

When the power motivation scores of the candidates and unselected psychology students were compared, there were indeed differences between the groups. Veroff (1957) found 65% of the candidates had high scores as compared with 26% of the unaroused psychology students. Evidently, the aspiring leaders thought more about power and control over other people and showed more emotional affect with regard to such issues. Thus, Veroff found preliminary evidence for the existence and measurability of the power motive.

INDIVIDUAL DIFFERENCES AND AROUSAL. The foregoing comparison is not definitive, however. Veroff (1957) assumed that the candidates' power motivation was aroused, and that the psychology students' was not. It could be that the former were initially higher in such concerns. In other words, the arousal and individual components of power motivation were "confounded," or inextricably mixed, in Veroff's study.

Fortunately, Veroff also investigated individual differences among the unaroused group of subjects. He had administered several psychological inventories in addition to the story test to these subjects and also had obtained ratings of classroom behavior from the students' instructors. His findings suggest that measurable individual differences in power motive do exist. High scorers on the story measure of power need were rated by their teachers as being high on "Argumentativeness" and also high on "Frequency of Trying to Convince Others."

POWER AS CONCERN ABOUT WEAKNESS. Further development of measurement techniques has been made by Veroff and others. In a nationwide survey, Veroff and his co-workers (1960) obtained thematic stories which were scored for the achievement, power, and affiliative motive. The patterns of power motivation in the different demographic groups surveyed in 1960 led Veroff (1972) to reinterpret the meaning of power motivation. He now feels that "the power motive measures should be interpreted as a *concern about weakness* [p. 281]." The observations that led to this new interpretation were that members of less powerful groups in society showed higher motive scores. Men with only a grade school education have higher power motives than do better-educated men. Black men also have higher power needs than white men. The findings of other studies are not altogether consistent with the "weakness" interpretation, but a new line of research with different measures (Winter, 1972) suggests that some people may have a strong fear of weakness; others, a strong desire for social leadership.

The new power motivation scoring system developed by David Winter (1972) differs from Veroff's scheme in its selection of the kinds of themes in imaginative stories that are judged indicative of the presence of the power motive (*n* Power). Winter's criteria emphasize concern about one's *impact;* a character in the story wants to establish, maintain, or restore his prestige or power in the eyes of the world. The actor may attempt to achieve this impact through direct, vigorous action, or by arousing the emotions of someone else. The actor's concern for his reputation may be expressed by a statement such as "He will lose the captaincy of the ship and will be bitter" or, "The young man knows the right spots in town to be seen in, and how to be seen in these spots."

Winter has conducted a variety of studies using his new *n* Power measure, which are reported in his recent book entitled *The Power Motive* (1973). Of interest is the delineation of what appears to be two distinct manifestations of the power motive. The person high in *n* Power often expresses this motive by seeking positions of leadership or *"organized social power."* This is the positive manifestation of the motive. The negatively oriented person's motive, on the other hand, seems to be more of a *fear of losing power.* He is concerned with his own reputation and is likely to engage in ostentatious expressions of his masculinity through such behaviors as drinking, exploitative sex, and the acquisition of prestige possessions.

Preliminary findings on the relation of power striving to political activism do not unequivocally support Lasswell's hypothesis about power concerns in the political man. Both Veroff and Winter have found some evidence of high *n* Power among student government officeholders. Green and Winter (1971) corroborated these findings among black student officeholders, as well. Evidence that political officeholders in the real world are higher than their fellows in *n* Power is sparse, however.

Personality and Motivational Factors

Motivation of Politicians

Browning and Jacob (1964) used Veroff's (1960) scoring of TAT (Thematic Apperception Test) [2] stories to compare the power needs of politicians with those of nonpoliticians. They also assessed affiliation and achievement motives from the same stories. Browning collected data from twenty-three politically active businessmen in an Eastern city and from eighteen nonpolitical businessmen, who matched eighteen of the actives in background characteristics and types of business. There were no differences between the groups in any of the motivation measurements.

Jacob also collected TAT stories from fifty elected officials in two Louisiana parishes (parishes roughly correspond to counties in other states). These Louisiana officials were lower on all three motives than were the politically active businessmen in the Eastern city. Browning and Jacob attributed these differences to the differences in opportunity for influence in the two geographical areas. Opportunities for gaining power and achievement through local political activity are poorer in Louisiana than in the East. Likewise, the opportunities for moving to higher offices from a parish office are demonstrably fewer than in the Eastern city. These differences in the realistic expectations for motive satisfaction are thought to account for differences between the two areas.

Some political offices do hold little power or achievement potential. A city clerk or a justice of the peace has relatively little basis for influence or achievement as compared with members of a city or parish council. Thus, one would expect differenecs among men who hold or campaign for high, as opposed to low, potential offices. These office differences were shown in the motive scores of men in both Louisiana and the East. While such after-the-fact comparisons are somewhat suspect, the findings do suggest important directions for future research.

In a more recent article, Browning (1968) summarized the Browning and Jacob (1964) findings. He concluded that motivation is related to the person's expectancies for satisfying his needs in a particular office. "Specifically," Browning (p. 97) noted, "higher average achievement and

[2] Strictly speaking, the term Thematic Apperception Test refers to a personality test which uses imaginative stories composed around a standard set of pictures (TAT pictures) (Murray, 1943). As used here, TAT stories refer to imaginative stories told in response to *any* set of pictures.

power and lower average affiliation motive scores were found among men who":

- initiated their own first political activity
- ran for offices with relatively high power and achievement opportunities
- reported vigorous policy-influencing behavior in office
- expressed explicit concern for achievement and power satisfactions in politics
- aspired to higher office

POWER AND OTHER MOTIVES. Research by Winter and his co-workers supported Browning and Jacob's (1964) finding that motives other than power may enter into motivation for political activity. Green and Winter (1971), for example, found that black undergraduate students who hold campus offices do indeed have higher power motivation than do students inactive in campus politics. However, the relationship between power motivation and activism was dependent upon the student's geographical origins. Northern-reared blacks with high power needs, for example, were more active in the black community outside the college and less trustful of the system than high n Power students with Southern backgrounds. For the Southerners, but not for Northerners, political outlooks were related to their level of need for achievement, as well as to their need for power.

The complexity of the relationships among activism, motivation, and the personal expectancies engendered by one's rearing are also shown in a study of New Left activists (Winter and Wiecking, 1971). These activists were full-time workers in New Left organizations. The male activists were found to be higher in achievement and lower in need for power than were the members of a control group. There were no differences between women activists and controls, although the radical women did tend to have higher affiliation needs ($p < .10$).[3]

Finally, Donley and Winter (1970) have shown that study of the motive patterns of politicians need not be limited to stories obtained in a test-like situation. They scored the first Inaugural Addresses of the twelve

---

[3] Read: "the probability is less than 10% that the obtained differences were due to chance." The criterion for "significant" differences in psychological research is usually 5% or a smaller chance probability.

U.S. Presidents who took office in the twentieth century for power and achievement imagery. Highest in power motivation were John F. Kennedy and Theodore Roosevelt, whereas Nixon's address expressed more concern over achievement than that of any other President. Comparative rankings are shown in Figure 5–2. It should be emphasized that these scores are not reliable estimates of Presidential motives since the Inaugural Address is a very limited sample of a President's preoccupations. However, the possibilities of the method for further research are provocative.

The importance of power in political affairs is undeniable, but my brief review of the personal concomitants of power shows that there is no one-to-one relationship between power motivation and behavior.

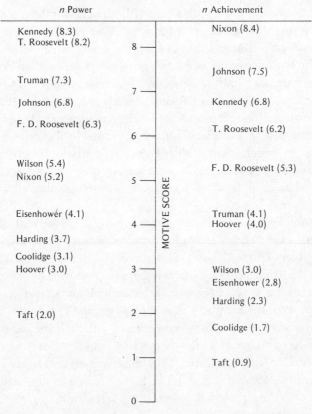

Figure 5–2 Power and achievement motivation expressed in the inaugural addresses of twentieth-century U. S. presidents—imagery per 1,000 words (Adapted from data reported by Richard E. Donley and David G. Winter, "Measuring motives of public officials at a distance: An exploratory study of American presidents," *Behavioral Science*, 1970, *15*, 227–36.)

The development of techniques for measuring the power motive, together with the emerging conception that the motive reflects both the seeking of control and of fear of weakness, promise further advances in our understanding. Other motives, especially achievement and affiliation, and the individual's concept of self will undoubtedly figure in future attempts at prediction. Also important are expectancies held by the individual about what he *can* accomplish in his personal and his political life. These expectancies are treated in the next section and in Chapter 10, which deals with the candidate.

POLITICAL MAN: MOTIVES, EXPECTANCIES, AND OPPORTUNITY

The relationship between motivational variables and the political behavior of the ordinary citizen can be no more than hinted at here. However, I would like to discuss why some people develop a sense of competence in dealing with the environment, while others develop a feeling of apathy or alienation. One needs only to look at his neighbors to observe these opposing tendencies. In politics, the range of involvement is marked —an appalling number of adult citizens in democracies do not participate at all. The usual turnout for municipal elections in Bangor, Maine, for example, is 30% of the registered voters. Since many adults are not registered to vote, the percentage voting in city elections is actually less than 25%. Participation in national elections is notably higher, but only about 56% of the voting-age populace cast ballots in the 1972 U.S. Presidential election.

The reasons for voting, however, do not necessarily include active seeking of control. Often, people vote out of a sense of duty or social conformity. Satisfaction of a need to deal competently with the problems of living seems to be important to only a minority of voters. Why, in a democratic society do people not have a strong need to effect the direction and course of their society?

Part of the answer to these questions lies in the socialization process in our society. There are profound social-class differences in socialization which affect both motive development and political activity. These differences relate to opportunities for motive development; differences in feelings of personal and political efficacy; and differences in knowledge of the opportunities for influence.

Personality and Motivational Factors

Opportunities for Motive Development

In recounting effectance theory, I have suggested that the motives such as power and achievement are rooted in the effectance need. What we term "motives" are systematic thought and behavior patterns that recur with enough regularity in a particular culture to be so termed. Thus, a person with a given set of innate aptitudes may become motivated to deal directly with the environment—either in a technical or in an artistic way. A talented musician may find the major expression of his effectance need in the manipulations of the physical vibrations, time sequences, and other natural phenomena. If he wins acclaim, the prestige thereby acquired will also be important, but the dominating "motive" remains his relationship to the physical universe and his effect upon it. Similarly, we can speak of a skilled craftsman's, or even a home handyman's, satisfaction in altering the environment in accordance with his predetermined plan.

In the United States, it is easy to see how effectance needs can be channeled into "motives" characterized by the seeking of either social prominence or social dominance. Lacking a fixed class structure, prestige in this country has revolved around accomplishment. Therefore, parents, schools, and other agents of socialization have emphasized the importance of achieving. As achievement is removed from the elementary victory over nature embodied in farming or invention, social accomplishments have become more important. It takes little elaboration to document the extent to which power or control over others is enshrined in American society. "Leadership," together with success in getting along with others, has become a primary yardstick of individual worth in family, neighborhood, and particularly in schools.

We assume that there are no appreciable class differences in the inborn tendency to seek competence in dealing with the environment. Motivational differences that occur later in life result from profound differences in the learning experiences of children in different families and social classes. Many examples of these learning experiences could be given, but consider just one example: the successes and failures experienced by a child seeking leadership on the school playground. He may have the requisite intelligence and physical strength to influence other children at play, but is handicapped because he is poorly dressed or has inadequate language skills. Motive development, that is, the beginning of a strong power motive, begins in social situations such as this: a child who learns that success follows certain kinds of activity in a particular situation is likely to persist in these kinds of activity.

Personal and Political Efficacy

There are also considerable differences in learning "what leads to what." In middle- and upper-class homes, for example, there is considerable direct training in how to control the environment. Campbell *et al.* (1960), in their study of *The American Voter,* found that people who have a strong sense of personal effectiveness also tend to feel politically effective. In turn, personal and political efficacy are strongly related to education. I discuss these findings in greater detail in later chapters, but here I want to suggest that the origin of efficacy is in the effectance need.

CONTROL EXPECTANCIES. An extensive series of investigations (Rotter, 1966) suggests that, in addition to specific motives, we develop generalized expectancies regarding our own ability to control the environment. Rotter speaks of these as expectancies for internal, as opposed to external, control of reinforcement. The person whose expectancies are *internal* believes that the good and bad things that happen to him are to his own credit or blame. If he is successful, he attributes his success to his own skills and abilities. A person whose expectancies are *external* believes that his outcomes result from the action of fate, chance, or the intervention of other people. For convenience, people who hold these types of expectations are often referred to simply as *internals* and *externals*. Of course, few people fall at either extreme, but there do seem to be important differences among people in their tendency to hold a large number, or very few, internal expectancies.

Considerable research supports the underlying theory of internal–external control. Rotter (1966) and his co-workers have developed a scale, for measuring the tendency to hold such expectations, called *the I–E scale*. It consists of pairs of statements such as:

a. Becoming a success is a matter of hard work; luck has little or nothing to do with it.
b. Getting a good job depends mainly on being in the right place at the right time [p. 11].

The person who chooses the first statement as the one in which he more strongly believes is making the internal response to this item. One's beliefs are relatively *internal* or *external* depending on the number of external choices one makes on the twenty-nine pairs composing the I–E scale. The test has shown considerable reliability and its validity has been demonstrated by studies such as those summarized in Rotter's paper and in the introduction to Seeman's (1967) study.

Seeman mentioned several findings regarding the external's actual attempts to control his environment. External tuberculosis patients were less likely than internals to take an active interest in their own treatment. The evidence for this lack of interest was the finding that the external patients had poorer knowledge of health matters than did internals (Seeman and Evans, 1962).

Another study showed that external Swedish workers had less political knowledge than internals (Seeman, 1966). The external's feelings of powerlessness (another name for external expectations) is evidently a self-fulfilling prophecy. That is, the individual who believes that he can do little to affect the "system" will behave in a way that actually does minimize his capacity for influence. Such a person neglects to learn how his environment works. He fails to pay attention to the daily news, reads few books, and makes no active attempts to learn from other people. Internal expectations, however, led reformatory inmates to acquire information about the rules for parole (Seeman, 1963) and led university students in Sweden to learn more about the political and nuclear test matters which concerned them (Seeman, 1967).

There have been a number of studies of internal–external expectancies and political participation; some of these studies are discussed in Chapter 9. Related conceptions, such as feelings of powerlessness and of personal and political efficacy, also appear in that chapter. The individual's personal feelings about his own *competence* interacts with his assessment of the enviromental possibilities. One needs knowledge about how one's society works in order to make any realistic attempts to affect it.

Knowledge of Opportunities for Influence

In addition to differences in motive development and in generalized expectancies for control, there are social-class differences in specific knowledge acquired about the means of influence. The child learns, or fails to learn, many specifics about the political process in the home. It stands to reason that information the parents possess *may* be imparted to the children. It also stands to reason that parents from lower socioeconomic backgrounds have different sorts of information to impart to their children than do parents of higher socioeconomic status. Contrasting opportunities for gaining such knowledge are dramatized by consideration of particularly stimulating home environments. Consider, for example, the discussion of political events and international affairs which reportedly were held in the Kennedy home while Jack, Robert, and Edward were growing up. Few children experience an atmosphere so filled with "knowledge of the opportunities for influence."

It should by no means be thought, however, that early experiences irrevocably shape the individual. The model of motivation I am employing allows for the development of new motives and expectancies in adulthood. David McClelland and his co-workers have amassed a good deal of evidence that strongly suggests that motives can be developed and changed in adulthood (McClelland and Winter, 1969). Their studies have revolved around the achievement motive, but there is no reason why their findings cannot be extended to the other competence motivations. The implications of the potential of motive development for broadening political participation have hardly begun to be explored. Some hint of the possible impact of broad-scale efforts to increase political motivation can be seen in the results of community organizing efforts in local poverty programs. The success of these efforts to organize the poor has been great enough to threaten entrenched interests. The threat was so great that Federal support for community organization and the concept of community control of poverty projects have been abandoned.

CONCLUSION

I have made no attempt to reconcile the uncertainties and inconsistencies that pervade the topic of motivation. There are tantalizing hints that certain motive and expectancy patterns do affect political activity, but the relationships cannot be neatly summarized.

My thesis in this chapter has been that the impetus to political activity can best be understood as an outgrowth of the effectance need, the innate tendency toward competence in dealing with the environment. The specific motives that relate to political behavior are numerous, but I have suggested the power motive as central. The degree to which an individual *wants* to influence others and the degree to which he perceives he *can* so influence seem to be the important determinants of political activity. Power cannot, admittedly, stand as the only motivational concept, since power, the desire for financial gain, and the desire for prestige are inextricably interwoven. As Murphy (1954) pointed out, these processes:

> . . . are bound to be interrelated because any one of them can be used to buy the other two. The coal magnate who wishes to be known as a patron of the arts may erect an art museum, essentially a flattering statue of himself; the financier may have a college or a fellowship named after him, or may buy his way into a controlling position in politics. Power is constantly being used by the "great" as a way of enhancing status; one "throws one's weight around." Power is likewise often directly used in the acquisition of material gain; the "big shot" becomes the "big time operator." Prestige likewise can command cash; one's recommendation of a toothpaste or a beer converts the prestige into a monetary value. And, from campus politics to those of the nation, prestige is easily siphoned into the power system [p. 624].

6

The Machiavellian

Things are seldom what they seem,
Skim milk masquerades as cream.

WILLIAM S. GILBERT,
H.M.S. Pinafore, Act II

To many citizens, the term *politician* has derogatory connotations. However the politician may argue his concern for the public good, they feel that he is not to be trusted. He will say anything to advance himself and his party. Even where such conscious derogation does not exist, a substantial portion of adults in the United States feels a vague distrust of politics and politicians.

Among the meanings of *politic,* according to Webster, are: "having practical wisdom; prudent; shrewd; diplomatic." The qualities mentioned are valued in the United States; paradoxically, the qualities of openness, honesty, and sincerity are also held to be exemplary. The person who speaks from the heart is admired, at least in the abstract. Such openness has been advocated as a way of life by some writers (e.g., Jourard, 1971); but, of course, one's true thoughts and beliefs may often be irritating to audiences or associates. Given these muddled values, the most successful politician will often be the man who seems most open while being most "diplomatic."

The term political also implies effort toward the accomplishment of some goal through joint action. I spoke earlier of the concept of working together in a common cause as a basic form of political behavior. Getting people to work together for some common objective (be it a candidate, the passage of a bill, or whatever) is a fundamental form of political activity.

Observers have long noted, however, that there are differences among citizen activists. Some are very cause oriented. Others seem more interested in running the show; that is, in organizing and directing other people. Thus, in the Prohibition movement, some workers were undoubtedly moved by moral outrage over the dealings in misery by purveyors of alcoholic beverages. Other Prohibitionists undoubtedly were most impressed by the fervor over an issue they could exploit in gaining some control over the movement. Of course, there were many middle types, people who were both morally aroused and who also derived some enjoyment from their power position in a popular movement.

TYPES OF POLITICAL CHARACTER

The usefulness of recognizing such differences in political role performance has been recognized by a number of authors. Lane (1953) suggested that these differences may result from differing political character types; he mentioned several such types that have been proposed. Lane's list, which brings together the conceptions of several important theorists, is reproduced in Table 6–1. A quick reading of the descriptions of the types shows certain common threads running through the ideas of different authors. For example, the automaton is similar to the indifferent, both being characterized by noninvolvement. Likewise, the psychopathological tendencies of the authoritarian personality have parallels in the anomic person described by Riesman (1950). The argument of this chapter, however, concerns the contrasting styles of Riesman's *moralizer* and his *inside-dopester*.

The Moralizer and the Inside-Dopester

Actually, a number of psychological tendencies are implied in the differentiation between the moralizer and the inside-dopester. The term *moralizer* implies a person who is overly concerned about a particular issue. His excess enthusiasm almost precludes his ability to work effectively for the cause. The notion that high affect arousal interferes with rational problem solving has been dealt with at length by psychologists; some of the relevant evidence is cited by Zajonc (1965) in his review of social facilitation. The moralizer's emotional involvement tends to preclude accurate perception of the situation, the paths to, and barriers against, successful accomplishment of his goals. Such lack of perspective, induced by strong emotional arousal, has been described by various

Table 6–1 A sampling of political character types

Automaton. A person who "escapes from freedom" by adopting culturally popular personality patterns, losing his sense of personal identity and responding to political stimuli without any individual or distinctive orientation (Fromm, 1941).

Pseudo–conservative. A person who adopts the conservative's ideology at the verbal level but, because of underlying personality disorders, subconsciously seeks radical solutions—for example, the lynching of agitators in the name of law and order (Adorno *et al.,* 1950).

Authoritarian personality. A person who (among other things) perceives the world as made up of a small, glorified in–group and despised out–groups, hierarchically arranged by power relationships, peopled by types rather than individuals. He cannot establish warm human relationships, judges people by exterior qualities, adopts a moralistic condemnatory tone toward deviant behavior, and so forth (Adorno *et al.,* 1950).

Political agitator. A political leader whose satisfactions are derived from arousing emotions in others and whose skills are greatest in this area of interpersonal contact (Lasswell, 1930).

Political administrator. A person whose skill lies in the manipulation of things and situations and whose displacement of affect upon less remote objects is associated with better adjustment to society (Lasswell, 1930).

Political theorist. A person whose skill lies in the manipulation of ideas and who has displaced his private motives and emotions upon a system of abstract concepts (Lasswell, 1930).

Bureaucratic personality. A person whose interpersonal relations have been habitually formalized by the demands of his work–life and whose responses to new situations are governed by overvaluation of rules (Merton, 1940).

Indifferent. A person either who has no emotional or mental relationship to politics or whose mobility or lack of orientation leads him to shun all political involvements (Riesman, 1950).

Moralizer (indignant or enthusiastic). A person whose responses to political situations are characterized by high affect and low competence (Riesman, 1950).

Inside-dopester. A person with controlled (and low) affect and great desire to know and/or use political phenomena for his amusement and advantage (Riesman, 1950).

Anomic. A person whose political style is inappropriate to the situations he faces and who shows other symptoms of disorientation (Riesman, 1950).

Autonomous. A person who is neither dominated by parentally instilled concientious views of politics nor by the concern for the opinions of peer groups; a person, therefore, free to choose his own political opinions (Riesman, 1950).

Source: Robert E. Lane, "Political character and political analysis," *Psychiatry,* 1953, *16,* 387–98. Copyright 1953 by *Psychiatry.* Used by permission.

writers as "tunnel vision." Flexibility in responding is reduced under high arousal; thus, the moralizer is often handicapped in making the creative or novel response many situations demand.

In contrast with the moralizer, the *inside-dopester* is not handicapped by "irrelevant affect." (Irrelevant affect is discussed later in this chapter.) Riesman described this character as one who is little concerned about the particular issues and goals involved. He seems to be more concerned with manipulating others through political expertise. Of course, neither the moralizer nor the inside-dopester represents the ideal democratic citizen since neither ineffective indignation nor manipulation of others for its own sake are valued in polite American society. Riesman's autonomous type would come closest to representing the ideal of most thoughtful democrats. A person who feels strongly about some issues, but who can work dispassionately for their accomplishment is, I think, an ideal type in our society.

Some of the issues brought up in this discussion of political types have been clarified by recent research on Machiavellian behavior. This research is described by Richard Christie and Florence Geis (1970) in *Studies in Machiavellianism*. Machiavellian and non-Machiavellian behavior, portrayed from empirical observations in the laboratory, bears remarkable similarities to that of the two political types I have been discussing.

MACHIAVELLIANISM

Niccolò Machiavelli, the man whose name has come to stand for the use of craft and deceit in political manipulation, was born in Florence, Italy, in 1469. During his lifetime, Italy was composed of many small states which were constantly at war with one another. Machiavelli served as diplomatic secretary for the Florentine rulers; in this capacity he traveled throughout Italy and visited France, Switzerland, and the Germanic states.

One of the many revolutions of the time brought an end to Machiavelli's political career. He was exiled to a small farm, where he spent the evenings studying and writing. His best-known book, *The Prince*, was written in 1513. Other political works by Machiavelli include a military treatise, a biography, a history, and two comedies. After several attempts to regain office, without success, Machiavelli died in 1527.

Machiavelli's counsel to Lorenzo the Magnificent, to whom *The Prince* was dedicated, consisted of advice regarding the tactics necessary for a prince to remain in power under differing circumstances. The tactics he recommended were based upon his cynical but pithy characterizations of human nature; for example (the pages cited refer to the Great Books Foundation edition of *The Prince*, 1955):

> . . . men in general . . . are ungrateful, voluble, dissemblers, anxious to avoid danger, and covetous of gain: as long as you benefit them, they are entirely yours; they offer you their blood, their goods, their life and their children as I have before said, when the necessity is remote; but when it approaches, they revolt [p. 55].

Furthermore, Machiavelli thought it permissible to take a life "when there is a proper justification and manifest reason for it." The prince should, however, "abstain from taking the property of others, for men forget more easily the death of their father than the loss of their patrimony [p. 56]." These cynical views of human nature formed the basis for the modern-day study of Machiavellian beliefs.

In the construction of the initial Machiavellianism scale, Christie (Christie and Geis, 1970) worked directly from Machiavelli's statements regarding human nature. In one item that has survived several versions of the scale, for example, only one word was changed from the translated version of the Great Manipulator's statement. "Men forget more easily the death of their father than the loss of their patrimony" became, in Christie's attitude scale: "Most men forget more easily the death of their father than the loss of their property [p. 8]." * In addition to Machiavelli's views on *human nature*, two other aspects of his thought dictated items for the original Machiavellianism (Mach) scale: his ideas about *interpersonal tactics* and abstractions regarding *generalized moral principles*.

Taken together, one's views on human nature and on the tactics that may properly be used in dealing with others, and one's generalized moral principles constitute the syndrome upon which one is classified as a Machiavellian or a non-Machiavellian. The former, for example, endorses cynical statements about human nature and advocates manipulative interpersonal tactics such as those represented in the Mach scale item: "The best way to handle people is to tell them what they want to hear." The

* Excerpts from R. Christie and F. L. Geis, *Studies in Machiavellianism*, copyright 1970 by Academic Press, are used by permission of the publisher and authors.

abstract moral principles advocated by Machiavelli are represented in the statement: "People suffering from incurable diseases should have the choice of being put painlessly to death." Christie noted that the fewest items were to be found in this last area since "the construction of items tended to follow Machiavelli's writings rather closely and Machiavelli was less concerned with abstractions and ethical judgments than with pragmatic advice [p. 14]."

In actual fact, reading of *The Prince* suggests that Machiavelli advocated no firm general principle, with the exception of the implicit idea that retaining and extending one's power was, for a prince at least, the highest good. He advocated the appearance of goodness where it is useful, but noted that a prince must "learn how not to be good." Machiavelli's discussion of various postures and strategies tended to emphasize the use of naked force. The prince must act with no qualms about taking the lives of others—friends as well as enemies. The use of cruel methods is justified if these tactics seem necessary to consolidation of the prince's power. War–making was advocated as the prince's major field of study: "War and its organization and discipline . . . is the only art that is necessary to one who commands [Machiavelli, 1955, p. 48]."

Thus, while Machiavelli's reputation as a proponent of craftiness and duplicity in interpersonal situations is well deserved, it should be obvious from the foregoing that he was writing from a perspective far different from that of twentieth-century Western democracy. In Machiavelli's Italy, the only forces for stability were the armed power of various princes and nobles and the power of the Church, which was often allied with one prince or another. He wrote in an era of constantly changing power fields based upon armed strength and the conquest of new territories. Although imperial ambitions and armed conflict still exist in the modern world, technological change and the growth of new institutions have profoundly changed the practice of world politics. Likewise, the governmental practices of contemporary Western democracies represent a profound departure from the world known to Machiavelli.

Christie and Geis (1970) did not deal with the relations between a prince and his subject, nor with international relations. Rather, they were concerned with interpersonal behavior, particularly the seeking of advantage by one person over another. Given this difference in the nature, the intensity, and the seriousness of the phenomena discussed, one wonders how far the analogy between Machiavellian power politics and interpersonal manipulative strategies can be taken. The questions, then, that

I address in the remaining pages of this chapter are: Is there a particular character type whose personal orientation seems largely the manipulation or control of other people? And, if such a character structure exists, is it properly called *the Machiavellian character?* Let us begin by examining the approach to these questions represented in the work of Richard Christie and his co-workers (Christie and Geis, 1970).

Development of the Mach Scales

Beginning with ideas gleaned from Machiavelli's essays, as well as ideas based on observations of university administrators, Christie conceived of a number of characteristics that were theoretically a part of the thinking of people who manipulated their way to success. His next task was to determine whether these characteristics did tend to cluster in certain individuals, but not in others. Thus, he embarked on a series of studies to see whether attitude statements chosen to reflect Machiavellian ideas could actually be used to form an attitude scale that would differentiate these two types of people. Choosing statements, or "items," from the three substantive areas already mentioned, that is, *interpersonal tactics, views on human nature,* and *abstract morality,* Christie obtained a pool of seventy-one items that comprised the preliminary version of the Mach scale. The questionnaire, in Likert format [1] for presentation to subjects with answers on a five-point agree–disagree scale, was termed the *"Mach II"* to differentiate it from the original, unedited pool of Mach items (Mach I). Some of the characteristic items under the three headings are shown in Table 6–2 under their appropriate headings. The three a priori statement categories did not exactly stand up under subsequent investigation, but they do reveal the initial conception of Machiavellianism.

There followed a much-refined twenty-item Likert scale version, the *Mach IV,* in which some items were reversed to control for response set (the tendency to agree with all items, regardless of what they say). This scale was used successfully in a number of studies. Even in this improved version, there remained the problem of social desirability in measuring Machiavellian tendencies. That is, statements reflecting antisocial tendencies were thought to have an indeterminate effect on the Mach scores. Would the Machiavellian be more likely to reveal his true

---

[1] In a Likert scale, the subject responds to statements such as those in Table 6–2 by checking his degree of agreement: agree very much, agree, undecided, disagree, or disagree very much.

Table 6–2 Sample items from an early version of the Machiavellianism scale (Mach II) *

Tactics

    1. A white lie is often a good thing.

  22. It is foolish to take a big risk unless you are willing to go the limit.

  45. The best way to handle people is to tell them what they want to hear.

  66. Just about anything one does can be justified after it is done.

Views of human nature

  20. Some of the best people have some of the worst vices.

  34. Most people don't know what is best for them.

  46. The biggest difference between most criminals and other people is that criminals are stupid enough to get caught.

  71. Most people are more concerned with making a good living than satisfying their conscience.

Abstract morality

  31. People suffering from incurable diseases should have the choice of being put painlessly to death.

  38. History teaches no moral lessons; evil and good have always been present.

---

* Only positive items (i.e., items on which Machiavellian tendencies are inferred from agreement) are listed.
Source: R. Christie and F. L. Geis, *Studies in Machiavellianism,* pp. 11–13. Copyright © 1970 by Academic Press. Used by permission of the publisher and the authors.

disdain of prevailing norms, or would he be more likely than the low Mach to conceal them? To solve this problem, a forced-choice form of the scale, *Mach V,* was developed.

Mach V, the much-refined scale for the measurement of Machiavellianism, employs triads of statements for each attitude item. The subject is asked to indicate which of the three is *most* like himself (i.e., most characteristic) and which is *least* like himself. Try it, with the following triad (Christie and Geis, 1970, p. 24):

  13. A. Generally speaking, men won't work hard unless they are forced to do so.

      B. Every person is entitled to a second chance, even after he commits a serious mistake.

      C. People who can't make up their minds are not worth bothering about.

Each triad contains two statements matched for social desirability. One of these statements is scored for Machiavellianism; the other is unrelated. The third statement is a buffer with a social desirability rating as different as possible from that of the other two.[2] This forced-choice format controls for the tendency to make socially desirable responses, and makes the scale markedly less transparent than it would otherwise be. Whether or not the control is perfect, the Mach V version does make it considerably more difficult for respondents to fake their scores according to the impression they would like to give. (Note that some college students might even fake in the socially undesirable direction if they wanted to appear hardened and worldly).[3]

Studies in Machiavellianism

In this section, I review a few of the many studies designed to illuminate the nature of the Machiavellian. Unfortunately, Christie and Geis (1970) did not proceed from a theory of Machiavellianism. They did not say whether the term refers to a basic character structure, a certain attitude syndrome, a value disposition, etc. Rather, they began with the observations that some people are more manipulative than others and that Machiavelli's ideas are perhaps representative of this manipulative orientation. They then proceeded to develop a test that seemed to have some internal consistency and that was successful in differentiating people. Examination of the behaviors of people who scored high and low has produced a somewhat more complete picture of the Machiavellian person. The characteristics that were observed in the behavior of experimental subjects has thus added to the initially vague ideas about those persons who adopt manipulation of others as a way of life. It should be noted, however, that all of the research, even when construed as an experiment, has been correlational in nature. That is, even though consistent differences may be found between people scoring high and low on the Mach scale, there still remains the possibility that both the ob-

[2] In the example, A and C are the matched items, and B is the buffer that has in this case a markedly higher social desirability rating than the other two. The Mach item is A.

[3] In practice, both the Mach IV and Mach V versions of the scale have seen considerable use; in order to learn more about the characteristics of the two scales, both were given in most of the studies described in the Christie–Geis volume. Unfortunately, little evidence is given regarding the behavior of subjects chosen as high and low on the Mach V alone. Correlations between Mach IV and V are moderate, at any rate, ranging from .60 to .67 in four subsamples of 1,744 subjects varying by sex and ethnicity (Christie and Geis, 1970, p. 32).

served behaviors and the Mach scale responses result from a third factor, such as an underlying personality disposition. Keeping this reservation in mind, let us examine some research findings.

THE MACHIAVELLIAN AS MANIPULATOR. Perhaps a good place to begin is with a study by Geis, Christie, and Nelson (in Christie and Geis, 1970, Chapter V). The subjects were instructed to manipulate, confuse, and distract another subject as part of an experiment. As in many of these experiments, potential subjects were first given the Mach IV and the Mach V scales. Those who scored high (above the median) on both tests were classified as *high Machs* and those who scored low on both tests were classified as *low Machs*. After the subject had completed a series of problems, the experimental situation was introduced to him as one in which he would serve as the experimenter. He was told that the experiment dealt with interpersonal power in addition to the study of problem solving. As experimenter, the subject was to be allowed to deliver rewards and punishments to another person as he saw fit. Moreover, he was told that he should use this power arbitrarily "to confuse or distract the subject who will be taking the test." While the subject–experimenter was required to give feedback to the next subject (actually a confederate of the real experimenter), he was also perfectly free to give incorrect answers; he was given "absolute power to use as you choose to use it." How the subject used his power was left "up to your imagination—and your conscience [p. 82]."

The experimenters' hypotheses were that high Mach subjects would:

1. Use more deception and a greater variety of deceptive manipulations than would low Machs.
2. Use more of the suggested deceptions than lows.
3. Be more inventive in devising new and additional distractions.
4. Be more likely to list manipulative reasons for enjoying the experiment.

All four of these hypotheses were confirmed. High Machs performed an average of 15.43 manipulative acts, while low Machs performed only 7.08 during their adiminstration of the test to their "subject." In terms of variety, high Machs also used significantly more different manipulations (lies, verbal and nonverbal distraction) than lows—twice as many (6.4 versus 3.1). Highs also used two out of the three suggested manipulative techniques, while the low Machs used only one. Inventive manipulations were also more frequent among the high Mach subjects, who devised an average of six innovative comments, as compared to an average of two such comments by low Mach subjects. Finally, in rating statements such as, "How much did you actually enjoy carrying out the experimental manipulations?" highs indicated significantly higher enjoyment (1970, p. 89).

The flavor of the innovative distractions employed by high Mach subjects is conveyed in the following list of manipulations performed by one of them:

> . . . rubs hands together in the stereotyped gesture of anticipation; bends over double, unties shoe, shakes foot, reties shoe; jingles contents of pocket noisily; pulls out chapstick and applies it while staring absent-mindedly at the ceiling; whistles; slaps leg and straightens up noisily and abruptly in chair; taps pencil rhythmically on table; hums; reaches around divider and carefully knocks it over (this produces a loud crash and sends papers on table flying in all directions); after a 10-sec. dead silence apologizes profusely to stooge for distracting him; erases vigorously on blank margin of stooge's score sheet (divider board prevents stooge from seeing that subject is not erasing actual marks); comments, with serious frown at one-way vision mirror, "I feel like I'm on TV, don't you?" (followed by grin at mirror as soon as stooge returns his attention to test booklet); holds match book in both hands above divider board in full view of stooge (pretending to ignore stop watch), tears out matches one by one, dropping each into ash tray; tears up empty matchbook cover and drops pieces ostentatiously into ash tray; dismantles his own ballpoint pen behind divider board, uses spring to shoot it, parts flying, across the room; jumps from chair, dashes across room to retrieve pen parts saying, "Sorry, I'm a little nervous" [Christie and Geis, 1970, p. 92].

The complex design of an "experiment" within an experiment was used to disarm the high Mach's suspicions. The greater suspiciousness of highs, which had been postulated, was confirmed in retrospective ratings by all subjects. In the first part of the experiment, when the person believed himself to be a subject in an experiment, high Machs reported significantly greater suspicion about both the experimenter's explanation and about the other student who was giving him the test than did low Machs. After the bogus explanation of the purpose of the experiment and the request to serve as experimenter, no significant differences were found—high Machs were no more suspicious of the experimenter or of the other students than were low Machs.

Personality and Motivational Factors

GAMES THE MACHIAVELLIAN PLAYS. A whole range of differences between high and low Mach subjects has been observed in laboratory situations. For example, highs, after having been implicated in cheating on a laboratory task, are more able to look the experimenter in the eye while denying the cheating. Interestingly enough, the high Machs also put up greater resistance than low Machs to the confederate's attempts to implicate them in the cheating in the first place (Exline, *et al.*, 1970). High Machs show the ability to gain the upper hand in three-man bargaining games, as shown by their winning of more points (see Chapter VII in Christie and Geis, 1970) and more money (Christie and Geis, 1970, Chapter IX) than either their low- or medium-scoring counterparts. Although introduction of money (1970, Chapter X) rewards in a variant of the Prisoner's Dilemma Game did not change participant's behavior overall from what it was with point rewards, the high Machs did become more cooperative when money reward was begun. When pennies or dollars replaced points, in the large incentive (dollar) condition, the high Machs became markedly less exploitive than the low Mach subjects. The authors interpreted this as the rational strategy in this particular game.

One experimental situation that bears distinct similarities to political life is the Legislative Game, whch was devised by James Coleman (see Christie and Geis, 1970, p. 191). This is an elaborately structured interaction situation in which subjects bargain for votes on the issues they sponsor. Issues determined to be emotion arousing for the student subjects (civil rights, draft, etc.), neutral issues (new postage stamps, appointments, procedures), and pork barrel issues are included. In one study (Geis, Weinheimer and Berger, 1970), the major hypothesis was that high Machs would win the games "when the issues under discussion were emotionally loaded, but not when they were neutral [Christie and Geis, 1970, p. 200]." This hypothesis was clearly supported, as demonstrated by the average points won by high and low Machs in the neutral-issues games (high, 9.32; low, 10.21), as opposed to the emotional-issues games (high, 11.24; low, 8.86). This outcome is plotted in Figure 6–1 to show that the posited interaction was obtained.

According to the authors, the poorer performance of lows on the emotional issues was not the result of any deficiency in understanding the game or any lesser adherence to principle. They lost to high Machs by the greatest margin on the issues they most strongly favored! These results, according to Geis and her co-authors: ". . . clearly support the notion that one of the significant advantages of high Machs in competi-

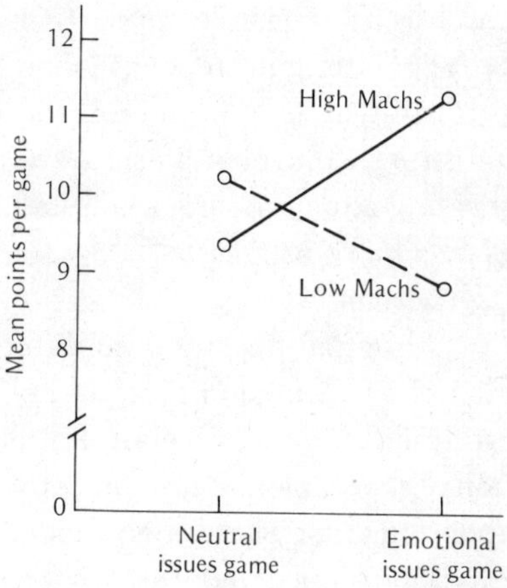

Figure 6–1 Scores attained by high and low Machiavellians on two types of issue in the Legislature Game (Adapted from Richard Christie and Florence L. Geis, *Studies in Machiavellianism*, p. 201. Copyright © 1970 by Academic Press. Used by permission of the publisher and authors.)

tive bargaining with lows is that the lows become distracted by potentially ego-involving elements in the bargaining context, while high Machs remain detached from such concerns and concentrate on winning [p. 209]."

GUILT AND COMPLIANCE. Although he is depicted as being amoral, the Machiavellian has not, as yet, been shown to have a less demanding superego than that of the non-Machiavellian. In an unpublished study by Hymoff (1970), however, it was posited that the high Mach would feel less guilt over transgression of the precepts of conventional morality than would the low Machiavellian subjects.

Hymoff's procedure for inducing "guilt" involved implicating the subject in cheating in the experiment. After talking in the waiting room with a supposed subject who described the test he had just taken, the experimental subject, either a high or low Machiavellian, met with the experimenter to receive his instructions. The experimenter stressed that much depended upon the subject having no previous knowledge of the test he was about to take. (Of the fifteen high and fifteen low Machs in the experimental condition, only one high and four lows confessed their prior knowledge of the test. This is not a significant difference.)

Theoretically, Hymoff assumed that greater feelings of guilt would lead to greater compliance with the experimenter's request for further assistance. Whether the measure was number of hours that the subject would be willing to serve, the choice of a personally uncomfortable experiment, as opposed to running rats, or actually appearing for a second appointment, there were no differences in compliance between high and low Machs. The sole support for the hypothesis that low Machs would suffer greater guilt feelings when implicated in cheating was in the verbal reports of subjects in the control condition. After the questions about volunteering, control subjects were asked to imagine that they were in the cheating situation, and requested to describe their probable feelings. Low Machs more often ($p < .05$) described feelings of guilt or anxiety than high Machs.

Although he found no differences between highs and lows in compliance as a function of guilt, Hymoff (1970) did find a number of interesting differences. Overall, low Machs volunteered more hours of additional experimental time and they were more apt to keep their second appointments. The same proportion of lows in experimental and control conditions appeared for the second appointment (approximately .75). Highs in the experimental condition, however, appeared less often (.25) than their counterparts in the no-cheating-induction control condition (.50). This finding suggests that the highs reacted to a feeling of being "conned" by the experimenter.

Further findings included Hymoff's observation that high Machiavellian subjects came more often from the ranks of social science and business students, while low Machs tended to be physical science and humanities majors. Highs were also closer to the real purposes when asked to guess the purpose of the experiment and were less likely to say that they had learned something of value about themselves from the experiment. The latter finding was interpreted by the author as indicating rationality on the part of high Machs since no real feedback had been given. The lows' assertion that they had learned something of value by their participation seems to be evidence of their desire to give the "proper" response.

Finally, in terms of Machiavellianism and political orientation, Hymoff's subjects were asked to identify their political beliefs as "liberal" or "conservative." No differences were found.[4] However, high Machiavellians did more often report that they differed from their parents' political views. Asked whether his political beliefs had changed from those of his family, 70% of the high Mach subjects replied in the affirmative; only 37% of the low Machs said their views had changed ($p < .05$). This observation is consistent with the idea that high Machs are inter-

---

[4] Christie and Geis (1970) also reported no ideological differences between high and low Machs; they also found no differences in political party affiliation.

ested in power and are flexible with regard to tactics. Thus, perception of prevailing trends among youth, for instance, might be more likely to influence the high Mach than the low. One of the routes to leadership is through accurate discernment of the directions in which the group wants to be led!

High Machs and Low Machs

Based upon the evidence reported in their book, Christie and Geis (1970) have reached some conclusions regarding the situations in which differences occur between high and low Machs. Three situation characteristics seem central, the maximal differences occurring when all three are present in the situation (Christie and Geis, 1970, pp. 286–88).

1. *Face-to-face interaction.* The low Mach tends to become emotionally involved and carried away in face-to-face interaction situations, in contrast to the high Mach, who remains cool and collected.
2. *Latitude for improvisation.* The high Mach seems to be at his best when the rules of the situation are not highly structured. An example is the greater innovativeness of the high in thinking up distractions for the subject when he served as experimenter.
3. *Arousing irrelevant affect.* The superiority of high Machs over lows in the Legislature game is attributed to the "irrelevant affect" aroused in the lows, but not in the highs, concerning issues that were important to each.

In studies where none of these characteristics was present in the experimental situation, no differences were found. Where all three were present, the predicted differences between high and low Machiavellian groups were found in every case examined by the authors (1970, pp. 290–91). Where only one or two of the factors were present, the results sometimes confirmed the hypotheses while sometimes they did not. The observation of these situationally determined differences in behavior, in conjunction with other findings, produced a more definite picture of the personalities of the high and the low Machiavellian.

THE COOL SYNDROME VERSUS THE SOFT TOUCH. These terms were used by Christie and Geis (1970) to summarize the dispositional differences between high and low Machs. The high Mach is calm and unemotional in his dealings with others; he is fact oriented, being unmoved either by emotional appeals or by his own desires in the matter. Thus, he is not moved by conformity pressures or by the urgings of another, unless the persuasion is backed up by convincing argument. He likes to achieve his own goals in competition with others. His success in doing so depends largely on his cool rationality and his initiative, particularly when the structure of the situation is loose.

The low Machiavellian, on the other hand, is a "soft touch" because he personalizes every situation. He is oriented to persons, rather than to abstract goals. His feelings tend to interfere with rational assessment of the situation. His emotional involvements cloud his vision, so to speak. Therefore, the low Mach is likely to be moved by emotional appeals or by pressure to conform. He does better when he can work in a well-defined situation; that is, one in which the rules are clear-cut. Thus, the major differences between highs and lows are most apt to be evidenced in situations in which they are engaged in face-to-face interaction.

The three situational factors are interrelated. For example, emotional affect is more likely to be aroused in a face-to-face situation where there is competition, rather than in an impersonal intellectual task. Although high Machs do not score higher on intelligence tests, they do tend to beat low Machs in games of skill involving interpersonal strategy. The affect aroused in the low Mach interferes with his performance. This affect is termed *irrelevant:* just as stress leads to stereotypy in the behavior of rats in experimental situations, irrelevant affect reduces the creativity or innovativeness of the low Machs in ambiguous or unstructured situations.

Christie and Geis (1970) illustrated the effect of emotional involvements on the bargaining behavior of subjects in the Legislature game previously mentioned. Although there were no differences on youth-relevant issues between high and low Mach college students (both types taking the expected positions favoring the Peace Corps and civil rights), the lows lost to highs on these affect-arousing issues:

> High and low Machs did not differ in success in lobbying on prosaic issues, but the highs won when the bargaining discussions revolved around such sensitive and affect-arousing issues as abolishing the Peace Corps, universal military conscription, etc. In this study the emotional detachment that led to the highs' winning was not coolness toward other people but detachment from their own ideological positions [Christie and Geis, 1970, p. 295].

THE MACHIAVELLIAN AS A POLITICAL TYPE

"High Machs are politic, not personal." So say the authors of *Studies in Machiavellianism*. I would like now to marshal fact and informed opinion to evaluate the importance of Machiavellianism to political psychology. Is the concept of Machiavellianism simply a concise way of describing what we mean by being "politic"; that is, diplomatic and effective in attaining goals? Does it imply nothing more than coolness, rationality, and unflappability in situations where these traits are advantageous? Or must the concept include the more antisocial traits that have been mentioned earlier, such as cynicism, suspiciousness of others, and, perhaps, hostility?

Previous conceptualizations of the political personality have focused on the underlying personality dynamics, rather than on specific behaviors. The conception of Machiavellianism, on the other hand, directs attention to effectiveness of the actor's behavior in specified situations. The picture of Woodrow Wilson presented by George and George (1956), for example, was intended to support their hypothesis regarding the effects of self-doubt upon political behavior. The man they described, however, fits very closely the behavioral description of the low Machiavellian, which has emerged from laboratory research.

In his most tragic hour, Woodrow Wilson failed to obtain approval from the Senate for the United States' entry into the League of Nations. The existence of irrelevant affect is undeniable. Instead of doing battle (and making compromises) in the face-to-face forum, that is, in conference with Senators of his own and the opposition party, Wilson chose to take his case to the people. Certainly, as President, he had plenty of room for improvisation; historians have suggested that rather minor compromises would have ensured ratification of the League. Instead of employing high Mach tactics of bargaining and compromise, Wilson insisted to the end that his plan for the League should be adopted without change.

Before we categorize him as a low Machiavellian, we must recognize that Woodrow Wilson was also capable of behaving like a high Mach. In his campaign for the Governorship of New Jersey, Wilson very coldly played reform Democrats against the machine. He successfully campaigned for the nomination and was elected Governor with the support of the old guard politicians, and then turned against these same men after his inauguration.

The applicability of the model of political man suggested by Machiavellian research is also limited by observations of great contrast in emotional constitution among successful politicians. At this time, the two most successful Democratic politicians from Maine present such a contrast. Senator Edmund Muskie, much admired and many times elected, is reputed to have a very hot temper (Lippman and Hansen, 1971). On the other hand Senator William Hathaway, who is undoubtedly the state's second-most popular Democrat, has a completely opposite disposition. I have never observed him angry, nor have I ever met anyone who has. My point is that we must go beyond emotional temperament in getting at core traits of the successful politician.

It would be premature to draw firm conclusions regarding the place of the modern conception of Machiavellianism in the psychology of politics. Without doubt, the research has added a new dimension for consideration of the relation of personality to politics. That the person holding Machiavellian beliefs does behave differently from others in the laboratory has been amply demonstrated, given the conditions of personal interaction that favor him. Whether the Machiavellian orientation will be found to be a major factor in political behavior remains to be seen.

Both theoretical analysis and further research is needed to clarify the possible relationship between Machiavellianism and real political activity. For instance, more needs to be known about the relationship of Machiavellianism to other psychological constructs. Witkin's (1954) notion of field dependence, for example, may be related to Machiavellianism. The field-independent, or analytic, person has some of the characteristics of the high Mach with regard to emotional control and the use of reason. Similarly, field-dependent people are similar to low Machs in that they are person oriented and emotionally labile. Finally, further research needs to be directed to the question of whether some more basic character disposition may underly the acquisition of Machiavellian beliefs. Likewise, the somewhat puzzling relationship between internal–external control and Machiavellianism reported by Christie and Geis ($r = +.43$) needs investigation. The correlation they reported indicates that the Machiavellian believes that his outcomes are determined by fate or luck, rather than by his own efforts!

Many applied investigations suggest themselves, as well. A longitudinal study of college students who are given the Mach scales upon entering college would answer some questions regarding the ability of the Mach scale to predict behavior in college politics, for example. Such studies are necessary to counter the possibility that Machiavellian beliefs develop along with growing interest and involvement in political situations. The reader himself can think of many more situations in which both the development of Mach attitudes and their predictive ability for political behavior can be studied.

7

Authoritarian and Democratic Personality Dispositions

> The serious threat to our democracy is not the existence of foreign totalitarian states. It is the existence within our own personal attitudes and within our own institutions of conditions which have given a victory to external authority, discipline, uniformity and dependence upon The Leader in foreign countries. The battlefield is also accordingly here—within ourselves and our institutions.
>
> JOHN DEWEY, *Freedom and Culture*, 1939

The term *democracy* is seldom used in a well-defined way in ordinary discourse about governmental systems. Likewise, its opposite, *dictatorship* is variously construed. It is possible, however, to use a small group of people, rather than a nation, as our model and to describe rather precisely the kinds of leader behavior and leader–follower relationships that constitute a democratic or authoritarian system [see Verba's (1962) *Small Groups and Political Behavior*]. Such definitions were used in an important series of studies by Lippitt and White (White and Lippitt, 1960).

Under the aegis of Kurt Lewin, Ronald Lippitt and Ralph White undertook a series of studies of the "group atmosphere" created by different styles of adult leader behavior in boys "clubs" created for the purpose. The three leadership styles employed are described by White and Lippitt (1960, pp. 26–27):

1. *Authoritarian.* All policy is determined by the leader; steps in activities are dictated one by one so that future steps are uncertain; the leader dictates tasks to be worked on and the co-workers; the leader personally praises and criticizes each member but remains aloof from active group participation.

2. *Laissez-faire.* Policy is determined completely by the individual members of the group; with minimum leader participation; he supplies materials and information when asked, but neither praises nor criticizes group members.

3. *Democratic.* All policy is a matter of group discussion and decision, with the active participation of the leader; procedures are outlined and alternatives suggested by the leader; members are free to work with whomever they choose; the leader is "objective" or "fact-minded" in his praise and criticism, and tries to be a group member in spirit, without doing too much of the work.

These different styles of leadership produced quite marked differences in member behavior. Boys in the authoritarian groups stuck to their assigned tasks—for example, operations in the manufacture of model airplanes—but were either sullenly apathetic or (in other groups) aggressively hostile toward each other. While they did not work as hard or continuously as the authoritarian group members, the boys in the democratic group atmosphere produced superior products. Also, there was much greater unity and "we feeling" in the democratic groups. Boys in laissez-faire groups produced few tangible products. Most of their time was spent in play.

Authoritarian and democratic group organization is defined for purposes of my discussion by the leader roles described by White and Lippitt. In the authoritarian model, direction comes from the leader, who oversees all activities of the group members and who may even dictate the interpersonal relationships possible in the group. Democratic group organization, on the other hand, provides for member participation in the decision-making process. While the democratic leader may make suggestions and give guidance, he is receptive to feedback from individuals in the group. A number of factors other than the behavior of the leader influences group atmosphere. Also important to group atmosphere are the structure of the group and the task facing the group. The purpose of this chapter, however, is to discuss individual differences in response to authoritarian and democratic group atmospheres.

AUTONOMY AND DEPENDENCE

Modern social psychology is replete with attempts to describe differences among people in their willingness to accept direction from others.

David Riesman and his co-workers (Riesman, 1950) suggested a historically changing system of orientation toward others, from tradition to inner direction to other direction. American society has evolved through the first two stages and is in the process of transition from inner to other direction. At the present time, according to Riesman, most people can be thought of as ranging between two polar types. The first type is the *inner-directed* person whose behavior is self-directed. He is autonomous from the point of view of contemporary influences, although his behavior *is* in accordance with internalized norms and values. The second type is the *other-directed* person whose behavioral direction is determined by his current milieu. His antennae are constantly set to receive the expectations of others; he is very responsive to situational pressures and current fads. Research conducted during he 1950s and early 1960s supported the notion that people could be meaningfully ranged along the inner–other continuum (Kassarjian, 1962). Further evidence of the concern with autonomy versus acceptance of the influence of other people is the vast literature on conformity (Hollander and Willis, 1967).

A somewhat different perspective, which developed in the 1930s, stemmed from the concern of social scientists over the rise of Nazism in Germany. In particular, some social scientists began to take the position that there is present in some people a deep-seated need not only to obey, but to adore and to offer complete submission to an all-powerful leader. An early publication of the Institute of Social Research (Horkheimer, 1936) on authority and the family suggested the concept of the "authoritarian personality" as a link between psychological dispositions and political leanings. In *Escape from Freedom*, Erich Fromm (1941), a contributor to the 1936 volume, furthered the notion of authoritarian character structure as a basic foundation of Fascism.

Aloneness and Authoritarianism

Fromm's thesis is that man, freed from primary group ties by the historical developments associated with the rise of capitalism, found himself alone, helpless, and isolated. The sense of anxiety over aloneness is experienced by everyone growing up in modern culture as an aspect of the development of selfhood. These unbearable feelings of isolation and powerlessness can be overcome by developing a loving relationship to one's fellow man and through development of one's capacity for productive work. Too often, however, man seeks to escape from the freedom that accompanies the process of individuation. This escape can be manifested by the use of any of a number of psychic mechanisms. Fromm (1941) described several such escape mechanisms, including authoritarianism, destructiveness, and automaton conformity. The discussion here focuses on the nature and origins of authoritarianism.

Authoritarianism arises from "the tendency to give up the independence of one's own individual self and to fuse one's self with somebody or something outside of oneself in order to acquire the strength which the individual self is lacking. Or, to put it in different words, to seek for new, 'secondary bonds' as a substitute for the primary bonds which have been lost [Fromm, 1941, p. 163]." These tendencies are based on deep-seated personality dynamics that developed, Fromm believed, from the interaction of cultural forces with man's basic needs for self-preservation and for relatedness to the world outside himself. The particular personality dynamics involved in the authoritarian character are sadistic and masochistic strivings. That is, the authoritarian wants to hurt and dominate others, while at the same time he wants to be hurt and dominated. These tendencies represent the individual's reactions to feelings of inferiority, powerlessness, and individual insignificance. Fromm preferred to talk in terms of sado-masochistic character structure, rather than simple power striving, since he felt that the latter terminology, as represented in Adler's thought, neglected unconscious personality dynamics.

Sadistic and masochistic impulses are present in everyone to some degree. Even though some people exhibit one of these tendencies to a marked extent, its opposite is always present. The individual, then, harbors both desires—to dominate and to be dominated. Fromm observed that these two tendencies may be complementary between persons. Symbiotic attachments are often formed between two people, for example, in which each, the sadist, as well as the masochist, is profoundly dependent upon the other. Fromm also suggested that a person whose personality is dominated by sadistic and masochistic traits may be, but is not necessarily, neurotic. He believed that certain cultural patterns could result in whole classes of people in whom the sado-masochistic character was typical, though the people involved were "normal." To designate this character type, Fromm suggested the term *authoritarian character*:

> This terminology is justified because the sado-masochistic person is always characterized by his attitude toward authority. He admires authority and tends to submit to it, but at the same time he wants to be an authority

himself and have others submit to him. There is an additional reason for choosing this term. The Fascist systems call themselves authoritarian because of the dominant role of authority in their social and political structure. By the term "authoritarian character," we imply that it represents the human basis of Fascism [Fromm, 1941, p. 186].

Fromm went much further in describing the authoritarian character structure, which is rooted in a basic feeling of powerlessness and characterized by a worship of power and power relations, together with a lack of love and human tenderness. Rather than pursue Fromm's intriguing theoretical analysis further, however, I now turn to the discussion of a famous empirical study that was in part stimulated by Fromm's theory. The study of *The Authoritarian Personality* has fueled controversy for over two decades, a controversy that has yet to be resolved to the satisfaction of many social scientists.

THE AUTHORITARIAN PERSONALITY

Toward the end of World War II a group of research workers in psychology and sociology concerned by the Nazi atrocities, began a study (supported by the American Jewish Committee) of the psychological factors underlying Fascism and anti-Semitism. The findings were published in 1950 in a thick volume entitled *The Authoritarian Personality*, authored by Adorno, Frenkel-Brunswik, Levinson, and Sanford.* Their methodology included both clinical and attitudinal approaches. They constructed, validated, and tested scales of anti-Semitism, ethnocentrism, politico-economic conservatism, and authoritarianism on hundreds of normal subjects. In addition, the investigators used projective tests and clinical interviews with smaller samples in their attempt to assess the underlying personality dynamics of Fascism-prone subjects.

A great deal of criticism has been generated by this study. In particular, the critics have questioned the validity of the findings of *The Authoritarian Personality* because of deficiencies in methodology. Before I discuss the criticisms, let me try to present as faithfully as possible the authors' conclusions about the origins and structure of the authoritarian character. Although a number of techniques were used in the study of authoritarianism, my focus in this discussion is on conclusions derived

---

* Excerpts reprinted by permission of Harper & Row, Publishers, Inc.

from one instrument, the F-Scale. This test was designed to measure the personality characteristics which underlie the acceptance of Fascist ideology and leadership. The justification of emphasizing the F-Scale is that all of the other techniques (attitude scales, projective tests, and clinical interviews) converged in the formation of this one device. Much of the continuing controversy has centered on the adequacy of the F-Scale as a measuring instrument.

The F-Scale

Central to the research effort on authoritarianism is the conception of a particular personality type that is prone to accept Fascist ideology and propaganda. The F-Scale is the instrument defining the core personality dispositions that lead to the acceptance of such anti-democratic attitudes. Although now called a measure of authoritarianism by most investigators, it was conceived by its authors as a measure of potential for Fascism and, therefore, was called the Fascism (F) Scale. The F-Scale went through several revisions; sample items from the final form are shown in Table 7–1. Typical statements, or items, are shown in the table under various cluster headings. In practice the scale was administered with the items in numerical order in a Likert scale format, that is with instructions to "mark each one in the left margin, according to the amount of your agreement or disagreement, by using the following scale [Adorno *et al.,* 1950, p. 68]":

+1: slight support, agreement —1: slight opposition, disagreement
+2: moderate support, " —2: moderate opposition, "
+3: strong support, " —3: strong opposition, "

The F-Scale clusters shown in Table 7–1 reflect the investigators' suppositions regarding the manifest beliefs of the authoritarian personality. *Conventionalism, authoritarian aggression, anti-intraception, superstition and stereotyped thinking, admiration for power and toughness, destructive and cynical attitudes,* and *projection of fears, aggression, and sexual urges* are characteristics derived from psychoanalytic theory and from the authors' previous studies of anti-Semitism and ethnocentric ideology. The character structure so manifested was thought to stem from childhood experiences, especially from subjection to harsh, inflexible discipline, together with a rather cold emotional climate in the home.

Personality and Motivational Factors

Table 7–1 Sample F-Scale items by clusters

(a) *Conventionalism:* Rigid adherence to conventional, middle-class values.
  12. A person who has bad manners, habits, and breeding can hardly expect to get along with decent people.
  41. The businessman and the manufacturer are much more important to society than the artist and the professor.

(b) *Authoritarian Submission:* Submissive, uncritical attitude toward idealized moral authorities of the ingroup.
  1. Obedience and respect for authority are the most important virtues children should learn.
  23. What this country needs most, more than laws and political programs, is a few courageous, tireless, devoted leaders in whom the people can put their faith.

(c) *Authoritarian Aggression:* Tendency to be on the lookout for, and to condemn, reject and punish people who violate conventional values.
  25. Sex crimes, such as rape and attacks on children, deserve more than mere imprisonment; such criminals ought to be publicly whipped, or worse.
  34. Most of our social problems would be solved if we could somehow get rid of the immoral, crooked, and feebleminded people.

(d) *Anti-intraception:* Opposition to the subjective, the imaginative, the tender-minded.
  9. When a person has a problem or worry, it is best for him not to think about it, but to keep busy with more cheerful things.
  31. Nowadays more and more people are prying into matters that should remain personal and private.

(e) *Superstition and Stereotypy:* The belief in mystical determinants of the individual's fate; the disposition to think in rigid categories.
  4. Science has its place, but there are many important things that can never possibly be understood by the human mind.
  16. Some people are born with an urge to jump from high places.

(f) *Power and "Toughness":* Preoccupation with the dominance–submission, strong–weak, leader–follower dimension; identification with power figures; overemphasis upon the conventionalized attributes of the ego; exaggerated assertion of strength and toughness.
  2. No weakness or difficulty can hold us back if we have enough will power.
  26. People can be divided into two distinct classes: the weak and the strong.

(g) *Destructiveness and Cynicism:* Generalized hostility, vilification of the human.
  6. Human nature being what it is, there will always be war and conflict.
  43. Familiarity breeds contempt.

Table 7–1 Cont.

(h) *Projectivity:* The disposition to believe that wild and dangerous things go on in the world; the projection outwards of unconscious emotional impulses.

    18. Nowadays when so many different kinds of people move around and mix together so much, a person has to protect himself especially carefully against catching an infection or disease from them.

    38. Most people don't realize how much our lives are controlled by plots hatched in secret places.

(i) *Sex:* Exaggerated concern with sexual "goings-on."

    35. The wild sex life of the old Greeks and Romans was tame compared to some of the goings-on in this country, even where people might least expect it.

    39. Homosexuals are hardly better than criminals and ought to be severely punished.

Source: T. W. Adorno, E. Frenkel-Brunswik, D. J. Levinson, and R. N. Sanford, *The Authoritarian Personality,* Table 7—F-Scale Clusters (Forms 45 and 40), pp. 255–57. Copyright 1950 by The American Jewish Committee. Used by permission of Harper & Row, Publishers, Inc.

Character Structure

The authoritarian character structure, which underlies the endorsement of the opinions represented in the F-Scale, may be briefly characterized. The framework is Freud's id–ego–superego structure of personality. Given that the primal impulses of the id are at first dominant and unchecked in the infant, the process of development is one of developing controls over the satisfaction of these urges. Through socialization, two control mechanisms for satisfaction and suppression of the sexual and aggressive impulses of the id are developed: the *ego* and the *superego*. The superego contains the standards that specify which gratifications are permissible and which must be prohibited. It develops through simple learning processes and operates to a large degree without the person's awareness. Such parental reactions as slapping the child who is handling his penis, spanking him for talking back, or grim silence in the face of questions regarding birth or reproduction contribute to superego growth without any necessary conscious representation.

The ego is the structure of personality whose job it is to deal rationally with society and to obtain the maximum of satisfaction of id impulses within the restrictions of that society. It must deal also with superego prohibitions. Therefore, the ego is often in the position of mediating between id demands and superego prohibitions, in addition to its dealings with the outside world.

Basically, the authoritarian character is typified by a harsh, punitive superego and a weak, or incompetent, ego. Because of parental punishment, internal mechanisms are not developed for direct satisfaction of id impulses. Rather, these impulses are denied and they are expressed through mechanisms that operate unconsciously. Thus, the authoritarian never consciously comes to grips with his sexual desires and hostile feelings. Since the authoritarian's superego is largely an internalization of parental authority, rather than independent values, he strongly adheres to conventional values. The same explanation applies to his submission to authority figures. Since the superego prohibits aggression against authority, and since the individual inevitably harbors aggressive feelings, the individual *displaces* his hostility onto minority groups or other targets. This seems similar to *scapegoating*, in which an individual or group in a frustrating and uncertain situation turns against some plausible source of its difficulties. The authoritarian, however, is *compelled* to attack people who are different. Authoritarian aggression results from deep-seated personality needs: "the authoritarian *must*, out of an inner necessity, turn his aggression against outgroups [Adorno *et al.*, 1950, p. 233]."

Because the authoritarian character structure requires denial, rather than acknowledgment, of impulses, various mechanisms are employed in the service of self-deception. *Anti-intraception*, for example, is an attitude of opposition to any close examination of one's own feelings and motives. A belief in external causes (superstition) likewise reduces the need for self-examination. The emphasis on power and toughness is also a form of denial, in this case the denial of one's lack of ego control. Finally, the utilitarian function of statements in the destructiveness, projectivity, and sex clusters can be discerned in light of the foregoing discussion. Projection, in particular, permeates all of these ideas; that is, the tendency to attribute (project) unacknowledged desires onto other people. Thus, Statement 6: "Human nature being what it is, there will always be war and conflict," is interpreted as projection of hostility: "A person can most freely express aggression when he believes that everybody is doing it and, hence, if he wants to be aggressive, he is disposed to believe that everybody *is* doing it, e.g., that it is 'human nature' to exploit and make war on one's neighbors [p. 239]." Similarly, endorsement of sexual items implies projection of repressed sexual impulses.

IS THERE AN AUTHORITARIAN PERSONALITY?

The research by Adorno and his co-workers (1950) has been criticized on many grounds. The basic conception has been challenged, as has the methodology on which the authors' conclusions rest. [*Studies in the Scope and Method of the Authoritarian Personality* (Christie and Jahoda, 1954) is devoted to the analysis of these criticisms.] In the work preceding the development of the F-Scale, for example, prejudiced and unprejudiced subjects were intensively interviewed and tested. The characteristics that differentiated the two groups form the basic clusters of characteristics shown in Table 7–1. These clusters are in question because the interviewers knew that the particular subject being interviewed belonged to either the prejudiced or unprejudiced group. Knowing these classifications and the theoretical hypotheses may have biased the interviewers' clinical interpretations.

A major criticism of the F-Scale itself is that all of the items are so worded that agreement contributes to a high F-score. Thus, a simple agreeing response set, which Bass (1955) termed *"acquiescence,"* could explain high scores on the F-Scale. It has indeed been determined that agreement with F-Scale items is only partly determined by the content of the statement.

Another criticism is that educational and intellectual differences seem to correlate with F-Scale scores. In *The Authoritarian Personality*, there are data showing a negative relationship between ethnocentrism (E) and both intelligence and years of education. Since ethnocentrism is highly correlated with F, the latter must also be related to intellectual attainment. That is, high F-Scale scores are more often achieved by persons of low intelligence and little schooling. While Adorno *et al.* minimized this relationship, the critics feel that it brings into question many of the supposed psychological dynamics underlying authoritarianism. Hyman and Sheatsley (in Christie and Jahoda, 1954), among others, have expressed concern that many of the findings relating to prejudice and authoritarianism are more simply explained by educational differences among the population. In other words, less educated people may show a tendency to endorse authoritarian or ethnocentric statements apart from any differences in personality. Hyman and Sheatsley reported data from a national survey on agreement with individual items on the F-Scale. On one ideological item central to the conception of authoritarianism, "There are two kinds of people in the world: the weak and the strong," only 30% agreement was recorded for college graduates, whereas 53% of the high school graduates, and 71% with no education beyond grammar school, agreed. The presence of such attitudinal tendencies has been referred to as "working class authoritarianism" (Lipset, 1959). Whether such beliefs stem from personality differences or from educational deprivation is a moot point; however, the lack of perspective they indicate is antithetical to democratic political norms.

Roger Brown (1965), in a balanced review of evidence pro and con the Adorno *et al.* conception of the origins of authoritarianism, concluded that perhaps both personality and educational factors are important. That is, in spite of the many acknowledged deficiencies in the original studies and even in subsequent reports, the positive statistical interrelationships among anti-Semitism, ethnocentrism, and authoritarian attitudes seem to appear consistently. While the evidence for the genesis of such attitudinal syndromes is less well confirmed, there is evidence that strict, rigid, and punitive parental discipline is correlated with prejudice and high F-Scale scores. Whether, indeed, the mediating factors are the set of personality dynamics characterized as the authoritarian personality is less easily demonstrated:

> On the level of interpretation, the level on which repression is supposed to lead to displacement, rationalization, and anti-intraception, things are less certain. These ideas about personality dynamics cannot be proved by correlation. Studies of an entirely different kind are needed. . . .
>
> The major alternative to the personality dynamic explanation of the covariation is the suggestion that the traits of the authoritarian cohere simply because they are the norms of people with little education and low SES [socioeconomic status]. For each particular trait one could work out some plausible derivation from one or another aspect of SES. The dynamic explanation would make the coherence tighter by showing how one trait supports another, not logically but in terms of the needs and defenses postulated by psychoanalytic theory. *It is likely that both sets of forces— the dynamic interrelations as well as the ties with status and education— cooperate to hold this mosaic together* [Brown, 1965, pp. 525–26; italics added].

AUTHORITARIANISM AND POLITICAL BEHAVIOR

The importance of authoritarianism to the understanding of political behavior lies in its utility in predicting such things as political participation, adoption of liberal or conservative ideology, and the like, as well as predicting the tendency to join Fascist political movements. In the last analysis, our assessment must be based on the actual existence of the "authoritarian personality." For the present, no definitive answer to this question is possible. We must be content, rather, to ask whether taking authoritarianism into account will allow us to make better explanations of political behavior. By "better," I mean, does the addition of authoritarianism allow us to make more accurate predictions than would be possible using only such factors as social class, economic marginality, self-conception, and similar psychological and sociological variables?

The problems in making such an assessment are numerous. First, as I have noted, much painstaking research is necessary to substantiate the existence of dynamic factors underlying the surface manifestations of prejudice and acquiescence to authority. There is no sign at present of an intense research effort along these lines. Second, many, if not most, of the findings regarding differences between authoritarians and nonauthoritarians may be explained by simpler (if more pedestrian and less elegant) concepts than that of an authoritarian personality structure. Given that many factors having to do with one's place in the social order manifestly *do* dictate one's perceptions of and reactions to social situations, at the least the authors of *The Authoritarian Personality* have overemphasized dynamic determinants. There are many empirical correlates of authoritarianism, however, as the hundreds of studies that have employed the F-Scale since 1950 demonstrate. Some examples are given in the following section.

Authoritarianism and Political Ideology

The authors of *The Authoritarian Personality* found authoritarianism to be related to political conservatism. That is, people with high F-Scale scores tend to have conservative attitudes. The conservatism of the authoritarian is not the traditional laissez-faire type, which advocates keeping things as they are. Rather, it seems to be a kind of "pseudoconservatism," which rejects the rights of minorities and deviants (Adorno *et al.*, 1950). This notion of authoritarianism as a right-wing phenomenon has been supported by Rokeach (1960), who found that English Fascists scored higher on the F-Scale than members of other groups. Rokeach argued however, that authritarianism is actually a cognitive style—it represents a closed-minded way of thinking about the world. The F-Scale measures only right-wing authoritarianism, according to Rokeach, whereas the Dogmatism scale is a relatively nonideological measure of authoritarianism. Eysenck (1954) has argued that both Communists and Fascists are high on authoritarianism; and while both Rokeach and Eysenck have furnished some data that purport to show that political people on both extremes are authoritarian, their contention is by no means proven.

Along the same lines, it has been suggested that partisan choice is related to authoritarianism. Leventhal, Jacobs, and Kudirka (1964) investigated this hypothesis in mock elections before the 1960 Presidential and 1962 Congressional elections. Students who scored high on the F-Scale preferred the Republican over the Democratic Party, and Nixon over Kennedy. In the 1960 study, the authoritarians more often chose the conservative over the liberal candidate, regardless of party label.

Authoritarian attitudes have also been shown to relate to specific policy preferences consistent with the "pseudoconservatism" postulated by Adorno *et al.* (1950). High F-Scale scorers, for example, supported General MacArthur in his dispute with President Truman. They disagreed with the statement that "MacArthur should have been dismissed" significantly more often than did subjects scoring low on the F-Scale (Gump, 1953). Similarly, authoritarians tested during the loyalty-oath controversy at the University of California were shown to favor such oaths for faculty members (Handlon and Squier, 1955). Opposition to socialized medicine is another of the many consistent correlates of authoritarian ideology as measured by the F-Scale (Mahler, 1953).

Williams (1963), in a study making use of an environmental event, found differences in response to an airplane hijacking between high and low authoritarians. The day after the hijacking of a plane to Cuba (July 1961), students in an introductory psychology course were asked to take the F-Scale and afterward to indicate agreement or disagreement with Florida's Senator Smathers. Speaking at a time when feelings against Castro's Communist regime in Cuba were running high, Smathers advocated telling Castro that "if the plane is not released in 24 hours we're coming after it." Students scoring high on the F-Scale were significantly more likely to agree with Smathers's position than were those in the lower half of the F-Scale score distribution: 77% of the high authoritarians, and only 43% of the lows, wanted to draw guns and ride on Cuba!

Behavior in Groups

Conformity and obedience to authority, of course, are central to the conception of the authoritarian personality. The tendency of the authoritarian to conform to peer pressures has been documented in several studies (e.g., Nadler, 1959). Obedience to authority was the focus of Milgram's (1963) now famous experiments on obedience. Subjects were brought into Milgram's laboratory and given a carefully constructed rationale about the learning experiment in which they were to participate as the "teacher." The subject was told that he would be delivering electric shocks to the "learner" (a confederate in the experiment) as punishment for incorrect responses. The shock intensity was to be increased step by step as the learner's mistakes continued. After receiving a few shocks, the learner, who was in an adjoining room, began making noises that indicated that the shocks were severely painful. At that point, many subjects were inclined to discontinue their participation in the experiment. They were told: "The experiment requires that you continue." Some subjects ended their participation anyway, but over half of those who participated in Milgram's initial experiment obeyed completely these commands. High F-Scale scorers showed such obedience significantly more often than did lows (Elms and Milgram, 1966).

It might be supposed that differences in authoritarianism as measured by the F-Scale would affect the individual's response to the leadership styles described at the beginning of this chapter. In terms of leader preference, Haythorne *et al.* (1956) found that authoritarians tended to prefer directive leaders. Low scorers more often chose leaders who were friendly and less directive. Shaw (1959) found that performance and satisfaction of group members related to their degree of authoritarianism and the structure of the group.

Shaw observed the response of authoritarians and nonauthoritarians to authoritarian and democratic group structures. In contrast with White and Lippitt's (1960) work with boy's groups, the group structures in Shaw's (1959) study were defined either by controlling communication patterns or the power differentials within the group. Shaw's subjects were characterized as high or low in acceptance to authority (AA), in

Wheel

Concom

Figure 7–1 Communication networks with restricted (wheel) and unrestricted (concom) communication patterns: the circles represent individual subjects and the lines represent two-way communication channels; four-person networks are shown to illustrate those used by Shaw (1969).

accordance with a scale devised by R. F. Bales (1958) containing many F-Scale items.

Shaw's first experiment utilized the communication nets devised by Bavelas (1950). The wheel pattern (see Figure 7–1) restricted communication patterns; all the written messages had to pass through a central person. The second pattern, the all-channel or concom pattern, allowed each of the four subjects to communicate with any of the others. Problem solving was fastest in the decentralized structure, but leader authoritarianism was an important factor: In the restricted (wheel) nets, groups led by high authoritarian (high AA) leaders did no better than those led by low AA leaders. In the more "democratic" concom structure, however, groups led by "democratic" (low AA) leaders did significantly better. These differences are shown in Table 7–2, which depicts the average times for problem solution (note that shortest times are best scores).

In Shaw's second experiment, groups were varied in that one person was given the final decision on the answer to be presented for the group's problem solution (leader power) in half the groups, and the group mem-

Table 7–2 Problem-solving mean-time scores as a function of leader authoritarianism (AA) and communication restrictions

| | | COMMUNICATION NETWORK | |
		Restricted (Wheel)	Unrestricted (Concom)
LEADER	High	9.0	8.7
AA SCORE	Low	9.1	6.6

Source: Computed by the author from data provided by M. E. Shaw in "Acceptance of authority, group structure, and the effectiveness of small groups," *Journal of Personality*, 1959, 27, 196–210.

bers were to decide by vote among themselves (group power) in the other half of the four-man groups. Here, the emphasis was on the response of groups varying in average level of authoritarianism. While the results were not entirely clear-cut, it is evident that the groups higher in authoritarianism were more involved and worked more conscientiously under leader power conditions. Low AA groups, on the other hand, worked better under group power.

Political Participation

In the realm of political participation, Sanford (1950, p. 168) reported that "authoritarians are not highly participant in political affairs, do not join many community groups, do not become officers in those groups they become members of." Sanford found significantly lower authoritarianism among political actives, as opposed to people who only voted. The voters, similarly, were lower in authoritarianism than the nonvoters among Sanford's respondents. Age, education, and economic status were not considered in Sanford's study, however, and another investigation in a more homogeneous population (college students) failed to find a relationship between authoritarianism, as measured by the F-Scale, and political apathy (Mussen and Wyszinski, 1952).

Finally, Janowitz and Marvick (1953) reported on an extensive sample survey that employed Sanford's (1950) scale to measure the authoritarianism of respondents. They considered age, education, and social class in relation to authoritarianism scores and political behavior. They found, first, that authoritarianism is not a middle-class or bourgeois phenomenon; overall incidence of high scores was almost as high in the lower class as in the middle class. When income was considered, however, the lower income group of the middle class was much more authoritarian than the upper income group of the middle class. Similarly, age and educational status were linked with authoritarianism; the younger and better educated within each social class were found to be less authoritarian than the older and less-educated respondents.

With regard to political beliefs and behavior, the high authoritarians tended to be more isolationist with regard to foreign affairs, to have a greater feeling of personal political ineffectiveness, and to be less likely to vote. Overall, authoritarianism did not explain candidate preference in the 1948 Presidential election (Truman versus Dewey). In the middle class, neither the group most disposed to authoritarianism (the poorly educated) nor the well-educated respondents voted differentially for Truman or Dewey. Although some 80% of the well-educated middle class did vote, as compared to only 44% of the poorly educated middle-class respondents, half of the voters in each group selected Dewey, the other half, Truman. In the poorly educated lower class, a group high in authoritarianism, the votes of the 40% who did vote were over three to one in favor of Truman. These data suggest that class interest in Truman's Fair Deal program, and not authoritarianism, determined voting patterns in the 1948 election.

CONCLUSION

Insofar as the "authoritarian character" is conceived as an attitudinal syndrome, its existence seems fairly well demonstrated. Numerous relationships between authoritarian attitudes and political opinion and behavior also seem established. Two important questions remain, however: First, does the authoritarian pattern actually constitute a character type, or can the attitudes best be explained on the basis of background factors such as age, social class, and educational attainment? The second question, if the first is given an affirmative answer, concerns the genesis of the authoritarian character. Does this type of character develop along the lines suggested by psychoanalytic theory, or is authoritarian character more fruitfully construed as a motivational syndrome which develops in the context of the individual's socialization experiences?

In the light of the evidence now available, I accept the existence of a coherent set of traits that fits the general notion of the authoritarian character. The same evidence suggests that we can also posit a "democratic character structure" characterized by freedom and spontaneity, which in general is the mirror image of the authoritarian. I shrink from total acceptance of the idea of any fixed character structure, however, since social psychologists have shown over and over again the effects of the situation in determining behavior. If a person or group of people is placed in an authoritarian structure and required to remain there, most people will adapt to the demands of that structure over a period of time, regardless of personality disposition.

With regard to formative influences, at least equal weight must be given to social structure, class, education, and income considerations, along with familial and dynamic determinants. It is my view that the theoretical origins of authoritarianism, as presented by the authors of *The Authoritarian Personality*, are far from established in any scientific sense.

Authoritarian attitudes *are* of importance to political psychology even though their basis in character structure is still in doubt. The existence in a democratic society of sizable numbers of citizens who exhibit antidemocratic ideology is a threat to that society. It seems likely, at the least, that authoritarianism represents a narrowness of perspective resulting from educational and social deprivation (Kelman and Barclay, 1963).

8

Liberalism–Conservatism

It has been customary to label gradations from one extreme [of opinion] to the other . . . these names refer to time aspects of the issue under consideration. The reactionary is regarded as one who prefers not the existing, but a past state of an institution; the conservative is assumed to have an attachment to things as they are: the liberal is said to prefer modifications of the *status quo* when they permit a building of the new into the pattern of the old; and the radical approves of and seeks drastic changes in the existing order.

CHARLES BIRD, *Social Psychology*, 1940

The liberal person's stands on social and political issues can be readily catalogued. Having opposed U.S. military involvement in Vietnam, he would reduce foreign military aid and overall defense expenditures; he favors programs to promote social integration; and he is for better welfare coverage. Further, the liberal supports labor unions, favors strict controls over industrial pollution, advocates the progressive income tax, is for the establishment of day-care centers for the children of working mothers, and is likely to support liberalization of laws relating to divorce, abortion, and marijuana.

Of course, there are a few exceptions. One of the issues used in the successful election campaign of the liberal President John F. Kennedy was the need for a stronger military posture. Kennedy charged, for example, that the Eisenhower administration had allowed a "missile gap" to develop between the United States and the Soviet Union. Another departure from uniformity in liberal positions is found within the Socialist Party in the United States. (The Socialist Party is now operating under the title Social Democrats, U.S.A.) The party strongly supports labor union prerogatives, efforts to ensure full equality for blacks, and liberal economic policies. At the same time, it has been hopelessly divided on the Vietnam war—to the extent that majority sentiment in the party has supported President Nixon's policies in Vietnam over strong minority opposition.

These examples suggest some difficulties regarding the traditional conception of a liberal–conservative continuum ranging from radical at one end through liberal and conservative positions to reactionary positions at the far right. Many political observers continue to think of liberal–conservative ideology as an important axis of political life, however, so there is a need to examine the usefulness of such a typology in describing the political mass man.

Psychologists in particular have stressed liberalism–conservatism as an important attitudinal structure. Bird (1940) described a number of early studies of "radicalism–conservatism," and the 1937 edition of *Experimental Social Psychology* (Murphy, Murphy, and Newcomb) has an extensive catalogue of such research. A number of scales are available for the measurement of left–right attitudinal tendencies, but none of them is commonly accepted as a fully adequate measure (see, for example, Shaw and Wright, 1967, pp. 302–24; and Robinson *et al.*, 1968, pp. 79–160). An English investigator of these problems, Hans Eysenck (1954), used existing attitude scales, as well as statements devised by himself and his students, to study radical–conservative attitudes. The results of his research have occasioned some controversy.

In the attitude scale upon which Eysenck has based many of his conclusions, the following statements represent radical positions: *

- Ultimately, private property should be abolished and complete socialism introduced.
- Men and women have the right to find out whether they are sexually suited before marriage (e.g., by trial marriage).
- Our treatment of criminals is too harsh; we should try to cure them, not punish them.

Conservative attitudinal orientations are represented in Eysenck's research by the following statements:

* Excerpts from H. J. Eysenck, *The Psychology of Politics*, copyright 1954 by Routledge & Kegan Paul Ltd., are used by permission.

- · Production and trade should be free from government interference.
- · "My country right or wrong" is a saying which expresses a fundamentally desirable attitude.
- · We should believe without question all that we are taught by the Church.

Of course, one can reveal radical beliefs by agreeing with radical statements and disagreeing with conservative statements, and vice versa for the conservative.

Do one's beliefs regarding private property, permissiveness toward sexual behavior, leniency toward criminals, patriotism, free trade, and conventional religion actually have anything in common? Eysenck's (1954) writings suggest that one's opinions on these matters do go together, such that they constitute attitude clusters, which in turn comprise liberal, conservative, or radical *ideologies*. Eysenck (1954) maintained that:

> There can be no doubt whatever that attitudes do not occur in splendid isolation but are closely linked with other attitudes in some kind of pattern or structure. Indeed, the very existence of parties and political labels implies as much; to say that a person is a Socialist or Conservative immediately suggests that he holds not just one particular opinion on one particular issue, but rather that his views and opinions on a large number of different issues will form a definite pattern [p. 107].

Eysenck used the scheme shown in Figure 8–1 to relate specific opinions or beliefs to habitual opinions of the individual and thence to his attitudes and ideology. Whatever level we consider, belief, opinion, or attitude, will relate to the left–right ideological dimension, Eysenck believed. Even specific beliefs on the social and economic issues mentioned have liberal–conservative ideological implications. Whether such broad ideological orientations do in fact exist has been questioned, as we consider later in the chapter. But let us look further into Eysenck's ideas before criticizing them.

PERSONALITY AND IDEOLOGY:
EYSENCK'S TWO-FACTOR THEORY

As I have suggested, Hans Eysenck believes that political ideology ranges along a left–right continuum. This continuum he labeled "R," for radical-

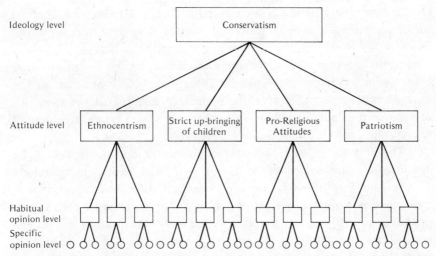

Figure 8–1 Diagram illustrating relation between opinion, attitude and ideology (Adapted from H. J. Eysenck, *The Psychology of Politics*, p. 112. Copyright 1954 by Routledge & Kegan Paul Ltd. Used by permission.)

ism, which is one extreme of the ideological scale running from radicalism to conservatism. In research dating back to the 1950s Eysenck has found differences in radicalism among English political parties and groups in the expected order: The Fascists rank lowest on radicalism, followed with some separation by members of the Conservative Party, and then the Liberal and Labor Parties respectively. Members of the Communist party, whose average scores anchored the scale on the left, were most radical. Such a pattern is commonly expected and is not particularly controversial. The aspect of Eysenck's work that does lead to controversy is his finding of strong similarities between Fascists and Communists. He believes that members of the two extreme groups are similar in terms of personality factors, which in turn are reflected in the attitudinal domain by a distinctive cognitive style. In order to understand Eysenck's argument, we must first examine this style, which he terms the T-dimension (tough–tender-mindedness).

Tough-Mindedness and Tender-Mindedness

Tough-mindedness and tender-mindedness are terms taken from William James's (1907) references to two opposing philosophical temperaments which lead to differing belief systems. The terminology was

Personality and Motivational Factors

chosen by Eysenck as the best characterization of the second attitudinal factor that emerged from his statistical analysis of the test scores achieved by his subjects. This factor was orthogonal to the radicalism dimension (*orthogonal* factors are independent; in this context, this means that being "tough-minded" does not imply any particular position on the radicalism dimension). That is, the points representing each statement's factor loadings could be plotted with reference to two axes at right angles to one another as shown in Figure 8–2.

The test items that indicate tough- or tender-mindedness (The T-dimension) are suggested in Figure 8–2. The items most strongly "loaded" on T are those farthest from the radicalism–conservatism axis. Eysenck originally thought of the T-factor in terms of a theoretical–practical dimension, but found a better conceptualization in James's work. James (1907) listed the characteristics of the two temperamental types as shown in Table 8–1.

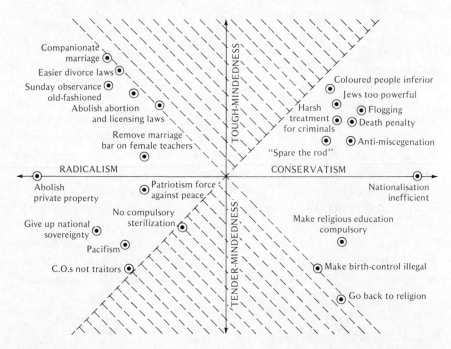

Figure 8–2 Distribution of attitudes with respect to tough-mindedness and radicalism (Adapted from H. J. Eysenck, *The Psychology of Politics*, p. 130. Copyright 1954 by Routledge & Kegan Paul Ltd. Used by permission.)

Table 8–1   Characteristics of the tender-minded and tough-minded person

The Tender-Minded	The Tough Minded
Rationalistic (going by "principles")	Empiricist (going by "facts")
Intellectualistic	Sensationalistic
Idealistic	Materialistic
Optimistic	Pessimistic
Religious	Irreligious
Free-willist	Fatalistic
Monistic	Pluralistic
Dogmatical	Sceptical

Source: William James, *Pragmatism,* New York: Longmans, Green, 1907, p. 12.

The tough-minded person favors capital punishment, divorce reform, harsh treatment of criminals, and so on. His counterpart is favorable to Sunday church attendance, pacifism, prohibition, and belief in God. In a paper originally written in 1944, Eysenck (1954) discussed the dichotomy represented by this second factor:

> Thus, on the one side we have the practical, materialistic, extraverted person, who deals with the environment either by force (soldier) or by manipulation (scientist). On the other side we have the theoretical, idealistic, introverted person, who deals with problems either by thinking (philosopher) or by believing (priest). The best way of describing this factor is perhaps by stressing the *practical–theoretical* dichotomy . . . this factor also seems to be connected closely with temperamental factors. The *practical* attitude is that of James's "tough-minded" man, of the extravert; the *theoretical* attitude is that of the "tender-minded" introvert [p. 119].

Eysenck (1954) has also discussed the parallel between the T-dimension and authoritarian–democratic ideology. He pointed out that authoritarians often take pride in the greater practicality of dictatorial regimes, looking down on the ". . . preoccupations of democracies with theoretical, legal, and religious problems and scruples. The very term 'Realpolitik' was originally coined to convey this impression of political behavior unhampered by extraneous considerations of a theoretical or philosophical ethico-religious character [p. 120]." James (1907) suggested that these temperamental differences have always been important parts of the philosophic atmosphere, and continue in importance today: The tough think of the tender as sentimentalists and softheads. The tender feel the tough to be unrefined, callous, or brutal [p. 113]." Modern science, James believed, has tended to favor the tough-minded.

> Ideals appear as inert by-products of physiology; what is higher is explained by what is lower and treated forever as a case of "Nothing but"— nothing but something else of a quite inferior sort. You get, in short, a materialistic universe in which only the tough-minded find themselves congenially at home [pp. 16–17].

PRIMARY ATTITUDES AND POLITICAL IDEOLOGY. According to Eysenck (1954), the combination of radicalism and tough-mindedness determines the individual's political preferences. To quote his summary with respect to this point:

> . . . Fascists were found to be a tough-minded conservative group, Communists a tough-minded radical group. Conservatives and Socialists were found to be conservative and radical respectively on the R-factor, and intermediate with respect to the T-factor. Liberals were found to be the most tender-minded group and to be intermediate between Socialists and Conservatives with respect to the Radicalism–Conservatism variable [p. 266].

Eysenck believes these relationships to be quite firmly established on the basis of several studies done by him and his students, a belief not shared by all psychologists (e.g., Christie, 1955, 1956, a, b). But we are getting ahead of the story. While there are serious criticisms of Eysenck's theory, before taking up these criticisms, I wish to discuss more thoroughly the relationships between personality and political attitudes as Eysenck sees them.

INTROVERSION–EXTRAVERSION AND THE T-FACTOR. Hans Eysenck is a clinical psychologist whose primary interest is in personality theory. One of his many books is *The Structure of Human Personality*, which was first published in 1951 and by 1970 was in its third edition. His research has primarily involved testing and the use of correlational approaches (factor analysis) to isolate fundamental dimensions of personality. According to Eysenck, one of the most important personality dimensions is introversion–extraversion. The contrasting personality styles of introversion and extraversion were first observed and reported by the Swiss psychoanalyst Carl Jung.

Both in Jung's writings and in the subsequent work by Eysenck, the introvert is presented as shy, self-conscious, tending to nervousness and feelings of inferiority, and moody. He tends to be oriented toward his own inner feelings and thoughts. The extravert, on the other hand, is more concerned about external objects and his relations to the world outside of himself. He is said to be outgoing, to prefer action to contemplation, and to see himself as lively and sociable.[1]

Eysenck considers introversion—extraversion to be a pervasive dimension of personality. The extensive differences in life style that characterize the two types are, he believes, the result of differences in their ability to form conditioned reflexes. The introvert conditions more easily and thus is prone to develop inhibitions, as well as sensitivities. The two other primary dimensions of personality proposed by Eysenck (neuroticism and psychoticism) need not concern us here, though they are important to a complete understanding of his personality theory.

The importance of introversion—extraversion in the present context is that this personality dimension is seen as underlying the T-factor in the ideological sphere. Tough—tender-mindedness is not, Eysenck has maintained, an attitudinal dimension in the same sense as radicalism—conservatism. Rather, T is the reflection of the personality dimension of extraversion—introversion. In Eysenck's (1954) words:

> While the R-factor could truly be called a major dimension of social attitudes, the T-factor was of a different character altogether. It appeared essentially as a *projection* onto the field of social attitudes of certain fundamental personality traits, in the sense that a person's social attitude (Radical, Conservative, or intermediate) would seek expression in terms of the fundamental personality variables so closely connected with the T-factor [p. 266].

He goes on to relate tough-mindedness with extraversion and tender-mindedness with introversion.

---

[1] Harvey, Hunt, and Schroeder (1961, pp. 202–3) listed extravert and introvert traits as follows:

Extravert	Introvert
Carefree	Sensitive
Insensitive	Personal
Free from inhibitions	Intellectual
Ascendant	Deep
Changeable	Persistent
Non-persistent	Obsessional
	Submissive

The Learning of Political Attitudes

In the final chapter of *The Psychology of Politics* (1954), Eysenck advanced "a theory of political action." In this chapter, he discussed the relationship between attitudes and action, stressing the importance of learning principles. Of special consequence for the theory I have been discussing is Eysenck's attempt to apply Hullian learning theory [2] to the development of political tendencies. Following O. H. Mowrer (1950), Eysenck distinguishes between *conditioning* and *learning*.

Conditioning involves automatic activities, the responses of the smooth muscles and glands, governing such activities as breathing, heart beat, etc. Learning, as Eysenck uses the term, involves the skeletal musculature and the so-called voluntary responses. The distinction between learning and conditioning was explained by Eysenck (1954) in the following way:

> Some types of learning are directly useful and produce results which are pleasant. We learn to ride a bicycle, play cricket, or make love, and the resulting pleasure "stamps in" the actions which have produced this result. On the other hand, we are afraid when we see a bear in the woods, or hear bullets whining overhead, or find a bus bearing down on us. These reactions are unpleasant and are conditioned rather than learned; in spite of being unpleasant, however, they are exceedingly useful. As Mowrer puts it, learning is parallel to what Freud has called the *pleasure principle*, whereas conditioning is more closely related to the *reality principle*. "In other words, living organisms acquire conditioned responses or emotions, not because it is pleasant to do so, but because it is *realistic*." It is certainly not pleasant to be afraid, for example, but it is very helpful from the standpoint of personal survival [p. 257].

The importance of these observations lies in Eysenck's assertion that radical and conservative attitudes are *learned*, whereas T-factor attitudes result from the conditioning process. I shall try to explain the reasoning underlying this interesting hypothesis.

Pointing to the considerable correlation between political philosophy and social class, status, and income, Eysenck has suggested that radical–

---

[2] After Clark L. Hull, an architect of modern learning theory. See Kimble, 1961, for a discussion of Hull's theory.

conservative attitudes are taught to the individual. That is, one is re-warded for expressing views in accordance with those of one's fellows. In addition, Eysenck has noted the tendency to expect definite benefits from the political party one supports. Thus, radical and conservative ori-entations are directly learned in consequence of the rewards they bring from one's associates. Such straightforward application of the pleasure principle does not account for tough-minded and tender-minded attitudes, however. These attitudes result from conditioning.

The evidence that the conditioning process underlies T-attitudes is at best indirect. Two variables are said to relate to the success of condi-tioning in society. These variables are the *amount* of conditioning im-posed by the child's parents and teachers and the relative *conditionability* of the child (that is, the speed with which he forms conditioned re-sponses). Granting that there are individual differences in condition-ability, there is no reason to believe that such differences vary with social class. Therefore, Eysenck (1954) suggested that there are social-class dif-ferences in the *amount* of conditioning imposed by parents. He has cited evidence "that there is a distinct tendency for middle-class children to be subjected to a considerably more prolonged and intensive conditioning process with respect to the suppression of directly aggressive and sexual modes of behavior [1954, p. 259]."

Having tentatively established such social-class differences in amount of conditioning, Eysenck then pointed to parallel differences in tender-mindedness. He noted that the tough-minded end of the T-dimen-sion contains items dealing with immediate satisfaction of aggressive (war, capital punishment) and sexual (birth control, abortion) impulses. Such tendencies toward impulse expression are thought to be more prev-alent in the lower socioeconomic strata. The ethical and moral restraints implied by the tender-minded test items, on the other hand—restraints "which since time immemorial have been part of the socialization proc-ess"—are thought to be more characteristic of middle and upper socio-economic class respondents. Thus, Eysenck asserted that the well-socialized middle-class person should be more tender-minded and the less-socialized lower-class person, more tough-minded. Such indeed is the case in his comparison of scores in the T-factor between working-class and middle-class Britons. In this finding there seems at least a rudi-mentary basis for the two-factor theory of the learning of political attitudes.

CRITIQUE OF EYSENCK'S TWO-FACTOR THEORY

Eysenck's analysis of the relations between personality and political ideology is beguiling to the student of political psychology. Obviously, the liberal–conservative dimension of attitudes is important; equally obvious is the fact that the attitudes represented by this dimension do not completely explain political activity or affiliation. So it seems reasonable to add another dimension that contrasts the practical, tough-minded approach with the idealistic, tender-minded approach to social questions. The T-dimension does seem to make sense, and Eysenck has presented a compelling argument for its psychological reality based both on theory and statistical evidence. The addition of introversion–extraversion to this scheme as the basis for variations in the T-factor attitudes completes the theory. The final product is a rather reasonable, simple, and credible theory for dealing with differences in political ideology.

In spite of the internal consistency and the theoretical attractiveness of Eysenck's R–T theory, supporting evidence has been slow to accumulate. Many commentators have been critical of the evidence offered by Eysenck in support of his theory (Christie, 1955, 1956a, b; Hanley and Rokeach, 1956; Rokeach and Hanley, 1956). In particular, the sampling procedures and the validity of the measuring instruments have been questioned. In a rather harsh judgment, Christie (1955) asserted that the evidence in support of the highly plausible argument, which I summarized in the preceding paragraph, was based ". . . upon samples which are at best atypical and at worst highly aberrant, upon the use of scales which do not measure what they are purported to measure, and upon a misleading analysis of results [p. 703]." Much of the criticism has focused upon the tender–tough-mindedness measure. The critics question whether, in fact, the T-factor does exist apart from R. Moreover, the critics have questioned Eysenck's assertion of similarities in personality between Communist and Fascist party members; that is, they question whether the members of these groups are equally tough-minded.

My reading of Eysenck's book and of a recently published paper by Eysenck and Coulter (1972) has convinced me that the foregoing criticisms are warranted. It should also be noted that although the evidence supporting the theory is weak, there is little contradictory evidence. The studies that have been done suggest that the operational measures of T are inadequate.

One piece of research, a dissertation completed at American University in 1958 by L. Schatz, did undertake to evaluate the R- and T-scales. Schatz found no relation, in a United States' sample, between extraversion and T (using the Edwards Personal Preference Scale to measure extraversion). Schatz questioned the psychological meaningfulness of T, both because of the lack of relation to extraversion and because of the correlation between T and R. Schatz found that one subset of T-items, religionism, correlated positively with conservatism. The second T-subset, humanitarianism, correlated significantly with radicalism. DeFronzo (1972) also used Eysenck's fourteen items for the measurement of tender-mindedness. The statements were divided into eight humanitarianism items and six religionism items. He found the same relationship between these subsets and political leanings as had Schatz. These studies lend some support to Argyle's (1958) contention that Eysenck's tender–tough-mindedness is actually a composite of several tendencies. These tendencies include authoritarianism–humanism and two types of religious orientation, which could be termed conventional religiosity and liberal religiosity.

There seem to be two main difficulties with Eysenck's theory apart from deficiencies in his research methodology. One concerns his unsupported assertion of a single dimension of radicalism–conservatism. Various investigations in the United States have called into question such unidimensionality of political ideology in the general population. Key (1961) noted that, "despite the obvious correlation between domestic liberalism and internationalism during the 1950's in Congress and among political activists, the two clusters seem to have been essentially unrelated in the general public, according to the 1952 and 1956 Survey Research Center Data [pp. 157–58]." Observations of the "populist" sentiments, which seem prevalent in some parts of the United States, also raise questions about the existence of a single radical–conservative axis underlying political attitudes. Populist ideology was characterized by Axelrod (1967) as a cluster of attitudes of mixed liberal–conservative content: favoring welfare, but opposing taxation, foreign involvements, and civil liberties.

The second major difficulty in Eysenck's theory is, of course, the questionable nature of the T-factor. Eysenck is the first to admit that no "pure" T-scale items can be found, but asserts that the T-loading derived from factor analysis can accurately measure differences in tender-mindedness. Among most observers, however, the lack of any T-items that measure tender-mindedness, while being neutral with regard to radicalism, weakens the case for T as an important politico-psychological dimension. However, the argument for the two-factor scheme has sufficient plausibility that additional research effort should be worthwhile. Particularly needed are alternative measures of tough–tender-mindedness or, alternatively, the idealistic–practical orientation.

A possible alternative measure of T is Machiavellianism (see Chapter 6), which may prove to be closer to what Eysenck means by T than the scale he used to measure tender-mindedness. Certainly, the Machiavellian has been shown to be "tough-minded" in his dealings with other people. Also, the content of the positive Mach items seems to evidence a practical, or tough-minded, approach. For example, the statement, "Barnum was right when he said there's a sucker born every minute," is endorsed by the Machiavellian.

Other observations support the idea of Mach scores as an alternative measure of the T-dimension. There is some reason, for instance, to believe that Machiavellianism is independent of liberalism–conservatism, a necessary requisite to overcome past criticisms of the tough–tender-minded dimension. This suggestion follows the evidence reported by Christie and Geis (1970, Chapter 3). Although the evidence is not direct, they did find that Mach scores were essentially unrelated to intelligence. Since intelligence is generally correlated with liberalism, we may infer that Machiavellianism is unrelated to liberalism–conservatism.[3]

In addition to the suggested *lack* of relation to radicalism, Machiavellianism has other correlates that suggest tough-mindedness. High Machs have been shown to be high in anomie, which would seem to parallel the cynicism of the tough-minded individual. Also high Machiavellians are more hostile, suspicious, have little faith in human nature, and show external control expectations. This evidence of tough-mindedness in the Machiavellian is not evidence of high authoritarianism, since Christie and Geis reported that correlations between Mach scale scores and the F-Scale are low or absent. Finally, there was no relationship between Mach scores and Presidential candidate preference in either 1960 or 1964.

There seem to be ample theoretical grounds, then, for considering

[3] An as-yet-unpublished study recently conducted by the author with Raymond Russ supported this line of reasoning. Tender-mindedness was found to be significantly correlated with radicalism, whereas Mach IV scale scores were uncorrelated with Eysenck's R.

the Mach scale as a possible measure for Eysenck's T-dimension. Such a relationship, if established, could breathe new life into Eysenck's two-factor theory. It would indeed be ironic if this suggested integration of Eysenck's and Christie's theories proved fruitful, after the rather bitter exchange that occurred between them nearly 20 years ago (see the exchange between Eysenck and Christie in the *Psychological Bulletin,* 1956, *53,* 411–51).

LIBERALISM–CONSERVATISM IN COGNITIVE SYSTEMS

Rokeach (1960) has dealt with liberalism–conservatism in terms of mental structure. In his book, *The Open and Closed Mind,* he characterized liberals and conservatives in terms of degree of opinionation. The strong liberal accepts opinionated statements on the left side of issues, whereas the conservative prefers his opinions on the right. In addition to opinionation, however, Rokeach also measures open- and closed-mindedness. By this he means the degree of dogmatism displayed by the respondent. Dogmatism, simply speaking, is authoritarianism with its right-wing political implications removed. There is relatively little evidence for Rokeach's notation of left-wing authoritarianism, however, so I leave the matter there (cf. Thompson and Michel, 1972).

Of greater concern with regard to the individual's cognitive functioning is the overriding question: Does liberalism–conservatism constitute a general, coherent, integrated system of beliefs? I have already pointed out some examples of contradiction, such as the Southern populist who is economically liberal and socially conservative. In spite of these contradictory instances, many people, such as the political scientist Herbert McCloskey, do believe that liberalism and conservatism exist as integrated ideologies. McCloskey's (1958) ideas are expressed in the following passage from his article on conservatism and personality:

> Many people of course, do not exhibit the patterns of mind and personality that are fully identified with either of the polar positions, but embrace elements of both. . . . Nevertheless, it is reasonable to believe that a conservative focus exists, not only because of . . . historical continuity . . . but also because liberal and conservative beliefs would not, in the absence of such focus, fall into pattern, but would instead be distributed

randomly throughout all sections of the population; *i.e.*, even if one knew some of the beliefs a given individual possessed, one could not predict by better than chance what other beliefs or values he held [p. 28].

And, I might add, there *is* some predictive value in knowing a person's liberal–conservative stance.

McCloskey's position, essentially, is that certain ideas *go together*. Whether liberal beliefs on sex are actually associated with liberal beliefs on welfare or foreign affairs is an empirical matter. But it has been fairly well demonstrated that there is some correspondence, keeping in mind the exceptions I have noted. Although the basis for this correspondence has not yet been determined, it could derive from logical interconnectedness, or from shared belief systems in primary groups, or from other sources. In any case, McCloskey's thesis is far from proven, as is shown by the response to national survey questions.

Ideology of the American Voter

People do seem able to characterize themselves on the liberal–conservative dimension. In early 1972, for example, pollster Louis Harris asked a cross-section sample: "How would you describe your own political philosophy—as conservative, middle of the road, liberal or radical?" A surprisingly large proportion did accept one of these labels, as shown in Table 8–2.

Table 8–2   Self-attributed political philosophy of the public

Position	Percentage Accepting Label
Conservative	29%
Middle-of-the-road	35
Liberal	19
Radical	4
Not sure	13
	100%

Source: Harris Survey, as reported in Bangor, Maine, *Daily News*, April 20, 1972, p. 25.

The surprising element in these poll results is the small number of voters who say they are "not sure" about their political philosophy. Such ex-tensive self-labeling is surprising in light of other surveys that show relatively little consistency across the issues generally thought to relate to such ideological positions. It is uncertain what a more careful study of such self-labeling might disclose, since few studies report the individual's own statements about his liberalism–conservatism. Rather, the investigator usually applies such labels to his respondents on the basis of the latter's answers to questions about government, welfare, and so on. More work needs to be done regarding the importance people attach to these ideological designations, as well as on the meaning people assign to them. The available evidence suggests that many people are uncertain of the meanings of the terms liberal and conservative (Converse, 1964).

After reviewing data amassed by the Survey Research Center, Converse concluded that people tend to lack comprehension of the terms "liberal" and "conservative." About 17% of the public has a rather so-phisticated understanding of liberalism–conservatism; their answers indicate an understanding of the breadth of reference of the distinction. On the other end of the spectrum, Converse found 37% who "are entirely vague as to its meaning." The 46% in between vary from persons who give a specific but limited meaning for the terms, for example, attributing thrift to conservatives and spendthrift tendencies to liberalism, to persons who demonstrate considerable uncertainty and guesswork in trying to define the terms. Of course, Converse's study is not completely definitive since we cannot be certain that the seeming lack of understanding of ideological terms is not more simply the lack of ability to articulate one's understanding.

The best guess at present, however, is that only a small percentage of the electorate can be classified on the liberal–conservative dimension on the basis of its position on issues. Converse (1964) presented considerable evidence to indicate that members of the mass public are consistent on party identification but on little else. His data came from reinterviews with the same respondents in 1958 and 1960. Usinug a correlation coefficient (tau–beta) that indicated the consistency of an individual's position over the intervening 2 years, he found party identification correlates about .72 (where 0 would indicate no consistency, and 1.00, perfect consistency). The average correlation on issues, however, was only about .35. This correlation indicated a very low tendency to respond the same way each time on issues such as Federal aid to education and foreign aid. Even the school desegregation issue failed to show much consistency across time (Converse, 1964, p. 240).

If such inconsistency does occur, and it is fairly well documented (see Sears, 1969), whence arises the conception of mass political activity oriented toward right–left positions on the issues? Certainly, commentators in the mass media make much of ideology, proposing swings to the left or right as explanations for voting behavior and other political phenomena. In discussing the poll cited earlier, Harris (1972) compared the differences between 1968 and 1972 and predicted on the basis of voter ideology:

> Talk that America has turned more conservative in recent years simply is not borne out by these results. By the same token, those who would claim an emerging liberal-radical majority have a long way to go before even approximating any dominance in American politics.
>
> In 1972, at least, the battle will be over the middle-of-the-road group, where Richard Nixon now holds a substantial lead. However, Nixon can vie for the centrist vote only after consolidating his conservative base [p. 25].

Perhaps the reason for the persistence of such ideological analysis lies in the fact that political ideology *is* a determinant for an important portion of the electorate. This portion represents a small elite, perhaps 10–20%, rather than the mass of voters. This elite, however, sets the dialogue for election campaigns, fights for control of the political parties, and so on. In turn, the elite "opinion leaders" influence some of the mass of ordinary voters. But such factors as group identification (class, union, religion, party), habit (tendency to stick with, to give the benefit of the doubt to the incumbent), perception of the candidate, and personally relevant issues are much more predictive of mass-voting response than is liberal–conservative ideology.

CONCLUSION

The idea that people can be meaningfully arranged along an ideological continuum from liberal to conservative has been with us for a long time. Hans Eysenck took up this idea and joined the procession of social scientists who have developed attitude scales to measure liberalism–conservatism. Eysenck's "R" (for *radicalism*) scale did differentiate among the members of five English political parties ranging from Communist to Fascist.

Eysenck's proposal that two attitudinal dimensions are necessary to describe a person's political ideology represents a unique contribution. He thought that these two dimensions, radicalism and tender-mindedness, were necessary to adequately describe the ideology of different political parties. A person who is extremely radical and tough-minded, for instance, would find the Communist Party attractive. Moreover, these attitudes are explicable in terms of simple learning principles and have foundations in the person's basic character structure. The evidence for these assertions is fragmentary, however, so the theory remains unsubstantiated.

There also remain questions about the number of people who actually hold integrated liberal or conservative ideologies. Survey studies that have been done in the United states certainly question the widespread distribution of such ideologies. It has been pointed out that attitudes toward various political issues are not consistent within individuals. Thus, the average ctizen's attitudes toward foreign policy and his attitudes about race relations or domestic economic policies often seem to vary independently of one another. Truly integrated ideological outlooks seem to be held mainly by the educated, or at least the politically thoughtful, members of society.

Nevertheless, the idea that everyone's attitudinal system has either a leftward or a rightward orientation has persisted. In part, this persistence results from the common currency of ideological terms among the educated segment of society. There also seems to be a strong conviction among social scientists that *some* such organizing tendencies exist. It is acknowledged that opinions about the fast-changing issues of the day may not adequately measure basic liberal–conservative orientations, but there may be other ways to get at them. Some authors suggest that these orientations might best be considered as basic dispositions toward change (cf. Robinson *et al.*, 1968, pp. 87–89), a suggestion that brings us back to Bird's emphasis on "time aspects," in the quote with which this chapter began.

It seems likely that adequate description of political ideology will require two or more factors, as Eysenck's scheme requires. I have suggested that Eysenck's theory merits further research if more adequate measures of radicalism and tender-mindedness can be found. The parallels between tough-mindedness and Machiavellianism, which I have pointed out, suggest possibilities for measuring the tender-minded dimension; the search for adequate measures of radicalism will likely involve similar departures from conventional conceptions of liberalism—conservatism.

PART IV

Political Action

9

The Psychology
of Participation

Three human desires that are deeply and uniquely frustrated by American culture:
1. The desire for *community*—the wish to live in trust and fraternal cooperation with one's fellows.
2. The desire for *engagement*—the wish to come directly to grips with social and interpersonal problems.
3. The desire for *dependence*—the wish to share responsibility.

SLATER, *The Pursuit of Loneliness,* 1970

"People need people" was the way one little girl put it to her father (Schutz, 1958). In the Oneida Community, people's needs for other people were satisfied. Life at Oneida provided the individual members with a genuine sense of involvement in personal relationships, in religious life, in work, and in the governance of the community. Originating perhaps in the need to deal effectively with one's environment, personal fulfillment does seem to require a meaningful relationship with others. This idea has been expressed by a number of psychologists, notably Alfred Adler, who felt that the development of *social interest* is a necessity for psychological health. The German word he used, *Gemeinschaftsgefühl,* has been translated as social feeling or social interest. To Adler, the ideas of cooperation, belongingness, and social responsibility all entered into this necessary attitude toward social living.

The central tasks of life, Adler (1938) wrote in his book *Social Interest,* are the establishment of meaningful answers to three major problems, "the problems of communal life, of work, and of love." Meaningful involvement in one's community, work, and intimate relations—true *ego involvement*—requires both a feeling of effectiveness in dealing with these life tasks and the realization of one's interdependence with others. Self-worth or self-esteem does involve one's own assessment of self, but as Ziller (1973) pointed out, it also involves one's relationship to others. We need to feel significant in the eyes of our contemporaries, to be valued and useful.

Philip Slater (1970), whose words began this chapter, feels that the pursuit of individualism has frustrated man's need for meaningful involvement in his community. Increased geographical mobility, technological change, and the ensuing social change have produced profound feelings of isolation and alienation from one's fellows. It should not be thought that alienation is exclusively a problem of the 1960s and 1970s, however; the problem of meaningful participation in a changing democratic society has concerned American psychologists for more than 50 years.

In 1944, for example, Gordon Allport (1960) addressed the Society for the Psychological Study of Social Issues on "The psychology of participation." His remarks were dedicated to John Dewey, "who," Allport said, ". . . more than any other scholar, past or present, has set forth as a psychological problem the common man's need to participate in his own destiny." This same "need to participate" has also been discussed by Robert W. White (1959) as *effectance motivation* (see Chaper 5 of this volume). White's conclusion that higher organisms have in common a need to interact competently with their environment is important to the understanding of participation as discussed in this chapter.

ACTIVITY VERSUS PARTICIPATION

Allport (1960) made what I think is a crucial distinction when he pointed out the difference between *activity* and *participation*. He noted that American psychologists have always been interested in observable motor activity, have founded whole systems (behaviorism) upon systematic ways of observing such activity, and have shown that active rehearsal is important in learning school subjects, as well as motor skills. He maintained that such activity is not the same thing as participation, however. To illustrate the difference Allport (1960) created "Citizen Sam," a resident of the Bronx, who:

. . . moves and has his being in the great activity wheel of New York City. . . . He wakens to grab the morning's milk left at the door by an agent of a vast dairy and distributing system, whose corporate maneuvers, so vital to his health, never consciously concern him. After paying hasty respects to his landlady, he dashes into the transportation system, whose mechanical and civic mysteries he does not comprehend. At the factory he becomes a cog for the day in a set of systems far beyond his ken. To him, as to everybody else, the company he works for is an abstraction. . . . A union official collects his dues; just why, Sam doesn't know. At noontime that corporate monstrosity, Horn and Hardart, swallows him up, much as he swallows one of its automatic pies [p. 187].

Citizen Sam arrives home at night to eat his dinner and perhaps doze in front of the television set. He is tired from the intense activity of the day. From the time he left home in the morning to his arrival at night, he has played a part:

. . . in dozens of impersonal cycles of behavior. He has brushed against scores of corporate personalities but has entered into intimate relations with no single human being. The people he has met are idler-gears like himself, meshed into systems of transmission and far too distracted to examine any one of the cycles in which they are engaged. Throughout the day, Sam is on the go, implicated in this task and that—but does he, in a psychological sense, *participate* in what he is doing? Although constantly *task-involved*, is he ever really *ego-involved* [p. 187]?

Sam, in other words, is "just going through the motions" in his everyday life. Contemporary accounts (Howe, 1972) support the observation that a great many working-class men in our society have very little ego involvement in their work. Moreover, many participate very little—if at all—in religion or in neighborhood or civic activites. If there is any real involvement or participation, it is likely to be in family recreational activities. Sports are particularly important leisure-time activities, although spectators undoubtedly outnumber participants. Involvement in the fortunes of the Bruins and the ego satisfaction of hooking a trout on dry fly are not to be disparaged, but they do not substitute for intense participation in a *cause*. An example of what I mean by a cause is the Civil Rights movement, which in recent years has been an important source of pride and personal satisfaction for many blacks in the United States.

Political involvement is of particular concern because participation in politics in a democratic society is the chief way in which people can have an effect on the social institutions that shape their lives. But there are many engaging activities besides politics. Many people think that the most important form of participation should be in *productive work*. They like to invoke the image of the old-time craftsman, making a clock, a cabinet, or a pair of shoes. It is anachronistic for most people, as it is for Citizen Sam, to invoke this image. There are satisfactions to be gained at one's place of work, however, from such things as having a realistic voice in determining the conditions of work and interacting with one's fellow workers.

WORK AND OTHER INVOLVEMENTS

In the pursuit of efficiency, industry has turned more and more to the techniques of mass production instituted by Henry Ford. This emphasis on efficiency has led to increasing labor specialization and the fragmentation of work processes. An auto worker may stand by the production line, day in and day out, bolting one fender after another onto Fords (or Chevrolets) as they pass by him.

Efficiency is good for business, and the unions have seen to it that production workers receive their share in terms of higher wages. However, the high wages received by unskilled workers in mass-production industries may not offset the high psychological costs to the worker. The work seems meaningless; the worker is frustrated and complains about the speed of the line or the need for more frequent breaks. In one of the most automated plants in the industry, the General Motors' Vega plant in Ohio, an automobile moves past the worker every 36 seconds. In 1972, employee discontent became evident in negligence and actual sabotage. Cars with ignition wires cut, with slits in the upholstery, and untightened bolts began coming off the line. This particular case led to employee firings, followed by a strike which lasted 22 days (cited by Kahn, 1973).

Although dissatisfaction with uninvolving work is seldom manifested in employee sabotage, there is ample evidence to indicate that worker dissatisfaction is widespread. Kahn (1973), for example, cited the replies of workers in various occupations to the question whether they would choose similar work if they were beginning their careers again. The results, compiled from a number of studies, were expressed

in terms of the percentages who answered that they would do so: Satisfaction by this index was high (around 90%) among professionals—
urban university professors, biologists, lawyers who worked for firms,
and school superintendents. About half (40–50%) of the skilled and
white-collar workers would choose a similar job. Less than a quarter of
the unskilled and blue-collar workers indicated satisfaction with their
work. Indeed, only 16% of unskilled auto workers—those who do the
routine assembly-line tasks—would again choose that line of work.

Of course, not even professional people are uniformly happy with
their jobs. Each individual does need to participate actively in some
areas of his life, however. Allport (1960) suggested, in addition to work,
the educational, recreational, political, religious, and domestic fields of
activity. Even individuals who are bachelors, or who hate sports, or the
agnostic, need, for a balanced life, participation in four or five of these
fields.

> Against some such norm we might test our present situation. Do we find
> Citizen Sam truly participating in some *one* political undertaking? In some
> *one* of his economic contacts—preferably, of course, in his job, where he
> spends most of his time? Is he really involved in *some* religious, educa-
> tional and recreational pursuits, and in family affairs? If we find that he is
> not actively involved in all these areas of participation, we may grant him
> a blind spot or two. *But unless he is in some areas ego-engaged and par-*
> *ticipant his life is crippled and his existence a blemish on democracy*
> [p. 194].

His final remark reflects Allport's concern with the democratic personality. Unless we engage in activities we deeply care about, unless we
are concerned about the events that shape our lives, we can hardly be
called a democratic people.

POLITICAL PARTICIPATION

Whereas lack of work involvement may be caused by factors beyond the
individual's control, participation in the political process would seem
not to depend on considerations of efficiency and productivity. It is possible, however, that the issues may be too complex for the average citizen
to understand. Long before the age of the computer, of nuclear weaponry,
and the interventionist foreign policy that led to the Vietnam war, the
psychologist John Dewey (1927) observed that:

The ramification of the issues before the public is so wide and intricate, the technical matters involved are so specialized, the details are so many and so shifting, that the public cannot for any length of time identify and hold itself. It is not that there is no public, no large body of persons having a common interest in the consequences of social transactions. There is too much public, a public too diffused and scattered and too intricate in composition [p. 137].

When this passage was written, women had just been granted their suffrage under the Nineteenth Amendment to the Constitution, which was adopted in 1920. In 1971, another group of new voters, men and women aged 18–20, was enfranchised by the Twenty-Sixth Amendment. Thus, as we approach 1976, the Bicentennial of United States independence, all citizens who have reached their eighteenth birthday are eligible to vote. In the 1972 elections, however, participation rates of those citizens enfranchised by the Twenty-Sixth Amendment, as for those franchised by the Twentieth, were considerably below the rates for older male citizens.

Levels of Participation

Voting in elections is the most prevalent and least ego-involving form of political participation. The most intense and ego-involving participation is the occupancy of any high political office, up to the most powerful position—the Presidency of the United States. Leaving aside for the moment the occupancy of high office, I find it helpful to think of ordinary citizens as ranged along a scale of increasing political participation or involvement, as shown in Table 9–1.

The five levels of participation shown in the table in general follow those used by social scientists in a cross-national study (Rokkan, 1960). Of course, it is rather difficult to *scale* degrees of involvement, but the scheme shown in Table 9–1 will serve as a rough guide for discussion. Admittedly, there are many exceptions to the generalizations I shall discuss: A retired businessman who has been sought out by the Republican City Committee as a candidate for the state legislature, for example, may be much less an active participant than an eager volunteer working in a Presidential campaign.

PRESIDENTIAL VOTING. The minimal possible political involvement, at Level 1 in Table 9–1, is voting in a Presidential election. Activity at this level, I assume, includes all citizens who participate at all. (I am also

Table 9–1   Levels of citizen involvement in the political processes in the United States

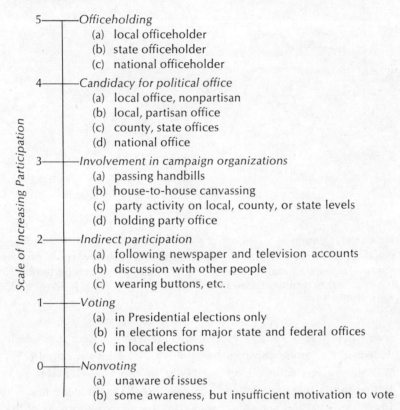

5———*Officeholding*	
	(a) local officeholder
	(b) state officeholder
	(c) national officeholder
4———*Candidacy for political office*	
	(a) local office, nonpartisan
	(b) local, partisan office
	(c) county, state offices
	(d) national office
3———*Involvement in campaign organizations*	
	(a) passing handbills
	(b) house-to-house canvassing
	(c) party activity on local, county, or state levels
	(d) holding party office
2———*Indirect participation*	
	(a) following newspaper and television accounts
	(b) discussion with other people
	(c) wearing buttons, etc.
1———*Voting*	
	(a) in Presidential elections only
	(b) in elections for major state and federal offices
	(c) in local elections
0———*Nonvoting*	
	(a) unaware of issues
	(b) some awareness, but insufficient motivation to vote

Scale of Increasing Participation

assuming that the scale shown in Table 9–1 is cumulative; by this I mean that a person who participates at the higher levels will engage in all the lower-numbered activities as well. The number of U.S. citizens who take this minimal step, voting in Presidential elections, is small compared with other democratic countries; about 56% of voting-age individuals made it to the polls in 1972. Comparable data for Canada and certain other democracies show much higher rates of participation. In Australia, Italy, and the Netherlands, which have "compulsory voting," 83–97% of the eligibles voted in 1972. Voting rates for four countries more comparable to the United States are plotted in Figure 9–1: West Germany (91%), France (82%, 1973 assembly election), Canada (74%), and Great Britain (71%). All of these countries make a greater effort to register voters than does the United States. "In Canada, for example, the gov-

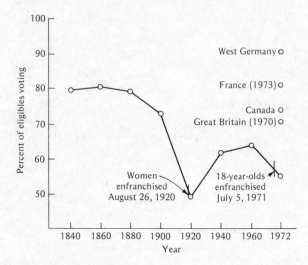

Figure 9–1 Voting as a percent of those eligible in United States presidential elections, 1840–1972, with 1972 comparisons for other Western democracies (Drawn from data supplied by The Library of Congress, as reported by Richard L. Strout, "The 'stunning' drop in U. S. voters," *The Christian Science Monitor*, April 20, 1973.)

ernment has an elaborate system of registering voters and conducts a door-to-door canvassing in urban polling divisions [Strout, 1973]."

Voting has dropped off markedly in the United States since the 1800s; the trends are plotted in Figure 9–1. The sharp decreases in the 1920s and 1972 represent changes in the base upon which the percentages were calculated. In 1920, for example, the electorate was doubled by the addition of women; because of the difficulties of registration, a relatively small proportion of these women registered in time to vote in 1920. Likewise, in 1972, the addition of previously ineligible young people expanded the number of potential voters.

There are wide differences among states in voter turnout. In 1960, for example, when the overall participation was 64%, only 26% of voting-age Mississippians went to the polls. In Idaho, on the other hand, the turnout was 81% (Dreyer and Rosenbaum, 1970, p. 451). There is a ready explanation for such interstate differences, in terms of differential barriers to voting (such barriers are discussed later in this chapter).

THE EXTENT OF POLITICAL INVOLVEMENT. The voting rates we have been discussing represent the *maximum* amount of popular participation that obtains in the United States—voting in Presidential elections. From these figures, one can make the following generalization about participation in politics in the United States: *Over one-third of the adult population in the United States has no political involvement whatsoever.* In non-Presidential years and in local elections, nonparticipation is even greater. The national turn-out for Congressional elections in non-Presidential years has not, since 1920, reached 50% of the eligible voters.

It is more difficult to estimate political participation at the higher levels shown in Table 9–1. In a comparative study of participation in Norway and the United States, Rokkan and Campbell (1960) found that 15% of Norwegian adults claimed membership in one or another of Norway's six political parties. Unlike Norway, where one joins the party of his choice and pays dues, party membership has an uncertain connotation in the United States. Such "membership" in the United States ranges from simply registering to vote in primaries to active campaigning. When asked about membership in political clubs or organizations, however, only 2–3% of the U.S. voters claimed such membership.

On the basis of the sample surveys, Rokkan and Campbell were able to make some estimates of participation at various levels shown in Table 9–1. I have reorganized their data somewhat to arrive at estimates for the various levels of participation outlined in Table 9–1. These participation estimates are shown in Table 9–2. Only the 14% at Level 3 could properly be called politically active. This figure is high as compared with other estimates. Lane (1959) has suggested that the number of volunteer workers never exceeds 5% in any one election, but my Level 3 includes giving money and attending rallies, in addition to belonging to a political organization or helping a candidate. The "indirect participation" (Level 2) percentages are guesses based upon reports from individuals who stated that they followed the campaign in at least three media. The differential in participation for men and women is a finding typical of other studies: Women do not participate in politics as frequently as do men.

Issue activism, of course, is another aspect of political participation. It is likely that there is a high overlap between party and candidate activity and issue activism. About the same percentage, at least, reported having served on a jury (16%), having ever written to a Congressman (19%), or having written a letter to the editor (16%) (1965 Gallup Poll cited by Rose, 1967, p. 466–67).

I generalize the findings of the relative frequencies of participation

Table 9–2 Estimated frequency of political participation among United States respondents in 1956

LEVEL OF PARTICIPATION	DESCRIPTION	PERCENTAGE OF RESPONDENTS		
		Total	Men	Women
3 (1 + 2 + 3)	Voted, indirect, direct participation	14%	16%	12%
2 (1 + 2)	Voted, indirect participation (followed news media)	14	15	13
1	Voted only	45	49	42
All levels	Either 1 or 2 or 3	73*	80	67
0	Nonvoting	27	20	33
		100%	100%	100%

* The 73% voting total is higher than the actual turnout in the 1956 election because it is based (a) on self-report, and (b) on the reports of people who were findable by the survey interviewers. "The Citizens not reached by sample surveys are exactly the citizens least likely to vote: this clearly biases the samples in the direction of higher turnout levels [Rokkan and Campbell, 1960]."

Source: Computed by the author from Survey Research Center data reported by S. Rokkan and A. Campbell, "Citizen participation in political life: Norway and the United States of America," *International Social Science Journal*, 1960, *12*, 69–99.

within the categories shown in Table 9–1 as follows: About 25% of the adult population never votes (Level 0); nearly two-thirds of the adults vote in any given Presidential election (Level 1), but fewer than 50% care enough to vote in Congressional elections; the figure dropped close to 25% in many elections confined to the local communities where Americans live. The frequency of political campaign involvement *or* active attempts to influence issues (Level 3) is no more than 15%, and intense participation is probably limited to well under 5% of adults. Another 15% of respondents report following political news closely in the news media. As to Levels 4 and 5, even if party offices were included, the proportion of the voting-age population that participates as candidates and officeholders is probably under 1%.

There are demographic factors related to participation. I have already mentioned the lower participation rates for women and young people, and the particularly low figures in some Southern states. The causes of these group differences can probably be attributed to psychological and environmental barriers to political participation.

Barriers to Political Participation

I have already suggested that complexity of the issues may be one factor that inhibits voting. Even at the local level, where debate may center on methods of funding needed improvements, considerable study may be necessary in order to understand the opposing points of view. I must confess to voting both yea and nay on bond issues with less-than-complete understanding of the implications of my vote. Although technical details may sometimes prohibit complete voter understanding, one can at least vote for candidates and parties who inspire confidence and seem best suited to represent one's interests. Even so, sizable numbers of potential voters stay away from the polls. The barriers to greater participation were analyzed by a special Commission on Registration and Voting Participation appointed by President Kennedy (see *Report of the President's Commission on Registration and Voting Participation.* Washington, D.C.: U.S. Government Printing Office, 1963, pp. 5–14).

The Commission's observations on "Psychological and Administrative Barriers to Voting" are of particular interest. Noting the relatively low turn-outs and the relatively greater electoral participation in most other Western democracies, the Commission asked: "What accounts for the widespread failure to exercise democracy's most fundamental and precious freedom? Why do so many Americans—in 1960, more than 25 million—not vote on Election Day? The answers to these questions fall in two main categories: psychological and legal."

In the psychological category, the Commission cited identification with a political party as most important. A person strongly identified with either major party is much more likely to vote than is the person with no party ties. This factor, together with the person's interest in a candidate or the issues, his concern about the outcome of the campaign, and his feeling that he can make a difference add up to what the authors of the Commission Report call the citizen's sense of *political involvement.* They noted that such involvement is lower in the young and among women.

Legal and administrative factors contributing to low voting turn-out include registration systems that make it doubly difficult to vote since the citizen must register and vote at separate times and places. In some states, registration must be completed a month or more prior to the election, before many voters have become interested in the campaign. Lengthy residence requirements bar newly resident voters in a country where large numbers of citizens change their residences every year. Restrictive absentee voting provisions may keep students, traveling businessmen, vacationers, and the ill or handicapped from voting. Finally, inconvenient polling arrangements may require long waits or insufficient time after working hours to get to the polls.

Laws aimed at erasing these legal and administrative barriers have been adopted by many states; a list of some of the measures that have been instituted appears in Table 9–3. A state-by-state tabulation based upon twelve such laws (Dreyer and Rosenbaum, 1970, p. 451) suggests that they may have an important effect on voting participation. Idaho, the state that in 1960 had the highest voter turn-out (81%), has laws incorporating eleven of the twelve provisions.

Mississippi, with the lowest turn-out (26%) for 1960, provided only two: permanent registration and precinct registration. Literacy tests have also been used to discourage black voter registration in some Southern states. The 1965 Voting Rights Bill passed by Congress provided for the suspension of such requirements. As of this writing, the U.S. Senate is considering setting up a new system of registration. This system would set up a uniform, nationwide registration by postcard for Federal elections, which, if passed, would likely be adopted by the states. The experience of other countries suggests that any measure that encourages voter registration will improve the rate of participation.

PSYCHOLOGICAL EXPLANATIONS OF VOTER APATHY. It is possible to elicit any number of "reasons" for participation in political campaigns and an equal number for refraining from such participation. The positive reasons are often couched in negative terms: "We must hold down tax increases;" "Stop the war!" and so on. Complaints about the existing situation sometimes appear to be more frequent energizers of political activity than more positive visions of the future. Nonparticipation is even more easily explained, "Because it really doesn't make any difference who wins." Often the poorly informed have little reticence in admitting their lack of criteria for intelligent voting decisions. The task is made more difficult by the tendency of the two major political parties to obscure, rather than to clarify, their differences.

Although personality seems unrelated to political party choice, there do seem to be underlying character dispositions toward political activity

Table 9–3 State election law provisions intended to facilitate political participation

---

A. *Registration Systems*
1. Permanent voter registration (as opposed to periodic re-registration).
2. Passing of a literacy test not required for registration.
3. Registration by mail permitted.
4. Registration closes no more than one month before an election.
5. Registration conducted in voting precinct rather than county office.

B. *Residence Requirements*
6. Less than one year's residence in state required for voting.
7. New residents (who otherwise have not met voting residence requirements) may vote for President.
8. Former residents (who have not established a new voting residence) may vote for President.
9. People who have moved within the state may vote by absentee ballot in their former precinct.

C. *Absentee Provisions*
10. Civilians as well as military personnel may vote by absentee ballot if absent from precinct on election day.
11. Handicapped, ill, or incapacitated people may vote by absentee ballot.
12. Absentee ballots may be obtained by mail.

D. *Election Day Provisions*
13. Polls must be open 12 hours or longer.
14. Polls must remain open until all in line have voted.
15. Number of polling places, voting booths, and so on must accord with number of voters registered.

---

or passivity. Campbell (1962) predicted that future understanding regarding personality-politics is more likely to be arrived at in connection with participation than with respect to party affiliation. "It seems to me" he wrote, "that while such [basic character] dimensions may not prove especially useful in the explanation of partisan choice, they have considerably more promise in the understanding of political interest or apathy [p. 11]."

Campbell's suggestion is supported by a study done by Mussen and Wyszinski (1952), which contrasted forty-five politically active University of Wisconsin students with thirty-seven who were classified as politically apathetic. All were from the middle social class. Activism was related to none of the ethnocentric scales (anti-Semitism, ethnocentrism, Fascism), nor to political and economic conservatism. "In brief," the authors (1952) concluded, "political participation seems to be independent of political, economic, or social ideology [p. 68]."

Other aspects of character were measured by Mussen and Wyszinski, using a series of ten projective questions. The questions were varied in content, including such things as, "What moods or feelings are most disturbing to you?" and, "What great people, living or dead, do you admire most?" The answers to these questions were categorized in terms of the "primary psychological content." Differences between actives and apathetics were found in a number of these response categories (those listed differentiated the two groups at the 5% level of significance). The apathetics reported difficulty in controlling desires to quit study and leave school; they were more embarrassed over social slips and violations of rules of etiquette. In child rearing, they were concerned with instilling good manners and obedience and wanted their children particularly to acquire skills toward successful interpersonal relations. When asked about desirable changes in their parents, the apathetic subjects more often asserted parental perfection.

Politically active students, more than apathetic students, tended to name social scientists and liberal political figures as the people they most admired. In answer to the question, "What could drive a person nuts?" eight actives listed problems codable as inability to adjust to situations or to face reality. None of the apathetics gave this response; they were more apt to list specific or generalized worries. Asked how they might spend the last 6 months of their lives, the actives listed activities oriented toward making some social contribution. They would instill in children "social consciousness" and "striving for maturity and independence," rather than stressing social adaptation.

In discussing their results, Mussen and Wyszinski (1952) stated their belief that "political apathy and activity are specific manifestations of more deep-lying, and pervasive passive and active orientations." Whereas the active individual seems concerned with understanding himself and with making a social contribution, the passive person seems generally passive, defensive, and conventional. In short, they found the actives to be concerned, socially conscious, and relatively spontaneous people. The passive or apathetic students, on the other hand, seemed more anxiety prone, more conventional in demeanor, and more defensive. These results suggest the possibility of conceiving two relatively pure types of political personality—the *active* and the *passive* political man.

CONTROL EXPECTANCIES AND
POLITICAL PARTICIPATION

In discussing "control expectancies" in Chapter 5, I pointed out that the individual's expectancies regarding his own ability to control the environment are logically related to political activity. With respect to Rotter's (1966) I–E Scale, the prediction is quite straightforward: Individuals who have a sense of personal control, the internals (I), are likely to be attracted to a theater in which they can have some effect on their own outcomes. They are likely, then, to become active in politics. The external (E) person, who attributes control to fate, luck, and the impersonal workings of the universe, is unlikely to waste much time trying to affect the system. Some research findings support this prediction.

Research with the I–E Scale, for example, shows that expectations that one can control the environment (*internal* orientation) do lead to activism in specific situations. Black Southern youth inclined toward activism are more internal (Gore and Rotter, 1963; Strickland, 1965). Furthemore, poor people who participate in self-help organizations are likely to develop internal expectations (Gottsfeld and Dozier, 1966; Levens, 1968). More traditional political activism, however, does not consistently relate to internal–external orientation. The findings relating I–E scores to political participation are contradictory.

Rosen and Salling (1971), for example, reported a study that explored the internal–external expectations and political activity of forty-five male undergraduates at the Santa Cruz campus of the University of California. The subjects completed a Political Activity Scale (the subjects were asked to report the number of activities they had participated in, from a list of ten activities), and a self-rating of political activity. Both political activism measures were significantly and negatively correlated with I–E scores ($-.57$ and $-.64$), meaning that activists are *internal*. These significant correlations support the logical prediction previously mentioned: persons who *expect* that their personal efforts can make a difference will be inclined to make such efforts. Another study published in the same year, however, produced opposite results.

Silvern and Nakamura (1971) studied students at the UCLA campus. Their sample was larger and included members of both sexes (89 men and 139 women). For the men, they found a low but significant *positive* correlation between I–E and activism ($r = +.19$). That is, male activists were more *external*. There was no significant relationship between I–E and activism for women. Silvern and Nakamura explained their findings in terms of the correlation of I–E with left-wing political views, the leftists being more external. Their argument, in brief, was that the results "primarily reflected the externality of left-wing activists and the internality of non-left-wing nonactivists." This argument seems particularly strained, however, in light of Rosen and Salling's contradictory findings.

Personal and Political Efficacy

It is obvious that expectancies for personal control cannot by themselves explain differences in political activity. One reason for the lack of consistent relationships between internal–external control and participation may lie in differences in knowledge of the opportunities for participation. A person who believes in his own personal effectiveness could conceivably be so unfamiliar with the political system that he feels ineffective in political matters. This explanation is supported by the findings regarding personal efficacy and political efficacy reported in *The American Voter* (Campbell *et al.*, 1964). The results of this investigation suggested that a person's sense of *political* effectiveness is a much better predictor of political involvement than are his or her feelings of *personal* effectiveness.

Angus Campbell and his co-workers (1964) examined the manifestations of what they called the "sense of political efficacy" in national survey samples. The five-item scale [1] measured feelings that "politics is a distant and complex realm that is beyond the power of the common citizen to affect, whereas to others the affairs of government can be understood and influenced by individual citizens [p. 58]." The political efficacy scale was given to a sample of respondents in a survey done after the 1956 election. In five categories varying from lowest to highest in political efficacy, 52%, 60%, 75%, 83%, and 91% voted in the election! Thus, not only was the increase in voting turn-out uniformly re-

---

[1] The five items composing the scale were: (1) I don't think public officials care what people like me think. (2) The way people vote is the main thing that decides how things are run in this country. (3) Voting is the only way people like me can have any say about how the government runs things. (4) People like me don't have any say about what the government does. (5) Sometimes politics and government seem so complicated that a person like me can't really understand what's going on.

lated to the person's political efficacy, but more than forty percentage points separated those who felt least from those who felt most effective.

The distinction between personal effectiveness and political effectiveness was supported by Mirels's (1970) factor analysis of Rotter's I–E Scale. Mirels's statistical investigation revealed two separate components of the expectancy for internal control: "a belief concerning felt mastery over the course of one's life, and a belief concerning the extent to which the individual citizen is deemed capable of exerting an impact on political institutions." These two separate sets of expectancies were measured by different questions on the I–E Scale, so that two separate scores can be obtained: Feelings of Personal Mastery (Factor I) and Feelings of Political Control (Factor II).

However, even when expectancy for political control is considered separately from personal control, the I–E Scale does not consistently predict political activity. In the Silvern and Nakamura (1971) study, no relationship was found between Mirels's (1970) political expectancy score and political action. Another study of voting by college students in the 1972 election found that women who held internal expectations regarding political activity (Mirels's Factor II) did vote more frequently than external women, but there was no relationship for men (Blanchard and Scarboro, 1973). It seems obvious from this brief survey that control expectancies alone do not predict political participation.

The reasons for these discrepant findings regarding control expectancies must lie partly in the distinction between one's beliefs and the tendency to act on those beliefs. The more academic studies do not enable us to understand the behavior of political involvement, and the applied studies, such as those reported in *The American Voter*, do not have a great deal of generality. (The latter study found that people who agree that "My Vote Counts" actually vote!). However, Campbell and his co-workers (1964) suggested *ego strength* as the more general disposition underlying political efficacy. I think that it is essential to consider the individual's whole self-structure, but we must also consider the situation since there may be very good reasons why internals are involved at certain times and places, and externals at others.

Personality and Control Expectancies

Some hints about the psychological factors that must be considered in addition to expectancies are contained in a dissertation by Alvin

Boderman (1964). This study was entitled *Feelings of Powerlessness and Political and Religious Extremism.* The term *powerlessness* is often used to indicate the opposite of efficacy; in the locus of control (I–E) research, the term *externality* is often used synonymously with powerlessness. Boderman used a political powerlessness scale, which contained a modified version of the Political Efficacy Scale (Campbell *et al.*, 1964; also see note 1 in this chapter). His hypothesis was that people low in political efficacy are likely to become involved in *either* extreme political *or* extreme religious movements. His reasoning went as follows: feelings of powerlessness (low expectancies for control) are likely to produce feelings of anxiety or aggression, though not necessarily both. When powerlessness is accompanied by aggression, the individual in whom they are conjoined will be likely to turn to political extremism. Such a person might join the John Birch Society or the Black Panthers, for example.

Powerlessness unaccompanied by aggressiveness, Bodeman suggested, will lead to religious extremism. Outward displays of aggression denote hostility directed toward the environment, which psychologists term *extrapunitiveness.* However, the absence of manifest hostility does not necessarily denote the absence of aggressive tendencies. With Freud, Boderman believed that an individual's guilt feelings could lead to self-blame or inwardly directed hostility, which is known as *intropunitiveness.* It is the latter tendency which will likely lead to acceptance of religious extremism. A powerless, intropunitive person, according to this reasoning, would find Protestant Fundamentalist religious sects attractive.

Boderman measured political extremism by means of a specially constructed attitude scale. He administered this scale, together with several personality tests, to two groups of adult male volunteers. The first was a group of eighty-seven men randomly selected from the community. The second group consisted of thirty-five men, members of either the Seventh-Day Adventist Church or a Jehovah's Witnesses congregation. Political extremism was defined as a high score on Boderman's attitude scale, rather than by actual activity in an extreme organization. Membership in one of the two religious groups mentioned constituted religious extremism.

The results supported Boderman's hypotheses. Political powerlessness was correlated with political extremism ($r = +.46$), and persons high on extremism were more hostile than persons low on the scale ($r = +.30$). The religious extremists were higher in powerlessness ($p < .05$) and were more intropunitive ($p < .001$) than members of more conventional religious groups. Boderman (1964) summarized his findings as follows:

> . . . feelings of political powerlessness are related to aggression, religious extremists (who also rank higher on political powerlessness than religious non-extremists) have significantly less aggressiveness and significantly more intropunitiveness than those who constitute political extremists for this study [pp. 85–86].

Boderman's study indicated some of the complexities involved in tracing the causal chain from control expectancies to political activity. Confirmation of the link between powerlessness (low expectancies for control, as indicated by the I–E Scale) and extremism was provided by a study of Los Angeles blacks interviewed shortly after the Watts riot (Ransford, 1968).

Ransford found that blacks who feel powerless are more favorable toward the use of violence than those with a stronger sense of social mastery. He found that the willingness to use violence was augmented by racial isolation (little intimate contact with whites) and by strong dissatisfaction with one's treatment as a black. The best prediction of being prone to violence could be derived from the cumulative effects of the three variables—powerlessness, isolation, and dissatisfaction.

I do not want to suggest that the investigation of "control expectancies" and political participation is a fruitless line of research. The sense of personal effectiveness and feelings of political effectiveness are indeed important foundations of political activity, but the relationship between them is not as simple as early investigators might have supposed. It is obvious, however, that many other personal and situational factors must be considered along with one's feelings of efficacy. Thus, I am essentially in agreement with M. B. Smith's (1971) prediction that: "Sense of personal control or efficacy, as a self-fulfilling source of initiative and political action is a psychological variable of which I predict we will be hearing much more [p. 43]."

SOCIAL INTEREST AND POLITICAL PARTICIPATION

Social interest is perhaps more an idealistic than a scientific term, but I think it does denote one of the most compelling forces toward political participation. Described by Nikelly (1962) as "belongingness, cooperation, and responsibility toward society," social interest reflects some of the most healthy tendencies in human behavior. Political activity can reflect such tendencies, as well as the search for personal power or aggrandizement. One's sense of involvement and belongingness may be restricted to narrow class, occupational, or racial groups. Social interest does involve such immediate group ties, but on occasion the boundaries of one's group involvements do expand, as in the following example.

A broadening of group feeling was evident in a student demonstration I observed at the University of Florida (April 15, 1971). The demonstration supported a list of long unmet demands made by the Black Student Union, a group promoting the interest of black students on campus. Although blacks have been present in appreciable numbers for only a few years on the Florida campus, and although most of the white students are Southerners, the sympathy of the majority for the blacks was unmistakable.

As I arrived on the scene, some two or three thousand students had crowded in and around the school's main administration building to protest the arrest of sixty-eight blacks, who had been pressing their demands through a sit-in at the President's office. The student body at the University of Florida is undeniably moderate-to-conservative, but there seemed great solidarity as I circulated through the crowd. This was even more surprising in that the demonstration leaders were expressing radical sentiments. Displeasure with the university president ranged from mild criticism to extreme anger. Moreover, this displeasure seemed almost universal among crowd participants, who ranged from longhairs to jocks and fraternity types on the masculine side and from the bra-less and jean-clad to the well-groomed and dainty sorority girls on the feminine side.

Common to all of the participants in this demonstration was the sense of a common reference group, namely, University of Florida students. This sense of we-feeling transcended differences in dress, hair style, and social origin. The second commonality was the strong and unambiguous perception that members of this reference group had been wronged. Of course, all of these events occurred in a context of past grievances, in an era of student activism, and in the immediate historical context of sympathy for the black rights movement to which even Southern youth had been exposed. My point is that these students were ego involved in an issue because members of a primary reference group were being unjustly treated. Their perception was ego involving, to the extent that the ego or self is defined by reference group identifications. Such involvement, I believe, is the core of *social interest*, which in turn is often a crucial determinant of political participation. There are some research findings that can be so interpreted.

Rossi (1966), in surveying voting behavior research, concluded that group ties were of primary importance in determining political loyalties. He illustrated the social determinants of partisan choice by citing the clear correlations between such choices and group membership. An example is the predominance of Democratic voters among Catholics, as opposed to Protestants. The most important ties, according to Rossi, are with primary groups—such as family or work groups. In fact, he asserted: "Primary groups . . . rather than personality structure or political ideology, provide the major sources for longstanding political loyalties."

Many people have recognized the relation of social interest to the problem of low participation in politics. John Dewey, among others, espoused what has come to be referred to as participatory democracy. He strongly emphasized the importance of face-to-face associations and the learning of democratic methods in school and neighborhood. In the same era, Mary Follett (1924), advocated small face-to-face groups as the basic unit of democratic society. These small groups would elect representatives who would again meet on a person-to-person basis for the discussion of problems.

These proposals bring to mind the New England town meeting, where, once a year, all adult residents meet for the day to discuss and vote on running the town for the next year. Even though many people look on the town meeting as the ideal form of direct democracy, more and more towns are abandoning these meetings (*Maine Sunday Telegram*, April 11, 1971). Their place is taken by an expert, the town manager, who receives his directions from a small elected council. One of the reasons for giving up the direct form of citizen control is the growing complexity of the problems facing a small town. The average citizen is not "omnicompetent." He is not equipped to make all of the complex decisions required in today's society, even in a small community of one or two thousand souls. Yet the key to the preservation of democratic society may lie in the notion of social interest and its impetus to community.

10

Leadership and Ambition

The successful leader must have membership-character in the group he is trying to lead. . . . In popular language this means that an individual must belong to the group he attempts to lead.

BROWN, *Psychology and the Social Order*, 1936

[Ambition for political office] develops with a specific situation, [as] a response to the possibilities which lie before the politician.

SCHLESINGER, *Ambition and Politics*, 1966

Dwight D. Eisenhower, two-term President of the United States, never held political office prior to his election in 1952. By virtue of his prominence as Supreme Allied Comander during World War II, however, Presidential opportunity presented itself. Although Eisenhower was elected as a Republican, it has been rumored that he was approached by both major parties in the early 1950s as a possible candidate, so nonpolitical had been his image. Surely, ambition for the office lurked within the General's breast, else he might have refused party blandishments (a genuine "draft" against the candidate's wishes being as yet unrecorded in American politics). Political *ambition*, in this case, might have gone unrecognized had not the *possibility* of election to high office (opportunity) become apparent.

As a political leader, Eisenhower reflected the aspirations of the American people for peace and stability. He was not an aggressive, "task-oriented" leader, ready with plans for changing the nation or the world. Rather, he was a passive President who inspired public confidence through calm sincerity and dedication to duty. In fact, some observers have questioned whether it *was* ambition which led him to accept the Republican nomination in 1952, noting that the idea that most persuaded Eisenhower was the argument that it was his *duty* to run for the Presidency (Barber, 1972, p. 160).

In this chapter, I discuss the two themes of leadership and candidate motivation. The topic of political leadership is approached from the perspective of social psychological research. The answers that this research offers to questions about the nature of leadership, the relationship of leaders to followers, and different leadership styles can contribute a great deal to the understanding of real-life political leaders such as Eisenhower, Kennedy, or Nixon. I also introduce the distinction between face-to-face and remote leadership as an aid to understanding the styles of different leaders.

I shall, moreover, discuss candidate motivation in more concrete terms than those previously employed. Power and effectance motives undoubtedly do underlie political ambition, but it seems necessary to tie motivation more directly to the candidate's political aspirations and his expectations of success. Thus, these two factors, ambition and the perception of opportunity for election, are presented here as inseparable components of candidacy decisions. My treatment owes much to political scientists who have pointed out that political ambition may not be revealed unless the prospective candidate perceives some possibility of success. Although in the present context I use terms that articulate more readily with social psychological theory, *motivation* and *expectancy*, it should not be forgotten that I am using them primarily to illuminate the phenomena of political ambition and opportunity.

Leadership and ambition can best be examined with reference to a real person. Therefore, I present an account of Congressman William Cohen's (R., Maine) career to date as an illustrative example to which we can return.

Bill Cohen is a young (age 32), attractive man with a record of political success in the small New England city in which he was born. The son of a self-made but now well-established small businessman, Bill attended the local high school. His success in school athletics accounts partly for the esteem in which he is held by older residents of the community and for his acceptance at a prominent private college. Both academically and athletically successful in college, Bill went on to law school and returned to practice in his home city.

After his law practice was securely founded, Cohen entered his first political contest, as a candidate for the City Council. He waged an aggressive campaign, capitalizing on his prominence a few years previously as a high school athletic star, and was easily elected. In the third year of his term, Bill Cohen was elected Chairman of the Council, a position of distinction—comparable to being Mayor of the city.

A 30-year-old man with such a successful record, a pretty wife, and two children might well aspire to further political office. In keeping with realistic political career expectations, we might have expected Mr. Cohen to aspire next to the State Legislature or to a post such as County Attorney. He eschewed such minor office, however, and instead entered the campaign for the Republican nomination for Congress. His candidacy was undertaken with the support of men prominent in state politics, who saw the opportunity to promote their party's interests through the advancement of an attractive and promising young candidate. Undoubtedly, there were other active party members who saw Cohen as stepping out of line in attempting to jump from a one-term nonpartisan office to the U.S. Congress.

Bill Cohen surprised many observers by taking his party's nomination in a serious contest with an older man. With the publicity he had gained in the primary, Bill was close to being on equal terms with his Democratic opponent, since the incumbent Congressman had vacated the post. Following an aggressive campaign, which included a walking tour of his district, Mr. Cohen easily defeated his opponent in the general election, to become one of the youngest members of the United States House of Representatives.

LEADERSHIP AND FOLLOWERSHIP

The study of leadership is a fairly well-developed area within social psychology, particularly as it concerns the leadership in small groups. There are certain logical coordinates between small-group and political phenomena, some of which were explored by Sidney Verba in his 1961 book entitled *Small Groups and Political Behavior: A Study of Leadership*. However, there are also certain dissimilarities between small-group and political leadership, which we need to explore here. The similarities and differences between political leadership and small-group leadership revolve around the degree of contact between leader and follower. I choose to designate two types of leadership situations: (1) *face-to-face* leadership and (2) *remote* leadership.

Face-to-face leadership involves immediate personal contact between leader and follower. This is the kind of leadership demonstrated in small groups, whether they be laboratory groups, bowling teams, neighborhood associations, or political committees. To a great degree, this is the basis upon which Bill Cohen's earlier political success was based. As a Councilman, he knew, or was personally known to, a large number of his followers, or "constituents," in his home city. Even people who did not know Bill personally knew of him in other contexts, or knew people who knew him. Any citizen who took the trouble to attend a meeting of the City Council had seen him in action.

As we move outward into larger political arenas, face-to-face or primary relations still play a part in political successes. Partly this owes to the friendships that develop through personal contact and to the work such friends will do to advance their candidate. Such support spreads because, as Milgram (1970) has noted, it is a "small world" in terms of chains of primary associations. That is, each of us has friends and acquaintances who have friends unknown to us. In this way we are linked to large numbers of other people. However, these chains of primary associations diminish in effectiveness as larger geographic units are involved, so that much political leadership is "remote" leadership. That is, the political candidate or leader must reach his audience through speeches, media presentations, and the advocacy of his workers.

Remote leadership is usefully distinguished from face-to-face leadership, even though both leadership processes are involved in political candidacy. A successful Presidential candidate, for example, must exercise face-to-face leadership with his core workers, as well as remote leadership in dealing with the masses of voters. Congressman Cohen's leadership was at first based on one-to-one relationships with his followers; he then had the problem of appealing to a larger constituency on a remote basis. The skills involved in the two kinds of leadership are different and often take time to develop. The time required to learn these skills is another reason for gradual progression to higher offices. Cohen had to learn fairly rapidly the skills necessary in appealing effectively to a larger constituency, skills he might have developed rather painlessly through a longer progression of offices. In the following sections I discuss these types of leadership in turn, beginning with the face-to-face situation.

The Face-to-Face Leadership Situation

I am concerned here with what has been called "emergent" leadership. Appointed or designated leaders have a role in political life, but we are interested in the leader who achieves his position through interaction with a group. In one type of small-group research, a group of, say, five to ten members is assigned a discussion problem, for which they are asked to arrive at a common decision or solution. Since no leader is assigned, various indicators of emergent leadership can be considered. The criteria might include the time spent speaking by each group member, ratings by group members or observers of the quality of ideas advanced by each group member, the number of suggestions made and/or accepted by the group, and so on. As time goes on, particularly if the group meets for several sessions, rather clear conclusions about the group's leadership can be formed.

A good deal of research has been accomplished using initially leaderless small groups. One prominent researcher, Robert F. Bales (1958), has studied the emergence of leadership in such groups. Bales's conclusions are generally accepted by other investigators. Most important among his findings is that two major types of leader function emerge in small-group interaction. These are the *task* function and the *social–emotional function*. These functions need some elaboration.

Task leadership involves moving the group toward its goal, whether this goal be solution of a human-relations problem or effective group action in opposition to a new zoning ordinance. The group member who makes the greatest contribution to achievement of the group goal, by furnishing information, ideas, or suggestions, is highest, according to Bales, in *task ability*. A school board member who has a good knowledge of the organization of his city's schools, of budgetary limitations, of trends in education, and so on, would have higher task ability than a member without this information. It is likely that the other board members would recognize such ability and its contribution to the board's purposes, perhaps by electing this person to the chairmanship. His election, however, might hinge on the second leadership function, the *social–emotional* function.

In his early writings, Bales referred to *likability* and *task ability*. Likability is part of the social–emotional side of group leadership. A group member who is liked is often one who pays attention to the more personal aspects of group life—the other members' feelings, rivalries, and hostilities. He is sensitive to the other members' emotions, as well as to their interpersonal interaction. Often, the task leader neglects this side of group life, he is so intent on "getting the job done." In such cases, it is often observed that two leaders emerge in small groups, the task specialist, who may not be especially well liked, and the social–emotional leader, who usually is the best-liked member.

The leader in face-to-face political interaction most likely will exercise both types of leadership. He has to cultivate friendships, make people feel that he is interested in them personally, *and* demonstrate competence with regard to the group's goals. The "group goals" may be difficult to define in politics because the groups involved tend to be less integrated and more disparate than the laboratory group. In a small town, the goals are likely to be low taxes and some minimal level of municipal services; the leader's competence in achieving these goals is readily assessed. In other settings, for example, in New York City, it becomes difficult to specify the goals, let alone the leader's competence in dealing with them.

A person like Congressman Cohen, or any one of us for that matter, lives his life in a succession of small groups. These groups differ in purpose, intimacy, size, and degree of permanence, but all are characterized by one-to-one interactions between members. For Cohen, some day-to-day group interactions would be with his family, his office staff, and the other Congressmen, lobbyists, and constituents he meets in the course of his day's work. Functioning in such groups is fundamental to political life, although such functioning does not necessarily involve the kind of gregarious behavior sometimes thought typical of the politician. A politician, as do other leaders, may appeal to his intimates on the basis of his dedication to shared causes or on the basis of his expertise. But whatever the basis for his ties with the group, the person's group ties provide the starting point for political leadership.

The interpersonal skills developed in face-to-face interactions provide the foundation for extending one's influence. Even in groups such as the Students for a Democratic Society (SDS), which at one time eschewed strong personal leadership roles, those members who had been most active, who had gained the trust and confidence of members, became spokesmen for the group when group goals required such leadership. It sometimes happens that a good within-group leader may not have the facility to extend his influence to larger spheres. A person may be liked, trusted, and respected within the small groups in which he exists, but he may not be able to exercise leadership in the larger political set-ting. I have already suggested the kinds of abilities that contribute to acceptance of leaders in small groups. Let us now turn to the settings where the aspirant must interact with larger audiences and must exercise what I have termed *remote leadership*.

What Do We Know about Remote Leadership?

Lenin, Gandhi, Franklin D. Roosevelt, John F. Kennedy—all ap-pealed to masses of people who did not know them personally. All ac-ceded to their positions by different routes. Each of these leaders, in his initial rise to prominence, dependend upon his ability to attract dedicated followers. Continued leadership success also depended on the man's ability to command loyalty and dedicated service from a comparatively small number of intimates. Beyond these face-to-face aspects of leader-ship, however, what are the factors that led to the broad appeal of Ma-hatma Gandhi or FDR?

The bases of the appeal of these leaders is little understood. Many provocative insights are provided in biographical and historical accounts of the careers of great men. These men obviously inspire confidence in their ability to lead, but the reasons for this confidence are still uncertain. Although both the Freudian perspective, which emphasizes the leader as a father figure, and the idea of the leader as a person who voices the ideological concerns of his followers are persuasive, there is relatively little social psychological research that bears on either hypothesis. There-fore, my observations on remote leadership should be seen as frag-mentary and tentative.

Leadership is thought by most contemporary observers to result from "a capable person being in the right place at the right time." This view emphasizes the situational aspects of leadership, as well as indi-vidual differences among people. In Brown's (1936) discussion of leader-ship, he noted that such questions as, "Should the leader be tall or short, thin or fat, of keen intelligence or only mediocre, honest or essentially dishonest, set in his mode of thinking or relatively changeable?" are meaningless considered apart from the particular situation. However, Brown acknowledged:

> It would be absurd to deny that two factors . . . are important in lead-ership, intelligence and psychosexual appeal. Of these, probably the more important is intelligence . . . [lack of which] . . . must lead to unsuc-

cessful leadership. . . . In addition personal charm in appearance, "sex appeal," is important in any field [pp. 346–47].

Both intelligence and personal charm contribute to the potential leader's ability to create a certain degree of affection from afar and an impression that he is competent to deal with the affairs of concern to his audience. While the creation of positive impressions may be the basis for election of a political candidate, continued tenure in office is also based on the impression that the officeholder is handling his job competently.

Let me illustrate the importance of such impressions. The newly elected Senator William D. Hathaway of Maine has a very liberal voting record. During his last term in the House of Representatives, he was often mentioned as one of the most liberal members of Congress. His constituents are moderately conservative, yet they returned him to Congress three times and, in 1972, elected him to the Senate. How did Hathaway do it? How did he, as a liberal Democrat, defeat the respected incumbent, Senator Margaret Chase Smith, in a conservative state? The answer lies in Hathaway's appeal to Republican and Independent voters in a state where the former have slightly more registrations than the Democrats. The basis for this appeal, I think, is twofold. First, Senator Hathaway has a strong following based upon personal relations: he is friendly in a quiet, nonobsequious way and has a good memory for names. Second, he has what might be described as a conservative demeanor. That is, he is tall, slightly jowly, has close-cropped hair, wears a grey suit and conservative ties, is slow spoken and thoughtful. It seems that this impression, rather than his liberal speeches and voting record, is carried in the minds of many voters.

There is another factor in any political leader's appeal, however, and that is familiarity. Senator Hathaway had been in the Congress for 8 years, which means that he had conducted four Congressional campaigns. Moreover, during those 8 years he made a great number of personal appearances in his home district, which encompasses half the state's population. He had also been interviewed many, many times, and had sent many newsletters bearing his words and likeness to his constituents. It is hard for newcomers to the political scene, who try to create familiarity on a crash basis through intensive campaigning and the use of mass-media presentations, to duplicate the exposure that an incumbent can achieve over time. There is little systematic evidence regarding the relative contributions of attractiveness, perceived competence, ideological agreement, and familiarity, but some recent work on "exposure" is suggestive particularly with reference to the unknown candidate.

Zajonc's (1968) work on the effects of frequent exposure on liking seems to have a bearing on the question of remote leadership. In an extended series of investigations, Zajonc studied the effects of *mere exposure* of several kinds of stimulus objects on the degree of positivity of the observer's attitude toward the object in question. He found, for instance, that words seen more frequently in print are rated as being more pleasant than rarer words. Even nonsense words and Chinese characters, shown varying numbers of times to subjects in the laboratory, became more pleasant with increasing exposure.

The most persuasive evidence that the familiarity–liking relationship may apply to politics was Zajonc's study using photographs of faces of men taken from a college yearbook. Some of the photos were never shown to subjects before they rated how much they might like the man pictured. Others were shown one, two, five, ten, or twenty-five times for 2 seconds each presentation. The result? Average liking scores increased with increasing familiarity. Scores were lowest for the pictures never seen before, higher for those seen once or twice, and so on, with the highest ratings being given to the photos seen twenty-five times previously. Zajonc (1970) concluded that "after repeated exposure, almost anything grows on you—even Spiro Agnew [p. 3]."

Do these results mean that all a political candidate need do to create a winning impression is to have his picture flashed on the television screen frequently? Most serious candidates would be loathe to try such an experiment, feeling that they should project more of themselves. And further research shows the politician is likely to be right. A later study (Perlman and Oskamp, 1971) demonstrated that the kinds of associations created between the person pictured and other people, ideas, and things are important.

Perlman and Oskamp showed pictures of men in positive, neutral, or negative situations (e.g., as a clergyman in a straight-on view of head and shoulders, or as a convict). They found, for both black and white stimulus persons, that "mere exposure" enhanced attitudes only when the person was in a positive or neutral situation. The greatest enhancement of liking with exposure occurred for men of both races in the positive setting. There was a tendency, particularly with black stimulus persons, for ratings of men in the negative situation to become more negative with increased exposure. Thus, the laboratory findings would seem to demonstrate that "mere exposure" is important, but that the context with which the exposed person is associated is also crucial.

In political terms, the current state of social psychological knowledge would support prevailing folk wisdom. That is, a prospective leader may establish himself with a constituency through repeated appearances while maintaining a "neutral" stance. However, in so doing, he leaves himself open for his opponents' attempts to smudge his image by creating negative connections. Therefore, the candidate is best advised, on the basis of this research, to try for maximum exposure along with as many associations as he can to people and issues that appeal to the voter.

There has, of course, been other research on the bases for the appeal of prospective leaders. There is some suggestion that leaders may be somewhat more intelligent, more flexible, better adjusted, and perhaps more interpersonally sensitive than those to whom they are appealing (Freedman, Carlsmith, and Sears, 1970, p. 158). But these factors seem to be of relatively small importance. In the small group, according to Freedman *et al.*, leaders are generally "more active, more talkative, more assertive, and not too different from the groups they lead." The latter assertion refers to the repeated observation that the most likely leader is seen as more competent than the average group member, but not way above the group.

We do not yet know what constitutes political charisma, but it is likely that charisma, far from being a magical quality, is composed of a number of ingredients, including those factors heretofore mentioned, as well as the current situation. Being in "the right place at the right time" is an important element in political leadership. I am not referring to plain blind luck, but to the fact that issues and voter concerns do change. The man whose image and eloquence on a certain set of issues might prevail at one time may be rejected in another situation. The prospective leader must be seen by his followers as being equal to the task.

Two theories of remote leadership that have appeared over and over again in the philosophical and popular, as well as the scientific, literature could be termed the *great man theory* and the *Zeitgeist* (referring to the particular historical situation existing—the "spirit of the times") *theory*. The first theory places the emphasis on the qualities of the man—a Napoleon, Gandhi, or a Franklin Roosevelt—who, by force of his own personality and abilities, is able to appeal to great numbers of people and to make significant accomplishments by reason of this personal force.

The Zeitgeist theory, on the other hand, places emphasis on the needs of the times. Given a particular historical and cultural situation, the theory asserts that some leader will emerge in response to the imperatives of the times and the prevailing mood of the people. The social psychologist's response to these alternative positions can by now be anticipated by the reader. Neither the great man theory, nor the Zeitgeist theory, alone is correct. Both the qualities of the person *and* the characteristics of the situation enter into the making of a leader.

THE CANDIDATE: MOTIVATION AND EXPECTANCY

Although President Eisenhower could be depicted as a reluctant candidate, his successors certainly could not. John F. Kennedy, Lyndon B. Johnson, and Richard M. Nixon were men with strong political ambitions. Each of them was a United States Senator, and the aspiration of each one toward the Presidency was obvious years before he reached his goal. Johnson and Nixon both served as Vice President, and Kennedy lost a strong bid for the Vice Presidential nomination in 1956. The sources of these driving ambitions undoubtedly differed. Kennedy was encouraged to enter politics by his wealthy father and was assisted by his family. Both Johnson and Nixon could be described as self-made men, although Johnson's career was aided by his friendship with Sam Rayburn and his support for President Franklin Roosevelt. Nixon, on the other hand, has been more of a loner, emphasizing hard work and solitary struggle (Barber, 1972).

Beyond the obvious presence of ambition, it is difficult to say just how Kennedy, Johnson, and Nixon differed motivationally. Of the three, Nixon seems best to fit the pattern described by Lasswell of self-doubt leading to the seeking for power. Johnson and Nixon had a great deal in common, however, according to James Barber, who calls them both *active-negative* Presidents. Their negativity, according to Barber, was discernible in their grim, rather compulsive, devotion to their duties. By comparison, an *active-positive* President like Kennedy seemed to find joy in his Presidential tasks.

The foregoing characterizations of Presidential behavior in terms of activity–passivity and positive–negative dispositions are explored at length in Barber's (1972) *Presidential Character*. This excellent historical analysis reveals, in case-study form, some interesting hypotheses about the personal forces that have driven twentieth-century Presidents. In this discussion, however, I want to explore the general phenomenon of political ambition as it can be discerned in candidates for lower-level office.

Motivation for Office

In Chapter 5, I cited Bertrand Russell's observations on man's desires for "power and glory," adding my own observations regarding the important motivations underlying political activity. In general, I characterized motives as learned "obsessions," based upon an underlying urge to deal competently with the environment. Effectance needs may have more-or-less direct expression in the behaviors leading to skillful interaction with the environment, as in sports, arts, or crafts. More commonly, we think of motives as particularly distinctive clusters of associations or ideas that are built up in the course of the individual's socialization. The power motive was discussed at some length as one of the most relevant to political behavior. The desire for ego enhancement and for manipulating others have also been suggested as important in understanding political orientations. All of these strivings could be subsumed under the headings of power (*n* power, Machiavellianism) and glory (ego enhancement).

Of interest in the present context is William C. Schutz's approach to interpersonal motivation. Schutz's (1955) early research dealt with the individual's basic orientations toward other people, focusing on two major types, the power-oriented and the personal-oriented type of individual. In practice, Schutz found that group leaders tended to be relatively dominant or assertive individuals, but that they were most effective in groups where their particular style of interaction was shared by most of their fellows.

In a later book, *FIRO* (Fundamental Interpersonal Relations Orientation), Schutz (1958) suggested that a person's interaction with other people could be predicted from knowledge of his needs for inclusion, control, and affection. How well the individual gets along in a particular group situation depends on the compatibility of his needs with those of the other group members. A person with a strong need to control the behavior of others, for example, is compatible with people who need to *be* controlled by others. Or, an individual with a strong need for affection will be compatible with persons who want to give affection.[1]

The interpersonal situations with which Schutz is concerned are those involving face-to-face relationships, situations in which the individual deals with others on a one-to-one basis. These interactions are important in determining the prospective candidate's desire to offer himself for a particular office. His interpersonal needs and the interactions based on these needs are also important determinants of the individual's *self-esteem*, which in turn seems to affect political aspirations. Schutz (1958) suggested the way in which early interactions set the pattern for adult social behavior in his hypothesis of *relational continuity:* "An individual's expressed interpersonal behavior will be similar to the behavior he experienced in his earliest interpersonal relations, usually with his parents. . . [p. 81]." Put more broadly, the candidate's behavior in political groups is likely to reflect his characteristic style of interaction with people, which developed through his earlier group experiences.

At times, the carry-over from childhood will find the adult acting, vis-à-vis others, in the way he behaved toward his parents. This idea is expressed in Schutz's *principle of constancy:* "When he perceives his adult position in an interpersonal situation to be similar to his own position in his parent–child relation, his adult behavior positively covaries with his childhood behavior toward his parents (or significant others) [p. 81]." In other words, the person, finding himself in a subordinate position in relation to another, behaves in a manner that is an extension of his habitual reactions to his parents.

A second possibility suggested by Schutz's relational continuity hypothesis is that the adult will take the role of the parent in interaction situations, as suggested by Freud's theory of identification. The *principle of identification* states that: "When he perceives his adult position in an interpersonal situation to be similar to his parent's position in his parent–child relation, his adult behavior positively covaries wth the behavior of

---

[1] Haythorne and Altman (see Haythorne, 1968) have found that compatibility in small groups is relative to the composition of the group. This relationship is quite complex, depending on the needs of the group members involved. A person high in dominance, for example, may find people low in dominance to be most compatible. A person whose prepotent motive is achievement, however, may function best in company with others like himself.

his parents (or significant others) toward him when he was a child [Schutz, 1958, p. 81]."

Schutz's argument may be summarized by stating that early experiences in groups shape the individual's later reactions in group situations. The learning process is not limited to family settings, however. The individual's successes and failures in other group settings in turn shape his later social relationships. One person may find success in relating to schoolmates on a friendly, egalitarian basis. Another, if he is so inclined by other factors, may find that he is able to influence the behavior of others. It seems likely, then, that face-to-face group settings do much to determine one's "motives" for further activity. That is, the individual's motivation for political candidacy is shaped by his experiences in primary group settings, as well as by his basic character.

It seems obvious, however, that we must go beyond the person's needs for face-to-face interaction to understand the sources of political ambition. In other words, it seems given that if a person's interpersonal needs were wholly met in the small-group setting, that is, in family, work, civic, and religious associations, he would be unlikely to undertake the rigors of political campaigning. I have suggested the existence of power motives, based on the effectance needs, and the need for "glory," which may be based on compensation for self-doubt, but there is little real data on the basis for the seeking of power and adulation in larger spheres of influence.[2]

Many candidates emerge from either successful or unsuccessful activity in support of a political cause. Whether this activity succeeded or not, the individual may derive some belief in his own special abilities and may actually have acquired political knowledge and previously unsuspected competencies. These newly acquired skills, in turn, may affect the individual's *expectancies* regarding possible successes in political endeavors. Our problem, in trying to assess latent motives relevant to political activity, is that they may never become apparent unless the

---

[2] To some extent paralleling this discussion is the approach taken by Rufus Browning (1968), who studied the relation of political involvement to affiliation, status, power, and achievement needs. He distinguished several types of political involvement and suggested that each is related to a particular need configuration (among other learning and social-system factors). An individual high only on affiliation need, for example, is likely to be a candidate only when requested by others and then is not eager to hold office. The zestful office seeker, on the other hand, tends to be high on the need for achievement, low on affiliation need, and often has high power motivation.

individual somehow becomes "turned on" by the realization that he can hope for success by reason of some special ability and/or by reason of opportunity. I agree with Lasswell (1948) that "yearning for power is not enough. It is essential to acquire and exercise appropriate skill with at least a minimum degree of effectiveness [p. 37]." In addition to *motivation* and *skill*, however, perception of *opportunity* is necessary for emergence of political ambition. We turn now to opportunity, that is, to the structure of expectancies held by the prospective candidate regarding his probability of success in a particular political undertaking.

Expectancies for Political Success

Whatever the original impulse—power, prestige, self-enhancement, or altruism—the prospective political candidate proceeds on the basis of the opportunities available to him. Psychologically speaking, he operates on the basis of *perceived* opportunities. (Of course, very strong motivation may distort one's perception. A strongly motivated candidate who objectively has little chance of success, may believe that he will win.) Although some people may campaign as a means of gaining individual prominence or to publicize a cause, in the main an individual becomes a candidate because he perceives some possibility of winning the office in question. The circumstances that produce such beliefs vary. The person may feel that he has a base of support in his church or religious group, or that he has some special oratorical or organizational skills. He may perceive an opening; that is, a special chance created by the retirement of a long-term incumbent. I have already mentioned the case of Congressman Cohen, who took advantage of such an opening. A similar case is that of the new Senator from Florida, Lawton Chiles. Previously a young State legislator with little statewide following or recognition, Chiles's opportunity came with the retirement of the long incumbent Senator Spessard Holland.

Many politicians begin their careers in local offices. There, on the local level, it is easy to observe the effects of perceived opportunity. Single positions, such as Clerk of Courts or County Attorney, often go uncontested (or at most only one person seeks the nomination of each party). A number of vacancies, however, on a city council or school board may bring forth a rash of contestants, particularly when there are no incumbents. A recent election of Superintending School Committee in Bangor, Maine, illustrates my point. The five-member board was to be elected for the first time in its entirety, following the change-over from an appointive to an elective school committee. This wide-open situation brought forth a total of sixteen candidates for the five positions.

AMBITION THEORY. The objective and subjective possibilities for election have been dealt with systematically by political scientists. Joseph Schlesinger, in *Ambition and Politics* (1966), spoke mainly of the objective prospects for election, assuming that personal ambitions for office develop in relation to one's expectation of success. Office ambition, wrote Schlesinger (1966):

> . . . develops with a specific situation, [as] a response to the possibilities which lie before the politician. A man in an office which may lead somewhere is more likely to have [higher] office ambitions than a man in an office which leads nowhere [p. 8].

Schlesinger's (1966) illustration of this proposition compares the relative prestige of gubernatorial offices:

> A New York Governor who does not make the Presidency has failed in a sense in which his counterpart in Mississippi or South Dakota cannot fail. Politics is, after all, a game of advancement, and a man succeeds only if he advances as far as his situation will permit [pp. 8–9].

Much of Schlesinger's work is devoted to an analysis of the structure of opportunities in the United States. Proceeding from the assumption that it is ambition for the office that moves politicians, the ambition theorist studies the careers of political leaders. From the electoral successes and failures of men already holding office, the structural conditions of opportunity can be determined:

> From the perspective of ambition theory . . . such mundane data as the tenure and turnover of officeholders, office succession, and the ages of elective officials take on major significance. The order which emerges from these data on political careers becomes "the structure of political opportunities." We assume that opportunities arouse expectations and, in turn, give direction to personal ambitions [Schlesinger, 1966, p. 15].

Ambition theory, in short, presupposes a rational assessment by the prospective candidate of his opportunities for success. It can be shown empirically that a person of a certain age, ethnic background, educational attainment, and who holds a particular office, is most likely to succeed in his campaign for a certain higher office. "My basic inference," wrote Schlesinger, "[is that] the ambitions of any politician flow from the expectations which are reasonable for a man in his position [p. 9]."

I find it difficult to think of man as a computer, assessing the objective probabilities of success in the various offices open to him. Two exceptions have already been noted in this chapter, Congressman Cohen and Senator Chiles, both of whom had little reason for ambition according to ambition theory. Senator Hathaway's case does fit the model, since by age, background, and tenure as a Congressman he could reasonably expect to attain higher office. A more adequate model of ambition would include personal motives and the desirability of the office. Although it has not to my knowledge been applied to politics, the motive expectancy theory of Atkinson and Feather (1966) is a more realistic model of the psychological dynamics of ambition. Their theory places much more emphasis than Schlesinger's (1966) on the subjectivity of one's expectations.

CANDIDATE MOTIVATION: MOTIVE × EXPECTANCY × INCENTIVE

According to this formulation, a candidate's ambition toward a particular office is a function of his own motives for power, esteem, or achievement, his expectations for achieving the office, and the value of the prize. That is, the prestige, power, or salary of the office must be considered. More exactly, in the terms employed by Atkinson and Feather (1966):

$$\text{Motivation} = f(\text{Motive} \times \text{Expectancy} \times \text{Incentive})$$

That is: "The strength of motivation to perform some act is assumed to be a multiplicative function of the strength of the motive, the expectancy (subjective probability) that the act will have as a consequence the attainment of an incentive, and the value of the incentive [p. 13]."

The Atkinson–Feather model, I believe, encompasses the critical factors for explaining the impulse to seek political office. By motivation I mean the net tendency to seek the office; the "motive" on the right-hand side of the equation is actually more than one stable disposition. Atkinson and Feather devote themselves to the achievement motive, but the same analysis could be applied to power, or whatever other motives are found to be important bases for political activity. The term *expectancy* has already been discussed in general terms; as Atkinson and Feather use the term, it refers to the person's perception of the probability that he can achieve the office in question. The probability of success (P_s) can vary from zero to unity (that is, from the belief that he has no chance of success to complete certainty of success).

INCENTIVE. Incentive refers to the value that the individual places on the office sought. In general, the inverse relation Atkinson and Feather posit between incentive and expectancy probably holds in the political realm. That is, an office that can be had simply for the asking (probability of success approaching 1.0) is likely to be little valued (incentive value approaching 0.0). On the other hand, the Presidency is so unlikely of attainment for most of us, and thus the incentive value of the office is so high, that many will pay large sums just to be associated with the successful aspirant.

FEAR OF FAILURE. Also included in the Atkinson–Feather scheme is the idea that behavior is directed away from failure, as well as being directed toward achievement, of a particular goal. While these authors are particularly concerned with the achievement motive, Winter (1973) has evidence for the existence of avoidance, as well as approach, motives for power (see Chapter 5 of this volume). Winter found two components of the power motive: fear of weakness and striving for social control.

Both motivation for success and motivation to avoid failure, which Atkinson (1966, p. 15) terms M_s and M_{af} respectively, can be discussed mathematically in relation to the probability of success (P_s). My present objective, however, is to illustrate their relevance to political candidacy in less rigorous terms. The key to understanding the relationship among motive, expectancy, and incentive lies in understanding that *the degree of elation following success or the degree of humiliation following failure depends upon the subjective expectations of the individual regarding his possibilities for attainment of a particular office.* Atkinson's (Atkinson and Feather, 1966) observation regarding levels of aspiration seem directly applicable:

> It is of some importance to recognize the dependence of incentive values intrinsic to achievement and failure upon the subjective probability of success. One cannot anticipate the thrill of a great accomplishment if, as a matter of fact, one faces what seems a very easy task. Nor does an individual experience only a minor sense of pride after some extraordinary feat against what seemed to him overwhelming odds [p. 15].

An equation similar to that given for success motivation applies to failure avoidance:

$$\text{Motivation to avoid failure} = (M_{af} \times P_f \times I_f)$$

The use of these simple notions, along with the more rigorous mathematical assumptions, allows explanation and prediction of otherwise perplexing behaviors. The "candidate" who indicates no interest in campaigning or otherwise exerting effort to achieve the office may have a motive to avoid failure (M_{af}) which is stronger than his motive to achieve success (M_s). This motive pattern ($M_{af} > M_s$) may result in the person's "leaving the field" in effect: "I lost because I didn't want to win and didn't try." The theory also predicts that this motive pattern will lead to selection of either very risky or very sure-win contests. That is, the politician who is more motivated by the need to avoid failure than to achieve success may choose to run for membership on his party's local committee ($P_s = .90$) or for Congress ($P_s = .10$).

When the P_s is such that the approach and avoidance motives are equal in strength, the individual is of course locked in to an approach–avoidance conflict situation with resultant motivation equal to zero. Most of the political examples that will come to mind will be of people with $M_s > M_{af}$; otherwise they would scarcely come to our attention. According to Atkinson and Feather's (1966) theory, the motivation for success (M_s) and the motivation to avoid failure (M_{af}) are strongest when P_s equals .50. Thus, a candidate with $M_s = 1$ and $M_{af} = 0$ would exert greatest effort when the probability of success is 50/50. In fact, a $P_s = .50$ (also $P_f = .50$) would in every case produce the highest motivation to undertake the task whenever $M_s > M_{af}$. However, exploratory experiments have suggested that another assumption, highly consistent with political experience, should be made: "the relative strength of a motive influences the subjective probability of the consequence consistent with that motive, i.e., biases it upwards. In other words, the stronger the achievement motive relative to the motive to avoid failure, the higher the subjective probability of success, given stated odds [Atkinson and Feather, 1966, pp. 23–24]." Similarly, a higher M_{af} will produce a higher subjective probability of failure. Simply stated, it now seems that the motivation toward success in a task is greatest when the objective probability is *less than* .50, perhaps around .33; anxiety about failure (M_{af}), on the other hand, is strongest when the probability of success is a little above 50/50 (say .60 or .65).

Expectancy and Audacity: An Overview of Candidacy Behavior

In this discussion of candidacy determination I have stressed two personal psychological bases: motivation and expectation. A person may have strong latent motives, which, if aroused, would lead him to actively enter politics at some level. As a matter of fact, it might be provocative to suppose that everyone has such latent tendencies. Their arousal depends upon the individual's perception of opportunity along with associated probability of success: an "expectancy."

Such expectancies, as I have noted, depend upon the person's perception of the political system, upon the particular opportunities apparent to him at a particular time, his knowledge of his own skills and abilities, and his expectancy of social support in a particular undertaking.

Expectancies for support of one's candidacy by others is an interesting topic, particularly in light of our romanticization of "candidacy by popular demand" in the United States. As a matter of fact, there are reasons to believe that the unambitious, public-spirited individual who runs only because of the urgings of supporters may be poorer both as a candidate and as an incumbent than the more frankly ambitious politician. Browning (1968), for example, found that candidates who were high in affiliation need had run only when urged to do so by friends and then did not seem to put their hearts into the campaign. Candidates high in achievement and power needs, on the other hand, are likely to put forth aggressive effort toward attaining political office and to be active in carrying out the duties of the office.

11

Changing Political Attitudes

In *The Selling of the President, 1968*, McGinnis (1970) presented evidence for the thesis that President Nixon was packaged and marketed to the American electorate through clever advertising techniques. According to McGinnis's account, the whole campaign was managed with the thought of controlling the impression Nixon made on the voters. Public opinion polling was used extensively to guide the image makers. Televised news conferences, where the candidate encounters newsmen in spontaneous dialogue, were replaced by carefully managed television sessions before preselected audiences. Needless questions about the candidate's temperament, knowledge, or competence were thereby avoided. In these sessions, Nixon was always in control of the situation.

The effectiveness of Madison Avenue techniques in politics can be overstated, however. While Nixon did win the 1968 election, his margin as projected from survey samples actually decreased between the party conventions and the November election. Following the internally divisive Democratic Convention, which nominated Hubert Humphrey, a Gallup poll taken September 3–7, 1968 (Bogart, 1972), showed Nixon favored by 43% of the voters to 31% for his major opponent (the remainder favoring the third party candidate, George Wallace). The official results of the November election, however, showed that Nixon's winning margin was less than 1% (Nixon, 43.4%; Humphrey, 42.7%, Wallace, 13.5%).

A candidate's image is but one factor in determining election outcomes. In the 1952 and 1956 Presidential elections it may have been decisive. Dwight D. Eisenhower, the distinguished World War II military commander, was a very popular figure who inspired the voter's confidence. His Democratic opponent in both Presidential campaigns was Adlai Stevenson, a learned, witty, and gentle former Illinois Governor. Voter surveys in the two elections showed that Eisenhower's image was important to the outcome of the 1952 election and probably was even more decisive in the 1956 election (Campbell *et al.*, 1964, pp. 269–74). The basis for the public's favorable response to Eisenhower was detailed by Campbell *et al.* (1964):

> General Eisenhower's record as a military hero had developed a strongly positive feeling toward him in all elements of the population before he had become associated in any way with partisan politics. Moreover, the Eisenhower candidacy seemed extraordinarily well suited to the demands of the time. Eisenhower's unparalleled reputation as a successful military leader gave promise of an answer to the desperate situation of Korea. And his freedom from association with the seamier aspects of party politics and his widely acknowledged personal integrity carried a special appeal to many people who were disturbed at the level of political morality in Washington [pp. 271–72].

In discussing the elections of the 1950s, the authors of *The American Voter* refer to "attitude toward Stevenson" or "attitude toward Eisenhower." There is nothing wrong with such usage, but I have been urging greater precision in terminology. As I outlined in Chapter 4, "attitudes" refer to relatively enduring tendencies in the person to respond to a general *class* of objects. Thus, a voter's evaluation of Eisenhower is colored by his attitude toward politicians, but also by his beliefs and feelings about the man. I am referring to the generally favorable or unfavorable impressions of a candidate as the candidate's *image*.

IMAGE AND IDEOLOGY

A candidate's image is a composite of beliefs, feelings, and judgments about the man as they exist in the minds of the voting public. An individual voter's image of Richard Nixon, for example, is composed of his beliefs about the President (he is a Quaker, an honest man, is married and has children), which are evaluated in the light of the voter's attitudes (Quakers are religious, conscientious, peaceful; politicians are dishonest; a man who leads a conventional family life is "normal"), and the voter's political ideology. By ideology, I refer to the integrated set of beliefs and attitudes by which a person is characterized as liberal, conservative, radical, or reactionary.

As a political figure is exposed more and more, a definite, integrated set of beliefs, and evaluations is formed in the mind of each individual voter. This integration, this *image*, will remain half-formed, impression-istic, and fuzzy to some voters who may receive little exposure to the candidate, who are little involved ideologically, and so on. Contrarily, the voter who is very attentive to the presentation of the candidate may form a very clear, definite image. Furthermore, the amount of actual in-formation needed by the voter varies; a person who is strongly ideologi-cally committed may need to know only the candidate's ideological position to take a very strong position for or against him.

Thus, a candidate's image is an end product and could be called an "attitude" were it not for its specificity. All three components of an attitude, at least, are present: (1) a set of beliefs about the object; (2) certain emotional feelings, favorable or unfavorable; and (3) a tendency to act favorably or unfavorably—to vote for or against. In spite of the similarity between attitude and image, I think it worthwhile to preserve the distinction between them since it is useful to consider an attitude as a part of the whole, which is the image. The elements that affect po-litical images—emotional feelings, beliefs, attitudes of all kinds which are relevant to the situation, and ideology—are not equally susceptible to change.

Various attempts have been made to measure the candidate's image as it is perceived by the voters. In the 1968 campaign, for instance, Nixon's campaign organization tried to assess the effectiveness of its efforts to build a new image for the candidate. This assessment involved the extensive use of public opinion polls. Traditional questions about both candidates were asked; in addition, modern measuring techniques such as Osgood's (Osgood *et al.*, 1957) *semantic differential* were used by the pollsters. Even the candidate took an interest in the success of the attempts to rework his image. Bogart (1972) reported that "Nixon per-sonally contributed 'semantic differential' scale items (shifty/direct, sin-cere /insincere) to compare his 'image' with Humphrey's [p. 38]."

The images of the 1968 candidates held by college students were explored in a study I conducted with John Arthur (1971). About three weeks before the November election, students were asked to judge the three candidates on sixteen different attributes. Their ratings were made on evaluative scales of the semantic differential. The first characteristic was "approve–disapprove." These two adjectives were ranged at the ends of the line marked with seven intermediate divisions:

Approve :___:___:___:___:___:___:___: Disapprove

Changing Political Attitudes

The respondent could indicate his feelings about the particular candidate by making a check mark at any of the seven points along the line. The other fifteen scales, which were responded to in the same way, are shown in Figure 11–1.

Each respondent received a booklet containing the semantic differential instructions (Osgood *et al.*, 1957) on the first page. The three succeeding pages each contained the set of scales shown in Figure 11–1. Each page was headed by the name of one of the three candidates: "Richard M. Nixon," "Hubert H. Humphrey," or "George C. Wallace." The questionnaires were scored from one to seven for each scale for each candidate. A seven indicates the positive end of each scale (approve,

```
     approve:     :      :    h:n    :      :  w  :        :disapprove
        wise:     :      :   hn:     :    :w   :           :unwise
    valuable:     :      :   hn:     :  w  :      :         :worthless
        kind:     :    :h   n  :     :     w:     :          :cruel
       clean:     :  h:n     :  w   :     :       :          :dirty
  beneficial:     :      :  hn  :     :    :w    :           :harmful
      honest:     :      :  hn  :   :w    :      :           :dishonest
        fair:     :    :  h n  :     :    :w    :           :unfair
        good:     :    :  h n  :     :  w  :      :          :bad
        nice:     :    :  h n  :     :  w  :      :          :awful
    pleasant:     :    :  h n  :     :  w  :      :          :unpleasant
 trustworthy:     :    :  h n  :     :  w  :      :          :untrustworthy
  attractive:     :      :    :  n h:  w   :      :          :unattractive
    agreeable:    :      :  h  :n    :    :w    :            :disagreeable
satisfactory:     :      :   h:n    :     :  w  :            :unsatisfactory
     sincere:     :    :  h   n:   w:     :      :           :insincere
```

Figure 11–1 Semantic differential scales used in rating the presidential candidates: Average pre-election ratings indicated for Nixon (n), Humphrey (h), and Wallace (w) (Adapted from William F. Stone and John D. Arthur, "Judging presidential candidates: Evaluative dimensions employed before and after the 1968 election," unpublished manuscript, 1971. Used by permission of the authors.)

wise, and so on) and a one, the negative end. The small letters in Figure 11–1 denote the mean scale positions assigned by our respondents. The profile so obtained can be spoken of as the candidate's image, insofar as these sixteen scales actually encompass the important dimensions of political images.

In general, Wallace's image, from the standpoint of our subjects (Maine college students), were very negative. His strong points were his relatively clean-cut appearance, his seeming sincerity, and to some extent his honesty. All of these characteristics were considerably below his opponents' ratings, however. It is likely that Wallace's whole profile was influenced by these Northern students' lack of "approval" of him. Of interest regarding the Nixon and Humphrey preelection profiles was the slightly more favorable image of Humphrey over Nixon. One seldom reads that people considered Hubert Humphrey "unattractive"—but this seems to have been a weak point in his image, at least among this group of students.

The study of candidate images holds promise for future research. At present there really is no way to say just how much of the variability in voting tendencies is accounted for by such images, in spite of the claims of advertising agencies. Further work needs to be done to see just what characteristics are most central in the judging of political candidates, since it has not been established that the sixteen scales listed in Figure 11–1 are the most important attributes.

Another question needing research concerns the way in which the candidate's image is established. Can such images be managed by clever use of television? The research on "mere exposure," which was cited in Chapter 10, suggests that such impression management is at least a possibility. However, the major image-building effort made on Nixon's behalf in 1968 seems to have been of limited effectiveness. Nixon, for example, spent 24.9 million dollars in the general election campaign, compared to Humphrey's 10.3 million dollars. Both the closeness of the 1968 election and the lack of pronounced differentiation in the candidates' images suggest that the extra 15 million dollars spent by Nixon had a relatively small return. On the other hand, it could be argued that he might have lost by a considerable margin without the expensive television exposure.

Many factors other than image enter into the evaluation of political candidates. A man who seems "right for the times," as did Eisenhower, may have an advantage over his opponent. But ideology and issue positions also contribute to electoral outcomes. In 1968, for example, Nixon emphasized ending the Vietnam war and made "law and order" a major issue. Wallace supporters, who differed from those of the other candidates in their racial attitudes, also responded to their candidate's emphasis on the law-and-order issue. Undeniably the liberal candidate on race and domestic issues (blacks overwhelmingly backed him), Humphrey was handicapped by his association with President Johnson and the unpopular Vietnam war. The relevance of ideology and ideological change to politics is explored in the following section.

Ideology and Change

The term *ideology* is used in several different ways. Generally, it refers to a relatively systematic set of cognitions that is shared by other people. "An *ideology*," Rokeach (1968) wrote, "is an organization of beliefs and attitudes—religious, political, or philosophical in nature— that is more or less institutionalized or shared with others, deriving from external authority [pp. 123–24]." There has been considerable debate about the importance of political ideologies in the contemporary world (cf. Bell, 1960), but I use the term here to describe any fairly coherent system of beliefs and attitudes held by an individual. This is the sense in which I discuss "liberal ideology" or "Communist ideology," without necessarily implying the well-integrated ideological systems associated with social movements.

Rooted as they are in a personal network of beliefs and attitudes, and often not consciously adopted, ideologies are rather stable. Substantial changes in the ideology of a mature person are rather rare. Older people may become somewhat more conservative, but there does not seem to be any substantial reordering of their convictions with age. The ideological change shown by Governor Ronald Reagan of California is remarkable because such change is so rare. Earlier in life a liberal Democrat and defender of the civil rights of fellow actors against the assaults of the House Un-American Activities Committee, Reagan now is widely acknowledged as a member of the right wing of the Republican Party. The explanation for his radical shift is not readily available, but the accounting probably would include personality factors, changes in group relatedness, and possibly even reinforcement theory.

Ideological conversion was the object of Communist "brainwashing" of American prisoners captured in Korea during the early 1950s.

Schein (1956) recounted the methods used by their Chinese captors in the attempt to convert the soldiers from Western capitalistic ideology to Communist beliefs. Dr. Schein interviewed twenty of the POWs for 2–4 hours upon their release in Inchon, Korea, or on the transport ship returning them to the United States. Based on these interviews, he assembled a coherent account of the techniques employed by the Chinese. The techniques included the disruption of normal group ties, rewards for learning Communist beliefs, and forced confessions.

In order to disrupt normal group ties, the Chinese separated officers from enlisted men and isolated any potentially emergent leaders. Mail from home was withheld from the prisoners, unless it contained bad news, for example a "Dear John" letter. Spying and informing by prisoners on one another was encouraged. Propaganda was disseminated daily by lecture, followed by required discussions. The Americans were rewarded for learning pro-Communist beliefs and practices. Confessions of wrongdoing were coerced by threats of punishment and promises of better treatment following confession.

There were no reports of the use of drugs, hypnosis, or other mysterious brainwashing practices. Rather, the Chinese relied on the simple methods described: heightened personal insecurity, reduced group ties, threats, and rational appeals, with rewards for compliance.

In the years following the Korean War, much misinformation was bandied about regarding the response of American prisoners to the attempted indoctrination. Expressions of alarm regarding the effectiveness of Communist techniques were voiced by some military sources; their fears regarding the extent of collaboration were heightened by sensationalistic accounts such as that of Kinkead (1959). The theme of Kinkead's book is reflected in the title, In Every War But One. That is, in every war but the Korean, American prisoners resisted the blandishments of their captors. This finding was attributed, among other causes, to lack of military discipline and to the soldiers' lack of indoctrination in democratic ideology. The armed forces responded to these fears with a new "Code of Conduct" [Executive Order 10631, August 17, 1955, reproduced in Biderman (1963, pp. 278–82)], and other steps to "inoculate" their men against possible indoctrination by enemy captors.

A more sober recent appraisal by a social scientist thoroughly familiar with the matter (Biderman, 1963), however, has raised questions about the effectiveness of brainwashing procedures. Some twenty-one prisoners, indeed, did elect to stay in China after over seven thousand of their fellows were repatriated, but these "successes" tended to be among poorly educated men, who, politically speaking, were naive. They could scarcely be said to have possessed well-developed political ideologies, so the result was more to create a system of political beliefs than to change one. Even so, the effort was not a success since all but seven of the twenty-one subsequently chose to return to their homeland following varying periods of residence in China (West, 1963).

CANDIDATE SUPPORT. Ideological agreement with a candidate has traditionally been thought to be an important basis for his support. Survey research results, however, have led some social scientists to question the importance of issues and ideology in determining the voters' choices. Sears (1969) reviewed the studies of voter behavior and came to the following conclusions, which I have paraphrased:

1. People are aware of only the most potent political stimuli. Everyday political issues and personalities are unknown to most voters.
2. Only a minority of the voting population actually applies ideological principles to its political choices. Sears suggested that this minority numbers about 30%.
3. Few voters have stable preferences as to concrete policy, and their attitudes on different policy issues seem generally disconnected.
4. Political commitments, in general, are to groups and not to issues.

In discussing the last point about political commitments, Sears noted that, "Even in presidential voting, with all the attendant publicity, a vast majority vote party; and in lesser elections [the number] is even greater [p. 347]."

The public's lack of interest may reflect the political system as it has developed in the United States. Candidates in the American two-party system tend to deemphasize ideological differences. The politician's appeals are often general and vague, with stress on his own image, rather than his partisan connection. The nonideological voter may be doing the best he can in a system that places so little emphasis on party policy positions. If the candidates began presenting clear policy choices, it is likely that the voter would become more sensitive to ideological differences. That ideology can be important in voting choices, all other things being equal, is suggested by research reported by Byrne *et al.,* (1969).

Byrne and his co-workers (1969) hypothesized, on the basis of Byrne's (1961) theory of attraction based upon similarity, that "when exposed to the views of two political candidates, (a) subjects vote for the candidate with whom they share the greater proportion of similar attitudes, and (b) attraction toward each candidate is a positive linear function of the proportion of that candidate's attitudes which are similar to those of the subject [p. 252]." The issues chosen for study were liberal–conservative in content.

The subjects, undergraduate students at Stanford University, were first given a fifty-six-item attitude scale to assess their own views on a series of topics. The critical topics for this study were views on military spending, nuclear arms, the admission of Red China to the United Nations, socialized medicine, welfare, and the income tax. Several weeks after taking the scale, the students were asked to take part in a research study on voting behavior. They were asked to choose between candidate A and candidate B. Each subject was given a list of statements made by the two candidates.

Candidates A and B were actual candidates in the 1966 election. The statements of their views on the six issues listed above were taken from the candidate's speeches. The liberal candidate's statements on the six issues were consistently liberal. For example he thought that:

> With the progress represented by Medicare, it should be possible to expand its coverage so that every man, woman, and child in this country would be guaranteed medical care throughout his lifetme with all costs paid by tax revenues as with the program in Great Britain [p. 254].

The conservative candidate supported a strong military posture, opposed to income tax in principle, and took other positions consistent with his ideology. His statement on medical care contrasts with that of the liberal:

> One of the most frightening prospects I can imagine is any form of socialized medicine in which the government assumes any influence over medical facilities, and the doctor–patient relationship becomes an impersonal interaction with a civil servant [p. 253].

The results of the voting and ratings clearly supported Byrne's predictions. The subject's vote was a function of the number of attitudes he held in common with each candidate, as was his attraction to each of them. Furthermore, it was shown that attraction was based on the six politically important issues; similarity of attitudes on irrelevant topics such as gardening or science fiction did not affect the subjects' responses to the candidates.

The correlation between voting and agreement with the candidate was particularly clear-cut. Those subjects who agreed with the conservative candidate on all six issues voted 100% for the conservative, as did subjects who agreed with him on five of the six matters. Subjects who agreed with the conservative on three, and the liberal on three, issues, however, split their votes 50/50 between the two. Subjects who agreed with none of the conservative's positions voted for his liberal opponent 93% of the time. A six-point attitude scale based on the subject's stand on the issues predicted his vote with a high degree of accuracy: The biserial correlation between attitudinal grouping and candidate choice was .87 ($p < .001$).

Further evidence for the importance of a candidate's issue stands was Byrne *et al.*'s findings that subjects who were similar to a candidate (agreed with him on at least four of the six issues) voted for that candidate 83% of the time. Those subjects who were in agreement with each candidate on three issues split 50/50, as I have noted. The important determinant for this latter group was party preference; 78% voted in accordance with their own affiliation. That is to say, Democrats voted for the liberal, and Republicans for the conservative, candidate.

The foregoing experimental study supports the idea that all other things being equal, voters will make their choices on the basis of issues and ideology. Of course, all other things seldom *are* equal, partly because politicians persist in taking the image approach and partly because of the absence of consistent ideology among most voters in the United States. Indeed, Byrne *et al.* (1969) noted that the winning strategy based on their mock voters would be to take the majority position on each issue:

> On the basis of the subjects' responses to the original attitude scale, the candidate who indicated that he was against the constant preparation for the possibility of war, opposed to the buildup of nuclear armaments, in favor of admitting Red China to the U.N., against socialized medicine, opposed to increased welfare legislation, and in favor of the income tax should easily defeat either of the consistent candidates [p. 259].

There are candidates who try to be everything to everyone, of course. And there are consistent ideologues, such as Barry Goldwater. In general, however, the politician tries to avoid the appearance of being chimerical; he tries to show that he has some principles, without seeming to be dogmatic. In the 1972 campaign, George McGovern found it impossible to make the shift from the liberal ideological approach, which succeeded so well in the primaries, to the broader appeal necessary to success in the general election.

A motion picture of 1972 depicted a candidate who was able to make the transition in which McGovern failed. *The Candidate* depicts the process of persuading voters to abandon a long-term incumbent California Senator in favor of a young, attractive, little-known lawyer. The younger man's sympathies were with the poor, the black, and the underprivileged. He also was concerned with the corporate disregard of environmental protection. Bill McKay, the young candidate, succeeded in his primary bid through speaking out on these issues. In the election campaign itself, his managers successfully persuaded Bill to minimize his discussion of such issues in favor of brief television appearances and innocuous generalities in his speech making.

If, indeed, present-day political campaigning *is* solely a matter of image making, then the principles of persuasion have little use. But so long as there are citizen elites who *are* concerned about issues—the reformers and environmentalists, as well as those promoting industrial and corporate interests—there will be a demand for candidates who appeal on issues. The rest of this chapter considers the possibility of changing opinions through such appeals. By way of a reminder, let me stress that opinions are verbal expressions of the beliefs and attitudes that a person holds. The expression of opinions depends not only on the person's beliefs and attitudes, but also on the situation, as demonstrated in Bill McKay's story. Thus, while changes in opinion *may* express changes in one's underlying convictions, such changes may simply express the person's perception of the necessities of the situation.

STABILITY AND CHANGE IN POLITICAL OPINION

In discussing the changing of political opinions, we are dealing with opinion formation, as well as with opinion change. That is, in any particular campaign, either for a policy or for a candidate, a considerable portion of the electorate has no well-formulated opinion. Consider, for example, the situation faced by the sponsors of a campaign designed to bring pressure upon a state legislature to pass legislation providing that polluters of waterways be assessed an amount based upon the volume of their dumping (the so-called "effluent charge"). They may find the public with no existing readiness to support *or* to oppose the measure. The promoters of effluent charges, then, must seek to *form* opinion on the matter. Their work may, of course, be made easier by existing attitudes regarding environmental protection, which may be associated with the specific measure proposed. Similarly, a previously unknown candidate like Bill McKay may arouse no strongly favorable or unfavorable sentiment among most voters. In his campaign, he tried to *create* favorable feelings or opinions, both by making himself familiar to the voters and by the creation of associations between himself and favorably evaluated people and programs.

It is easier, of course, to *create* a favorable impression about either a candidate or a program than it is to *change* an unfavorable opinion to a favorable one. Politicians well know that there are certain segments of the electorate, in the two-party system of the United States, which are irrevocably committed to one party or the other. Therefore, much campaign effort is directed toward the uncommitted voter, the so-called Independent. Indeed, the closeness of many recent Presidential elections attests to the importance of such concentration.

In a similar vein, attitude change researchers (Sherif, Sherif, and Nebergall, 1965) have established the generality of the principle that moderate attitudes are much more susceptible to change than extreme ones, either pro or con. In part, this difference in changeability seems to result from the higher intensity of feelings associated with extreme stands. An example will help to clarify this point. The current movement for women's liberation can be characterized as an attempt to move opinion along a continuum ranging from extremely antiegalitarian statements to extremely proegalitarian sentiments. Toward one end of this continuum are beliefs favoring the traditional distinction between men's and women's roles: "A woman's place is in the home"; or, "For the most part, a college education is wasted on a woman." Near the other extreme are statements of opinion favoring complete equality of sexes. Either direct statements of the principle such as, "Husband and wife should share equally in all the tasks related to child rearing and the home," or statements in support of abortion reform are likely to be favored by strong women's lib advocates.

Somewhere between these two extremes are to be found positions representing the "moderate" view with regard to women's liberation. One study (Stone, 1966), for example, found statements such as the following to represent the "middle ground" among college student respondents:

- "Women are not biologically inferior, but they *are* different in many important ways, therefore it is foolish to talk of complete equality."
- "A woman is happiest as a wife, mother and homemaker."

Converts to the cause of women's liberation are most likely to come from among the endorsers of these moderate positions. The moderates are most likely to listen to and evaluate more extreme views, whereas men and women who hold antiegalitarian views are likely to reject most statements favoring women's rights out of hand. However, the interconnectedness of the attitudes and beliefs that make up one's cognitive system should be noted. The readiness of an attitude to change will be affected by other attitudes that the person holds. In general, moderates (on the women's lib issue) who hold a liberal ideology are more susceptible to change in the proliberation direction than are moderates on women's lib who are also politically conservative.

OPINION CHANGE: THE STATE OF THE ART

Social psychologists have been interested in attitude measurement, the effects of propaganda, and public opinion for most of the twentieth century. The experimental study of attitude change or opinion change (a clear distinction is seldom made) has received its greatest attention since World War II. A particularly active program of research was conducted at Yale University in the 1940s and 1950s. A series of books came out of the Yale Communication and Attitude Change Program, the first of which was *Communication and Persuasion* (Hovland *et al.*, 1953).

The research on opinion change discussed in *Communication and Persuasion* was organized along the lines suggested by the formula of *who* says *what* to *whom* with *what effect* (Smith *et al.*, 1946). In discussing the current state of opinion change research, I use this formula, from which follow these four headings:

1. The communicator (who says)
2. The message (what)
3. The recipient of the communication (to whom)
4. The effects of the communication (with what effect)

In discussing the research findings, I focus on their political implications.

The Communicator

Political opinions are subject to influence from *primary* sources and from *secondary* sources. Primary influence on the formation and change of opinion is exerted by one's face-to-face intimates and acquaintances. Secondary influence stems from the mass media and various forms of political advertising.

It has been maintained (Lazarsfeld *et al.*, 1948), based on studies done before the widespread use of television in political campaigns, that most influence on political opinion is primary; that is it originates in face-to-face contact. The important contacts for most voters are with community "opinion leaders," people who pay a great deal of attention to political news and who engage in a good deal of political discussion, although they may not be leaders in any formal sense. According to Lazarsfeld and his co-workers, political influence is a two-stage process. Their hypothesis of a "two-step flow of communication" was supported by the findings that opinion leaders reported the formal media as being more effective in shaping their opinions, whereas the majority of people listed personal relationships as being the formative influences. "This suggests that ideas often flow *from* radio and print *to* the opinion leaders and *from* them to the less active sections of the population [p. 151]."

Personal contacts undoubtedly *are* very important in determining political choices. Lazarsfeld and his co-workers (1948) documented this importance in *The People's Choice* by repeated quotes from their respondents' reasons for making their decision on the 1940 election. For example, a woman who until mid-campaign planned to vote for Roosevelt (she voted for Willkie) said:

> I have always been a Democrat and I think Roosevelt has been all right. But my family are all for Willkie. They think he would make the best president and they have been putting the pressure on me [p. 155].

The influence need not be so overt or intentional, however, as exemplified by the waitress in a restaurant who decided against Willkie (Lazarsfeld *et al.*, 1948):

> I had done a little newspaper reading against Willkie, but the real reason I changed my mind was from *hearsay*. So many people don't like Willkie. Many customers in the restaurant said Willkie would be no good [p. 153].

The authors noted that such overheard conversation can be particularly effective because no persuasive intent is perceived.

Although personal contacts may not be as important as they were before the advent of television, they undoubtedly play a primary role in shaping political opinion. What one's family, friends, and co-workers are saying is difficult to ignore, unless one has become firmly committed to divergent positions. The importance of primary influence, however, does not mean that the media have no effect—they do affect what people talk about. In particular, the mass media influence the conversations of those people who have been spoken of as opinion leaders.

The *communicator* may be a political candidate, the Republican National Committee, or the spokesman for an interest group such as the National Association of Manufacturers or the Sierra Club. The persuasive intent of these spokesmen is usually evident to their listeners, who may thereby guard against being influenced by what that person has to say. Communicators who are believed to be impartial sources of information, however, may not be so hampered. Thus, even the reporting of news may have persuasive effects. Although the journalistic profession tries to maintain its objectivity, partisan observers will inevitably sense a bias in news reporting. These partisans charge that the media present more facts favoring one side of an issue than the other. In recent history, Vice President Spiro Agnew has attacked the "liberal" ideological inclinations of the media in its reporting of the Vietnam war.

Undoubtedly, the reports of the daily newspapers and radio and television news programs are believed by a large proportion of their audience. In other words, the media have high *credibility*. The term credibility refers both to *expertness* (the ability to understand and interpret current events) and to *trustworthiness* (inclined to give fair, unbiased presentation of issues). The communicator is more effective in producing opinion change if he has high credibility. After a period of time has elapsed, however, members of the audience tend to separate the message from the communicator so that credibility is less a factor.

Suppose, for example, that the issue is "withdrawal of troops from Europe." Let us suppose that two different audiences are exposed to identical arguments advocating the withdrawal of American troops now stationed in Europe. One audience hears the arguments in a speech made by the respected Senator from Montana, Mike Mansfield. The second audience hears the same views, expressed with equal force, by Charles Smith, a local businessman. Each speaker's presentation is likely to produce some change in any uncommitted audience member's opinions. More change will occur, however, when a highly credible communicator

(Senator Mansfield) advocates withdrawal of troops than when a person with lower credibility (Mr. Smith) takes the same stand. However, two or three weeks *after* hearing the speech, the amount of change is likely to be the same regardless of the communicator. The audience members who heard Mr. Smith speak to the issue are apt to increase in the degree to which they favor his position, and those who heard the Senator, to decrease in their support for the position. This phenomenon, dubbed the "sleeper effect" by Hovland and his co-workers (1953), seems to be a rather general one. The graph in Figure 11–2 shows actual results obtained in an experiment by Hovland and Weiss (1951). A later experiment by Kelman and Hovland (1953) demonstrated that the sleeper effect results from separation or dissociation of the content of the message from the source. When Kelman and Hovland reminded their subjects, 3 weeks after the initial persuasive messages, of the linkage between the persuader and the message, their subjects showed opinion change no different from that which had been measured immediately following persuasion. The investigators referred to this reconnection as a "reinstatement" of the communicator.

The political implications of the sleeper effect are important. Political smears or unfounded charges against a political candidate are likely to be remembered long after the questionable source of these charges is forgotten. Current in the news as I write, for example, are headline stories about the possible role of President Nixon in trying to "cover up" the Watergate bugging case. Although these stories are based on rumor and "leaks" from grand jury and Congressional hearings, the charges are likely to be remembered in spite of their low credibility sources.

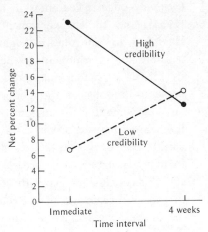

Figure 11–2 "Retention" of opinion: Changes in extent of agreement with position advanced by "high credibility" and "low credibility" sources (Adapted from C. I. Hovland and W. Weiss, "The influence of source credibility on communication effectiveness," *Public Opion Quarterly*, 1951, *15*, 646. Copyright 1951 by The Public Opinion Quarterly. Used by permission.)

The persuader's effectiveness can also be enhanced or diminished by the style of presentation he adopts. For example, he may take a "plain folks" position early in his talk, emphasizing points of similarity between himself and his audience. Such "softening up" for the forthcoming persuasion has been noted by many authors. Furthermore, the audience's reaction to the communicator may be affected by its response to his message. This point has been made in detail by Osgood and Tannenbaum (1955), who noted that a highly credible communicator may be able to influence his audience on an unpopular issue. The less credible communicator, however, is more likely to have his own image tarnished. Dwight D. Eisenhower could criticize the military establishment with some effect, whereas a Senator or Congressman with less glowing military credentials might have hurt himself by attacking the military.

The Message

Much discussion and research has been devoted to the question of whether a persuasive speaker should present only his own position or something on both sides. For example, should an advocate of public power mention some of the benefits of leaving electrical power distribution in the hands of private companies? Experimental research suggests that he should present both sides if the audience initially disagrees with him, or if it is likely to hear the private power case from the opposition. All other things being equal, the proponent should present his own position last, since the most recent message is more effective. Under some conditions, however, the first argument may be more effective (*primacy effect*). Presentation of both sides is advocated by McGuire (1964), since the speaker can prepare his hearers for counterarguments. He refers to "inoculation" against persuasion by presentation of the possible counterarguments to the communicator's position.

If the persuader does present both sides of an issue, or even if he presents a number of arguments on his own side, it is sometimes dangerous to assume that the audience will "draw its own conclusions." Rather, the hearers may be left in a state of uncertainty and confusion with regard to the conclusion that the speaker believes to be implicitly obvious. In many situations, therefore, the communicator is better advised to state his conclusions explicitly: for example, "The facts I have presented to you with regard to power rates, industry, and community needs lead me to the conclusion that a publicly operated power plant is needed."

The choice of explicit versus implicit conclusion drawing must be made on the basis of the audience, however, since the speaker may better leave the conclusion drawing up to an intelligent and informed audience.

Fear appeals were used very effectively by the Democrats in the 1964 Presidential campaign in the United States. Barry Goldwater, the conservative Republican candidate, advocated that the United States maintain a strong military posture in Vietnam and throughout the world. The electorate's fear of the possibility of war and of nuclear devastation was successfully exploited by his opponent, Lyndon Johnson, who convinced the voters that their fears could be lessened by voting for Johnson. While emotional appeals sometimes do not work, in this case the results accorded with the laboratory findings that fear arousal produces change when the action to be taken to reduce the fear is both clear-cut and possible (vote for Johnson).

The Recipient of the Communication

I have already noted the need for tailoring persuasive appeals to one's audience. An appeal for support of fluoridation of water supplies directed to an audience of chemists would not be suitable for the general public. The educational level of the communicator's audience, its specialized interests, and even the members' intelligence are factors to be considered. Emotional, as well as intellectual, differences among the recipients may enter into the consideration of the most effective means of communicating the message to them. Self-esteem and other personality factors seem to have a bearing on persuasibility; persons with low self-esteem have been found to be more persuasible. Personality dynamics may lead to the development of certain attitudes and affect the susceptibility to change. Opposition to water fluoridation, for example, may stem from the anti-scientific attitudes which seem to be typical of the authoritarian personality.

Finally, the personal commitments of members of the prospective audience will affect receptivity to persuasive communications. Such commitment may lead to self-selection such that the only people who listen to the message are those who already agree with it. As Zimbardo and Ebbeson (1969) put it: "The people you may want most in your audience are often least likely to be there [p. 22]." If the likely listeners are at all aware of the purpose of the persuasive communication, meeting, program, etc., the ones who agree are likely to "tune in"; those disagreeing or uninterested to "tune out or turn off." The commitment that leads to self-selection is often a very deeply felt, ego-involved commitment.

In Maine, many voters are very *ego involved* in the individualistic values of hunting, fishing, and other outdoor sports. Their involvement leads to strong opposition to any proposed gun-control legislation. One of the ways to change such strongly held opinions is through active role playing. For example, an opponent to gun control might be led to support handgun-control legislation through participating in role playing the part of a distraught father whose teenage daughter had been shot by a gun bought by an unbalanced boyfriend the day before. It is difficult to imagine how the person could be induced to participate in such role playing, however. Whenever an individual is forewarned of a persuasive attempt, he tends to avoid or resist the message.

The most important sources of social stability are the individual's multiple connections with various *reference groups,* the groups of which he is a member or to which he aspires. Paradoxically, social change is also closely related to the individual's group ties. All kinds of interpersonal relatedness must be considered, ranging from close primary-group ties to superficial relationships with strangers. In matters of great importance to a group, such as gun ownership for members of a fish and game club, opposition to gun-control legislation is a strongly entrenched norm of behavior from which few members dare deviate. In matters of lesser importance, the individual may deviate alone or with minimal support from one or two of his fellows.

Thoreau spoke of the individual who "hears a different drummer." That is, some people question the opinions of others around them. Few march to that different drumbeat, however, because of the strong rewards and pressures that groups can bring to bear in favor of the existing "social reality." A social or political movement begins when a number of individuals become aware of their mutually deviant tendencies. Thus, for most people, a new group affiliation must be available before they can abandon the old one. As Asch (1952) has shown, the presence of even one supporter will strengthen the tendency to hold onto a deviant opinion. One persuasive example of this phenomenon is to be found in the accounts of jury deliberations, in which a single hold-out sometimes attracts other jury members who have doubts regarding the majority opinion. The result can be a deadlock or even reversal of the position initially favored by the majority. A particularly fascinating account of the personal interactions which led to deadlock of the Harrisburg Conspiracy trial of Father Philip Berrigan and his co-defenders illustrates this point (Schulman *et al.,* 1973).

The Effects of the Communication

It goes without saying that an effective communication is one which produces opinion change. Recently in my social psychology class, I brought up the possibility of adopting the parliamentary system of government in the United States. I asked one-half of the class to indicate their opinion about making such a change, then gave a short lecture on the advantages of parliamentary government. I pointed out that the parliamentary system would likely be more responsive and more responsible, that the governing party could be changed immediately if people lost confidence in it, and gave an account using the names of current party leaders and how the system would work with Richard Nixon as Prime Minister, rather than President. After the talk, the other half of the class members responded to the opinion question. The before–after comparison showed a change from negative to slightly positive attitudes toward a parliamentary government in the United States.

Even though attitude change may be readily produced in some circumstances, the change is unlikely to persist. The individual member of the audience is likely to backslide to his previous opinion *unless* he hears more of the issue. In politics, of course, we are likely to encounter a prolonged campaign, rather than a single exposure to an issue. In other words, durable opinion change is likely to require repetition. Research also suggests that an advocated opinion change bolstered by many facts is more likely to persist than one which is supported only by a simple persuasive message. Active participation by members of the audience, as happens in role playing, also results in longer-lasting change.

The most important factor in the retention of opinion change, however, is the provision of social support for the new opinion. This is best accomplished by working with groups of people, so that the members can mutually support each other's changed views. Any method by which the individual can be kept informed that others support his position will be effective in maintaining the change.

Current research places a great deal of stress on the arousal of inconsistency as a consequence of the communication, which in turn is thought to produce lasting changes in opinion. The *consistency theory* approach to opinion change has been stated in a number of different ways [dissonance theory (Festinger, 1957); congruity theory (Osgood and Tannenbaum, 1955); and consistency theory (Rosenberg, 1960) are some of the major variations]. Common to the consistency theories are the ideas that inconsistency among one's beliefs, attitudes, and feelings is uncomfortable; and an important means of reducing this discomfort is to change one's opinions toward greater self-consistency. A strong Republican who admires President Nixon will be troubled by information indicating that the President countenanced dishonest campaign practices. In order to reduce this inconsistency in his attitude system, he may reject the new information as untrue, or he may change his opinion about the President. Another possibility is that he may use "psycho-logic" (Osgood, 1960) to reduce the inconsistency. Such psycho-logic might run as follows: "The President did use dishonest means to gain reelection, *but* all politicians are dishonest, and further it was very important for the President to be reelected because he had so many important things left to accomplish. And besides, his opponent was an incompetent."

Similar processes are suggested when one's behavior differs from his cherished attitudes. Festinger (1957) has referred to cognitive dissonance, the state that ensues when one's beliefs and behavior are contradictory. Festinger has suggested that the smaller the justification for an act that contradicts an important belief, the more likely that belief itself will change. Consider, for example, the case of Jane Smith, an uncommitted prospective voter from a Republican family. Her existing attitudes are moderately conservative, in line with her family's Republicanism. However, she is persuaded to register as a Democrat by a friend and to vote in the state primary election for a Presidential candidate popular with youth. Jane's political attitudes and opinions are likely to change in accordance with her declaration as a Democrat, in inverse proportion to the concrete inducement for her act. She is most likely to change her beliefs if she registered with little persuasion, less likely if her friend offered her five dollars to do so. It is interesting to speculate regarding the amount of change if the friend were also her fiancé. She could, on the one hand, say, "the reason I registered Democrat was to please my future husband" (large inducement, little change) or, "I really wanted to register as a Democrat, anyway, Jim and I agree on these things" (small inducement, large change). Such are the possible applications of the findings of Festinger and Carlsmith (1959) and of later researchers.

This completes my survey of the state of the art in social psychological research on opinion change. Our understanding is far from complete, but there does exist a sizable body of knowledge, and research is continuing. Will such knowledge lead to "mind control" of the kind described in George Orwell's novel *1984*? I think not. One purpose of this volume is to expose the reader to current knowledge regarding the influences that operate to determine his opinions. I believe in the paradox posed by Edward Lee Thorndike (1959) that man is most free when he is most aware of how lawfully his behavior is determined:

> For strange as it may sound man is free only in a world whose every event he can understand and foresee. Only so can he guide it. We are captains of our own souls only in so far as they act in perfect law so that we can understand and foresee . . . only so can we control our own selves [p. 362].

CONCLUSION

The topic of attitude change has occupied American social physchologists for many years. There is considerable knowledge about factors that can influence individual opinions, but changes in ideology seem much more difficult to accomplish. Candidate preferences are affected by one's partisan preferences, by one's image of the candidate, and by ideological agreement with the candidate. Campaign tactics generally involve attempts to create a favorable image of the candidate. Such tactics often include presentation of popular stands on issues of the day. Attempts to actually sway opinion on such issues are infrequent, although they may be made by an incumbent officeholder who finds that his actions or policy stands have been unpopular.

At the present stage of knowledge, it is unwarranted to attribute electoral outcomes to any specific cognitive factors. It is a mistake to assume that a candidate won because of the image that he projected or that he won because the voters agreed with his stands on the issues. The voter is responding to the limited choices available to him, and, as Key (1966) has noted, the candidate may win *in spite of* his tactics, rather than because of them. "If the people can choose only from among rascals, they are certain to choose a rascal [p. 3]."

Thus, while I have argued that issues, ideology, and image are important aspects of a candidate's appeal, there is no way of weighing the contribution of each factor. There is a tendency to believe that a winning candidate used the correct techniques and the loser, the incorrect ones. The real effect of the campaign tactics may have been to obscure any reasonable basis for choice, so that the voter was actually choosing the lesser "rascal."

> It thus can be mischievous error to assume, because a candidate wins, that a majority of the electorate shares his views on public questions, approves his past actions, or has specific expectations about his future conduct. Nor does victory establish that the candidate's campaign strategy, his image, his television style, or his fearless stand against cancer and polio turned the trick. The election returns establish only that the winner attracted a majority of the votes—assuming the existence of a modicum of rectitude in election administration. They tell us precious little about why the plurality was his [Key, 1966, p. 2].

12

Political Choice

Under the definition of political behavior advanced in earlier chapters of this volume, many different kinds of human behavior can be classified. I have suggested, for example, that many of man's cooperative activities, as well as antagonistic ones, can be considered political behavior. Similarly, *refusal* to participate in the ordinary activities of a society is a kind of political act—I am thinking here of the young members of the counter-culture, who refuse to be caught up in the "rat race" of competition, working at a steady job, dressing in conventional ways. Many of these young people abstain from voting or otherwise participating in conventional political institutions.

In spite of my attempt to extend the definition of politics, I keep returning to the topic of participation in conventional political institutions. Since I am mainly discussing the United States, we return to the most widespread political act in that country—the act of voting. The reason for my concentration on voting, after having tried to broaden the definition of political behavior, is simply the availability of empirical data. Much research has been done on voting behavior, whereas relatively little attention has been given to noninstitutionalized forms of political behavior.

Voting may be thought of as choice behavior. The voting decision usually involves a choice between two alternatives: Candidate A and Candidate B. Note that we can speak of a choice only when there is some degree of comparability between alternatives. In general, the individual will choose the most attractive of two alternatives, but where one possibility is highly attractive and the other highly unattractive, it is not very meaningful to speak of a decision being made. Restle (cited in Festinger, 1964, p. 2) observed that:

> The answer is very simple if the choice is merely between something the person likes and something he dislikes. Some doubt arises when the choice is more difficult, as when it is between two things which the individual

likes and his preference is relatively slight. The question becomes difficult and interesting when the alternatives offered are complex, each involving some pleasant and some unpleasant aspects, or where the person chooses without being certain as to the outcome he will receive.

Choices among political personages inevitably involve both pleasant and unpleasant aspects of the person (he is a very fine speaker, but I disagree with his stand on marijuana penalties), as well as uncertainty about outcomes for the voter (will taxes go up if Smith is elected Governor?). How does the citizen evaluate the effect on his own economic well-being of the election of Smith over Jones, for instance?

IMPORTANCE OF THE CHOICE

Generally speaking, the importance to the individual of a political decision varies in direct relation to the stature of the office involved. We know, for example, that voter turn-out is much greater in Presidential elections than in elections for local office. Similarly, off-year Congressional elections draw fewer voters than do those held in Presidential years. We know from laboratory studies that the more important a decision is to the individual, the more time he will take to make up his mind, and the more information he will require before making his choice. These observations are supported by experiments on choice reaction times (Woodworth and Schlosberg, 1955) and by studies of information seeking in decision-making tasks (Lanzetta and Driscoll, 1968; see also Rhine, 1967).

Differences in the time or space allotted by the news media to the various political races reflect editorial judgments regarding the importance of contests at the various levels. For example, nearly everything a Presidential candidate has to say will be aired by the media; he has a corps of reporters following his campaign, ready to report any significant utterance. In contrast, candidates for local office receive next to nothing in the way of press coverage even if they try to advocate new or startling positions. Relative inattention by the news media extends often to Congressional candidates. For example, one investigator who was interested in analyzing stories about Congressional candidates found too few articles to be of use (Converse, 1962). Of course, the relative neglect of candidates below the Presidential level may not be entirely the fault of news editors. Lack of voter interest in even congressional races is indicated by Miller and Stokes's (1966) findings in a study of contested Congressional districts in 1958. Only 24% of the prospective voters in these districts had "read or heard something" about both the incumbent Congressman and his challenger.

More direct evidence of lack of interest in candidates for minor positions is shown by sparse attendance at "meet the candidates" affairs for city council or school board candidates. The City Clerk of a Maine community of 40,000 reported on one such meeting for City Council candidates, a well-organized presentation of the League of Women Voters: "After you subtract the number of candidates and their relatives, there were six voters there," he said. Such observations seem to indicate that poor coverage by the media reflects low demand from readers. It is likely that the media, spurred by notions (and F.C.C. rules, in the case of broadcast journalism) of *public interest*, program far more political coverage than is sought by most of their audience.

Choices in 1972

The 1972 Presidential campaign pitted Senator George McGovern against the incumbent President Richard Nixon. In August of that year, with the primary campaigns over and the nominees named by party conventions, the November election results were foreseeable. The Democratic nominee was some twenty percentage points behind the President in mid-August opinion polls.

The campaign promised excitement, however, because of the rags-to-riches saga of McGovern's campaign for his party's nomination. Favored by only 5% of his party's voters in January of 1972, McGovern went on to capture the Democratic nomination in July. There were precedents for upset victories, and it was expected that many of the Democrats who opposed McGovern's nomination would "come home" to vote for him in November.

Policy differences between the two 1972 candidates also held promise for a spirited campaign. McGovern, an attractive if somewhat professorial candidate, favored immediate withdrawal from Vietnam. He argued for reductions in military appropriations and for stronger efforts on the domestic welfare front. His suggestions for a guaranteed annual income for the poor led to charges of radicalism by Hubert Humphrey in the California primary campaign. Each of the policies advocated by

McGovern could be contrasted sharply with the policies that had been pursued during the first Nixon administration.

As President, Nixon's leadership in foreign affairs had been dramatized in many directions. He broke with the long-standing U.S. policy that had isolated the People's Republic of China from the West. His historic visits to Peking and to Moscow drew much favorable attention. Nixon had not ended U.S. involvement in Vietnam, but his policy of Vietnamization [1] and his continued bombing of North Vietnam appeared to have the support of the American people. Domestically, Nixon had followed policies acceptable to extreme conservatives. His domestic conservatism was evident in his Supreme Court appointments and his antagonism to court decisions requiring busing for school integration, both of which signaled an end to aggressive Federal action in support of equal rights for black Americans. Decreased support for individual civil rights was also evident in the Nixon administration's use of wiretapping and the seeking of even greater authority for the use of wiretaps by Federal agencies.

These dramatic differences between Nixon and McGovern held promise for an interesting campaign. Although McGovern was relatively unknown, he had come from nowhere and been successful in his campaign for the nomination. He might be able to do the same thing in closing the gap between himself and Nixon before November. How reasonable was it to expect voters to shift their preference from the incumbent President to the challenger?

The results of past voting research suggested that neither spirited discussion of issues, nor increasing familiarity with the Democratic challenger, would be likely to change many voters' intentions. It was expected that Democrats who may have been leaning toward Nixon would "come home" in terms of their preexisting loyalties to the Democratic Party. As Rossi (1966) has noted, "electoral campaigns do not accomplish dramatic shifts among the electorate and have as their main function the reactivation of long-standing party loyalties [p. 71]." The Democratic Party, being in a majority position, seemed likely to close the 20% gap, though such "reactivation" was unlikely to provide a winning margin.

The results of the 1972 election did not bear out the prediction of a "closing of the gap." Nixon maintained his August advantage, winning

---

[1] Vietnamization referred to the announced Nixon policy of gradually turning over to the South Vietnamese the combat role once held by U. S. troops.

by over 20% of the votes cast. He was reelected with 60.8% of the popular vote, compared with McGovern's 38%. The challenger carried only Massachusetts and the District of Columbia. Nixon had the distinction of being one of three Presidents to win election by over 60% of the popular vote.[2] The reasons for such dramatic support for the President included a number of factors—his incumbency, his dramatic foreign trips, and his decisive actions in Vietnam. It is also likely that many votes were cast *against* his opponent. McGovern could not shake the image of radicalism and indecisiveness that many voters attributed to him. Further knowledge of the dynamics of electoral choice in 1972 will await analysis of opinion surveys taken before and after the election.

ELECTORAL CHANGE

The usual survey of voter opinion is taken with a different random sample of voters each time, so there is no way of telling just how people's minds are changing. In the past 30 years, however, voting research has made use of the "panel study" to investigate the stability of an individual's voting intentions over the course of an electoral campaign. In a panel study, the *same* voters are interviewed time after time so that the responses of each individual panel member can be tracked. By this means, the individual's voting intention in July can be compared with his proclivity in September and his reported vote in November. Rossi's (1966) survey of voting behavior research over 30 years (1933–63) led him to some conclusions about the processes by which voters make up their minds:

> Elaborate panel studies in the 1940, 1948 and 1956 elections have amply documented the fact that in presidential campaigns few voters shift their allegiances from one to another candidate in the course of the campaign. Furthermore, contrary to the expectation that voters who shifted would be those most sensitive to the issue differences among candidates, analyses uniformly showed that the voters who shifted were the least politically motivated and least knowledgeable concerning the issues and candidates [p. 73].

---

[2] Since 1824, the earliest election for which accurate totals are available, Roosevelt (1936) received 60.8% and Johnson (1964) received 61.1% of the popular vote (Associated Press *Almanac*, 1973).

Over against the pessimism reflected by Rossi is the more optimistic note found in V. O. Key's (1966) final work, *The Responsible Electorate.*[3] As might be gathered from his title, Key found much more occasion to be optimistic about the rationality of the voter than did Rossi. Using different data sources (the Gallup polls over the years), Key found changes in issue concerns in the electorate which presaged electoral changes: that is, the Presidential candidate whose stand best reflected voter concerns tended to be elected. In surveying elections from 1932 to 1960, Key found evidence for his thesis that governmental change followed the concerns of the electorate. It is difficult to resolve these contradictory findings. Whereas panel studies and surveys of opinion on various social and economic issues tend to show a rather inattentive and nonknowledgeable public, Key found that electoral results follow public opinion changes. An examination of the extent of party-line voting may help us to resolve this contradiction.

Partisan Predispositions

In the first place, it should be noted that the American electorate is divided into three parties—Democratic, Republican, and Independent. We give "party" status to no-preference voters since some people assert a good deal of pride in their status as Independent voters. Of these three parties then, the Democrats and Republicans vote quite consistently for candidates nominated by their own party. In the Presidential contests of 1952 and 1956, for example, in which a candidate of the minority Republican Party won election, some 80–85% of the partisan voters voted for the candidate of their own party. In the Congressional election of 1958, nearly 90% voted party (Sears, 1969, p. 344).

Party registration figures are difficult to interpret since the states vary in their procedures for party enrollment. Some show huge numbers of Independent voters (e.g., Alaska, with about 53%); many others such as Florida, Oklahoma, and Oregon list only 2% or 3% Independents. Some other states do not even have registration by party (Barone *et al.*, 1972). Averages for states that *do* report party registrations show a large margin of Democrats over Republicans. Overall, the available registration figures for the United States give the Democrats about 50%

[3] While Key's book was not entirely complete at the time of his death, enough of the manuscript was extant to allow editing, by M. C. Cummings, Jr., and posthumous publication of the work and Key's tentative conclusions.

and the Republicans about 35%. These figures, however, are subject to distortions occasioned by registration practices and historical factors within each state. Therefore, estimates of party loyalties based upon survey samples are more likely reliable than voter registration figures. The Survey Research Center at the University of Michigan has been asking respondents about their party preferences for some time. In 1968, for example, 45% of the respondents saw themselves as Democrats. Twenty-four percent called themselves republicans, and an even larger number (29%) labeled themselves Independent (Dreyer and Rosenbaum, 1970, p. 12).

Another factor of importance is the voter's *commitment* to his party. Some voters may be very strongly committed to a particular party; others may have relatively little commitment. In addition to asking its respondents about party identification, the Survey Research Center has asked about the strength of partisan commitments. Those who classify themselves as Independents have been asked about their partisan leanings. The eight categories resulting from the answers to these questions and the percentages in each category for the first Eisenhower election year (1952) and for the year 1968, which is generally regarded as the beginning of the "new politics" era, appear in Table 12–1. The hard-core party

Table 12–1 Party identification as revealed by Survey Research Center interviews in October of 1952 and 1968

Identification Category	1952	1968
Strong Republican	13%	10%
Weak Republican	14	14
Independent Republican	7	9
Independent	5	10
Independent Democrat	10	10
Weak Democrat	25	25
Strong Democrat	22	20
Apolitical, don't know	4	2
	100%	100%
Number of cases	1,614	1,557

Source: Adapted from Survey Research Center data, as reported by E. C. Dreyer and W. A. Rosenbaum, *Public Opinion and Behavior,* 2nd Ed., Belmont, Calif., 1979, p. 12.

vote lies among those voters who classify themselves as "strong" Republican or "strong" Democrat. Among the strong party identifiers, 82% reported in 1956 that they always voted for the same party. A majority, 60%, of the weak party identifiers do the same (Campbell *et al.*, 1964). Those most likely to alternate in their Presidential party vote, then, are the Independents. Switch voting occurs with decreasing probability as party commitment increases. This is shown graphically in Figure 12–1. The figure is based on reports by older voters that they have voted for the Presidential candidates of different parties in past elections: 89% of Independent voters reported such switches from election to election, while only 20% of the strong party identifiers reported having done so. Although the gradients are shown as symmetrical, it is likely that Democrats and Republicans differ in their tendencies toward straight-ticket voting.

Presidential election outcomes are disproportionately determined by the voters in the middle of Figure 12–1, the Independents and weak party identifiers. The number of possible switchers is important when

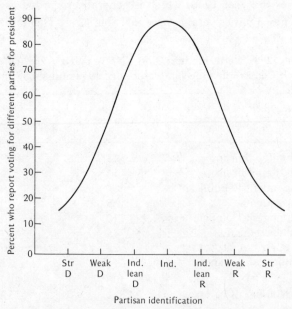

Figure 12–1 Relation between party identification and self-report of variability of party voting in presidential years, for voters age 35 and older (Drawn from Survey Research Center data as reported by Angus Campbell *et al., The American Voter: An Abridgement,* p. 71, New York: Wiley, 1964.)

we consider the closeness of many Presidential elections. Small electoral margins are the rule rather than the exception in U.S. Presidential elections. In the nineteen elections held since 1900, only four winners received as much as 60% of the total popular vote. In 1920, the Republican candidate, Warren Harding, took 60% of the vote in what has been interpreted as a reaction against Woodrow Wilson's idealism and a desire to return to normalcy following the end of World War I. In 1936, the New Deal policies of Franklin Roosevelt gained him 61% of the vote in his bid for reelection (*Associated Press Almanac*, 1973). Similar percentages of the popular vote were gained by Johnson in 1964 and Nixon in 1972 against opponents who were seen as extremists by the voters. These historical observations suggest that in the absence of an overriding issue, such as the economic Depression of the 1930s, or fear of Goldwater's warlike posture in 1964, the switching of a few votes may make a difference in the outcome of the election.

Group Loyalties

Strong attachments to political parties, as we have seen, include strong loyalties to the candidates of the respective adherent's party. Each of us has various attachments to other groups, however—attachments that may often be stronger than those to political parties. Catholics, for example, feel a bond to their coreligionists, as blacks identify with others of their race. Added to these ties are the traditional identification of some religious and occupational groups with political parties. Catholics, for example, have usually seen their interests to lie with the Democratic Party, farmers by and large (except in the South) have voted Republican, and trade unionists, Democratic. Black voters, interestingly enough, have changed over the years from Republican to Democratic Party loyalties as the respective party positions have changed. In 1972, for example, George McGovern received about 79% of the black vote.

While Catholics have strong tendencies toward Democratic voting, it does not follow that all Democrats are sympathetic to that religion. On the contrary, many Protestant Democrats in the past have given evidence of anti-Catholic feeling. For example, some observers have attributed the narrowness of the late President Kennedy's victory margin over Richard Nixon to such feelings. Donald Stokes (1966) took a closer look at the effect of religious loyalty on perceptions of the 1960 candidates. The joint effects of religious and party loyalties on the perception of John F. Kennedy by the voters who were questioned prior to the 1960 election will serve as an example. Stokes (1966) wrote:

> Because Kennedy was the Democratic candidate, voters identifying with the Democratic party tended to view him more favorably than did voters identifying with the Republican party. But Kennedy was seen by the electorate not only as a Democrat; he was seen as a Catholic as well. As a result, at every point along the party identification continuum, Catholics tended to perceive Kennedy in a more favorable light than did Protestants [p. 23].

These effects are shown in more detail in Figure 12–2.

In Figure 12–2, the 1960 sample of voters is categorized in terms of a standard party identification scale into five groups, in order: Strong Republicans, Weak Republicans, Independents, Weak Democrats and

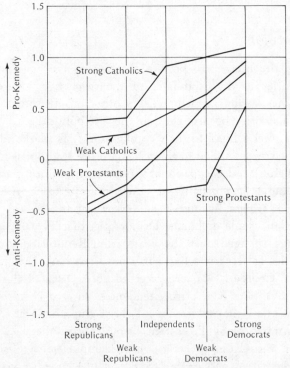

Figure 12–2 Influence of party and religious identifications on perceptions of Kennedy (Adapted from D. E. Stokes, "Some dynamic elements of contests for the presidency," *American Political Science Review*, 1966, 60, 24. Copyright © 1966 by The American Political Science Association. Used by permission.)

Strong Democrats. Religious adherents, Protestant and Catholic, were also divided in terms of the strength of their psychological identification with their respective churches. The candidate responses of voters in each of the twenty categories, defined by taking the respondents' religion and party together, are plotted to yield the rather distinctive curves that appear in the figure.

The conjoint effect of party and religion on the positivity of the voter's perception of Kennedy are clearly demonstrated in Figure 12–2. Overall, the impressions are favorable (pro-Kennedy). That is, the net impression he had on most voters was positive. Protestant Republicans, however, tended to negative evaluations, as compared to their Catholic counterparts. Strong group ties in either instance tended to override weaker affiliations; note that for weak adherents to either faith, party loyalty is linearly related to positivity of the candidate's image. Where strong religious orientations are involved, as in the Strong Protestant category, strong conflicting group loyalties were necessary to overcome traditional anti-Catholicism. That is, among the "Strong Protestants" *only* those who were also "Strong Democrats" had a net positive orientation to Kennedy as a candidate.

Many group loyalties figure in voting patterns. A shift in voting patterns, such as the one that occurred in 1972, when many traditionally Democratic votes went to President Nixon, undoubtedly involved group loyalties. That is, members of large subgroups (e.g., some labor unions) and smaller primary groupings come to share misgivings about the Democratic candidate's competence to fulfill the duties of the Presidency. In order to break from traditional loyalties, the Catholic Democrat or union member Democrat must perceive that many of his fellows share his deviant inclinations. Even with such group support, it is unlikely that many "Strong Democrats" voted for the Republican candidate.

EFFECTS OF THE MASS MEDIA
ON VOTING BEHAVIOR

In these days of instant communication, it is difficult to imagine how the citizens of yesteryear got enough information to make a voting decision. In the days of Washington or Jefferson, circular letters, travelers' tales, testimony of friends about letters from their friends, and similar word-of-mouth testimonials were very important. In the days before trains and telegraphic communication arrived upon the American scene, primary- and interest-group influences must have been even more potent than today. The influence of opinion leaders must have been immense, because they often had exclusive sources of information. Those individuals who could read and write automatically held positions of influence in colonial days.

Newspapers

Newspapers have been an important source of information throughout the history of the United States. Today, newspapers are available to nearly everyone, but they are not uniformly read by the adult populace. In their study of the 1948 election, *Voting: A Study of Opinion Formation in a Presidential Election,* Berelson and his co-workers (1954, p. 240) found that only 50% of the Elmira, New York, voters queried could actually name at least one of "the last two items (about the election) that you read in the newspaper." Of course, newspaper readership is higher than 50%, but we know that many people have little interest in politics or world affairs, reading only the comics, sports, and the "Dear Abby" column.

The actual influence of the newspapers on the voting choices of Americans is debatable. There have been many complaints about newspaper bias by both liberals and conservatives. It is rather widely acknowledged, however, that newspaper managements tend to identify with business interests and thereby with the Republican party. In their 1948 study, Berelson, *et al.* did not find a strong bias in terms of numbers of favorable news stories about the two candidates in the three papers serving Elmira. In one paper, 62% of the stories were favorable to Dewey, the Republican candidate, in another, 55%, and in the third, 52% of the stories favored Dewey. Undeniably, there was *some* bias, as shown by the contrast between the coverage and the campaign activity. For instance, the Democratic candidate (Truman) made more speeches (twenty-three as compared to seventeen by Dewey in September and October) and also spent more time discussing issues. Nevertheless, it can be argued that the percentages of stories about each candidate in the Elmira papers represented a "reasonable" balance of coverage. Editorially, of course, the newspapers (all under the same publisher) exercised their prerogatives. The same three papers' editorial comments were 93%, 88%, and 100% pro-Dewey.

It can be argued that as long as news coverage is reasonably balanced, newspapers have little impact on voting intentions. While correlations may be found between newspaper policy and electoral outcomes (61% of the Elmira panel voted Republican in 1968), such correspondence may simply show that newspapers reflect the milieu in which they operate. Just as Democratic newspapers *do* exist in many strongly Democratic areas of the country, it could be argued that the Republican bias of the papers serving Elmira reflect the Republican character of that part of upstate New York. A recent study by John Robinson of the Institute for Social Research, however, suggests that newspapers actually do influence voting choices. Robinson (1972) contended that newspaper support for Nixon was a significant factor in the President's close (0.7%) 1968 victory over Hubert Humphrey. He found, based on a national sample of 1,346 Americans 21 years of age or older, that "the largely pro-Nixon coverage carried by the newspapers in 1968 was associated with some shift in the vote in Nixon's favor [p. 241]."

Robinson's findings were based upon the interviewee's perception of bias toward the Republicans or the Democrats in the newspaper he regularly read. These perceptions were 90% accurate, taking as a standard the reports of actual newspaper positions reported by the trade journal *Editor and Publisher*. While his sample of voters said that television was the most important source of campaign news, Robinson reported that "In terms of voting behavior . . . far more people report having voted for the candidate espoused by the newspaper than by the other media [p. 245]." The public saw newspapers as more partisan than other media: 50% of the respondents believed that the papers took sides, whereas only 29% saw such bias in magazines, and 22% in television news programming.

Recognizing the complexity of voting determinants, Robinson controlled statistically for party identification, preelection voting intent (the survey that assessed actual votes was taken 1–6 weeks after the election of Nixon on November 5, 1968), and other factors.[4] With such adjustments, Robinson's computations showed that voters who read pro-Nixon newspapers were 6% less likely to vote for Humphrey than were voters whose newspapers advocated the Democratic candidate. The greatest in-

[4] Control variables included the respondent's sex, region, city size, age, education, income, party identification, preelection vote intention, professed concern over the election outcome, personal efficacy, and opinion giving and receiving for any of the three candidates.

fluence of newspaper endorsement was, as the reader will have guessed, on the voters who had least loyalty to either major party. Independent Democrats and pure Independents, in particular, were most likely to vote for the candidate endorsed by their local paper. Similarly, those listed as "undecided" in the preelection survey were most likely to vote as their newspaper suggested. "The most significant differentials exist among the Undecideds, 75 percent of whom exposed to newspaper support for Humphrey voted for Humphrey compared to only 33% exposed to a newspaper supporting Nixon [p. 244]," Robinson (1972) reported.

Robinson's findings alone bring into question the conclusion of some students of voting behavior (Rossi, 1966; Sears, 1969) that the mass media are relatively ineffective influences on voting. His study shows that newspapers likely *do* have an effect, particularly in a close election, where the issues may not be clearly defined in the minds of many voters. Because of its more dramatic impact, however, current controversy has centered on the impact of *television* coverage of the campaigns and the effects of the tremendous sums of money now spent on television advertising in Presidential contests.

Television and Politics

I have already made extensive reference to candidate images and to the effects of repeated exposure to such images. Undoubtedly, television plays a major role in national campaigns. Through television exposure a previously little-known individual can quickly become a national figure. As long ago as 1952, television was credited with transforming Adlai Stevenson from an unknown to an established political personage. The review by Weiss (1969) suggested that there still is little hard evidence about the effects of television on voting decisions. A particularly well-studied campaign was the 1960 contest between Nixon and Kennedy, which aroused special interest because of the four televised debates held between the candidates (Kraus, 1962). The consensus seems to be that Kennedy benefited more from the debates than the better-known Nixon. However, the beneficial effects seem mainly to come from a firming-up of the voting intentions of previously weakly committed Democrats. An intriguing perspective on these debates is provided by the controversial writing of Marshall McLuhan (1965).

McLuhan's phrase, "The medium is the message," has been interpreted in many ways, but at least as applied to television, it refers to a dramatic change in the communication environment. " 'The medium is the message,' he wrote, "means, in terms of the electronic age, that a totally new environment has been created [1965, p. vii]." This environment is distinctively different from that provided by radio or the print media. These earlier forms were "hot" media, in McLuhan's terms, meaning that they presented sharp, well-defined messages that intruded upon the recipient's consciousness. A "cool" medium—television—is more subtle. Television, rather than imposing itself on the viewer, might be said to draw him in, thereby producing high involvement. The nature of the television medium is that images, speaking metaphorically, are not sharp, but fuzzy and indistinct. The viewer must exert effort to draw meaning from these images; He *participates* in the communication process. According to McLuhan (1965):

> Earlier, it was mentioned how the school drop-out situation will get very much worse because of the frustration of the student's need for participation in the learning process. This situation concerns also the problem of "the culturally disadvantaged child." This child exists not only in the slums but increasingly in the suburbs of the upper-income homes. The culturally disadvantaged child is the TV child. *For TV has provided a new environment of low visual orientation and high involvement that makes accommodation to our older educational establishment quite difficult* [p. ix, italics added].

The impact of television on modern life in the United States is seldom questioned. The exact nature of the effects is uncertain, however, as shown by the still unresolved controversy over the effects of televised violence on the children who view it. In the realm of politics, there is no great certainty either, though many millions of dollars are spent by political candidates for television exposure. Robinson's (1972) survey of media users, discussed in the preceding section, did find television ranked first by the public as its most important source of campaign news, and McGinnis (1970) credited Nixon's victory in the 1968 Presidential campaign to adroit use of the medium.

McLuhan's views regarding the effects of television on our political life are quite in accord with speculation recorded previously about the effects of "image" factors on political campaigns. After observing the series of televised debates between Richard Nixon and John F. Kennedy in 1960, McLuhan predicted, as he noted retrospectively (1965, p. 325), that "TV would inevitably be a disaster for a sharp intense image like Nixon's, and a boon for the blurry, shaggy texture of Kennedy." He referred to an article by Philip Deane that appeared in the *Toronto Globe and Mail* on October 15, 1960. Deane's story, headlined "The Sheriff and the Lawyer," explained McLuhan's views on the impact of the debates on the election:

> Now the press had tended to say that Mr. Nixon has been gaining in the last two debates and that he was bad in the first. Professor McLuhan thinks that Mr. Nixon has been sounding progressively more definite; regardless of the value of the Vice-President's views and principles, he has been defending them with too much flourish for the TV medium. Mr. Kennedy's rather sharp responses have been a mistake, but he still presents an image closer to the TV hero, Professor McLuhan says—something like the shy young Sheriff—while Mr. Nixon with his very dark eyes that tend to stare, with his slicker circumlocution, has resembled more the railway lawyer who signs leases that are not in the interests of the folks in the little town.
>
> In fact, by counterattacking and claiming for himself, as he does in the TV debates, the same goals as the Democrats have, Mr. Nixon may be helping his opponent by blurring the Kennedy image, by confusing what exactly it is that Mr. Kennedy wants to change.
>
> Mr. Kennedy is thus not handicapped by clear-cut issues; he is visually a less well-defined image, and appears more nonchalant. He seems less anxious to sell himself than does Mr. Nixon. So far, then, Professor McLuhan gives Mr. Kennedy the lead without underestimating Mr. Nixon's formidable appeal to the vast conservative forces of the United States [cited in McLuhan, 1965, p. 330].

I present McLuhan's analyses more for their flavor than as an explanation of his views. Upon reading the foregoing passages, one of my graduate students commented, "I never understood what the SOB was talking about, and I don't now!" However speculative and obscure McLuhan's presentation, I think that he may be on the track of some of the interesting and crucial differences between the print, radio, and television media.

Of course, a candidate does not agree to televised debates with his opponents unless he feels he can benefit thereby. An incumbent President, for example, has a great advantage over his opponent in terms of exposure; neither Johnson in 1964, nor Nixon in 1972, was interested in debating his lesser-known opponent. In each case, to do so would have involved the likely possibility that the encounter would be a net gain for the challenger (based on the principle of "mere exposure" discussed previously).

I have surveyed a multitude of possible influences on political choice. Many factors in the individual's day-to-day environment undoubtedly do affect his vote, but we have only begun to sort them out. Of major importance is party identification—the individual votes for his party according to the strength of his commitment to it. Second, primary- and membership-group ties—family, friends, religious, work, and fraternal groups—have an important effect on voting decisions. Finally, the mass media surely affect voting though we are not fully able to ascertain its extent. Indeed, the media likely have a decisive effect on some elections in the United States because of the great impact of television, radio, and newspapers on the undecided, uncommitted, or "independent" voter, upon whom the results in most elections depend.

CONCLUSION

Innumerable problems face the United States in the last quarter of the twentieth century. Can the great powers live in peace, or is war and nuclear annihilation inevitable? Can disparities of wealth within the United States and among the U.S. and other nations continue to exist? How long can the depletion of our natural resources and the pollution of the environment continue? Is it possible to recapture the lost sense of community? Can citizens have faith in their government? Will the fear of thieves and murderers on our city streets and of subversive elements lead to a police state and loss of freedom?

Informed, concerned, participating citizens can work with elected officials toward the solution of the problems facing our country. Unfortunately, this is not the picture of the democratic citizen which emerges from our survey of political action in the United States. Rather, we are presented with a citizen whose participation is limited and whose concerns are circumscribed. The average voter seems poorly informed about the alternative policies available, and his capacity for making intelligent decisions about the people to whom he turns over the making of decisions seems limited.

There are, of course, severe limitations on the applicability of the psychological approach to social problems. Within any nation, there are a number of different social strata whose "psychology" must be considered in understanding the country's political structure. Terhune (1970) discussed these strata or subgroups within a society as the *loci* that must be distinguished in discussing national behavior.

The four loci Terhune distinguished are: the masses; the elites; the national leaders; and any significant dissident minority. In the United States, we tend to reject such differentiations, but in terms of our discussion of political participation, the *masses* could be conceived as the relatively large body of people who have little understanding of the way their government works or of the policies it pursues. Also, there are many influential groupings in the United States; that is, there are many elites. Members of one or another elite may be intellectuals, businessmen, union officials, or the military, to name a few. The distinction between the mass man and a member of the elite is in terms of the relative power of each to affect the society in which he lives. To some extent, the blacks constitute America's "dissident minority."

Differences between the character of the masses and that of the elites are more clearly seen in another country than one's own. Terhune (1970), for example, pointed out the differences between the masses and the elite in the U.S.S.R. In terms of national policy, the Soviet Union's behavior from 1945 to 1949 was seen by many observers as being "overbearing, truculent, and aggressively Communistic." These tendencies were presumed to result from the aggressive orientation of the Russian leaders, rather than that of the mass of Russian people. The Russian people were seen as basically friendly: "the great majority of individuals in the U.S.S.R.—certainly in what was formerly European Russia—were friendly, peace-loving, and not members of the Communist Party [Platt, 1961, in Terhune, 1970, p. 241]."

Inkeles and his co-workers (1958, cited in Terhune, 1970, p. 241) supported Platt's findings of friendliness and low hostility in the Russian people. The Russians in their sample semed to be high in need for affiliation and were described as having "emotional aliveness and expressiveness . . . and strong and secure feeling of relatedness to [others] . . . and great capacity to enjoy such relationships [pp. 11–12]." In view of these findings, it seems impossible that the cold war waged by the Soviet Union in the fifties and early sixties can be attributed to the temperament of the Russian people.

There is, then, ample evidence of a gap in many countries between the politically influential elites and the average citizen. In the United States, one "elite" consists of the better-educated citizens who support democratic ideals of equality, free speech, and citizen involvement. Little comfort can be taken in the beneficial effects of such elitism, however, because the governing of the many by the few diverges so far from the ideal democracy. In many concrete instances, for example income tax loopholes which benefit the wealthy, the interests of the influential citizens diverge from those of the less affluent masses.

In an earlier time, the current back-to-nature movement might hold promise. Love, meaningful work, and a feeling of common purpose with others in intentional communities certainly held some promise in the 1800s, to judge by the number of people who were moved to try such new life styles. The Oneida Community proved successful for a long period of time, but it existed in semi-isolation from the larger society that tolerated it. As an example of the good life, such a community or many such communities might in the long run influence the society that shelters them. But in general, the isolation of such communities minimizes their impact on the larger society.

How would we go about designing a society more suited to man's nature? Little guidance is given by this account, since the behavioral approach of modern psychology has little to say about the basic "nature" of man. The scientific approach to psychological problems simply does not reveal the data necessary to answer such questions. Then too, there are questions about the generality of the psychological findings we do possess. Gergen (1973), in his discussion of "social psychology as history," questions whether the limited knowledge we have acquired about face-to-face interaction has either generality or timelessness.

Nevertheless, there do seem to be certain recurring themes that could serve as at least a hypothetical model of man and his needs. As expressed by Fromm (1941), Adler (1938), and Reich (1970), these recurring themes include love, work, friendship, and understanding. Lane (1972) has suggested a model of a good citizen which emphasizes the striving for one's *own self-interest*. Lane's suggestion does not necessarily conflict with the more altruistic-sounding strivings if we think of the self as inevitably *including* other people.

The theme of self in community stresses the interdependence of individual people. One's concept of self includes one's relations with others. This self-conception includes one's sense of competence in one's work, as well as in dealing with other people. It involves one's own comparisons between self and others, and the evaluations reflected from other people. Psychological security first of all means the absence of threat to one's own existence, then the stability of one's relationships with others. My existence, my *self* involves *my* children, *my* family, *my* job, *my* community, and *my* country. Insecurity implies the lack of ability to understand and control possible threats to this extended self.

The specific directions that such self-oriented striving takes are dependent upon the particular cultural setting in which the person lives. In the United States, for example, people are relatively well off as compared with the citizens of underdeveloped countries. As compared to others in their own country, however, these people are relatively deprived in terms of their own security. The relatively deprived person, who sees himself as powerless, his work as meaningless, and his status threatened, is likely to be an ineffective and unconcerned citizen.

The relatively deprived person has little sense of living in a community. His ties with other people are tenuous, his own existence is threatened, his comparisons of himself with other people are unfavorable. Such a person is unlikely to develop a clear understanding of the society in which he lives. He will tend to have a relatively limited, dogmatic conception of his own group and his country. Such a simplistic view of his own interest may make him ripe for extremist movements. He develops no clear ideology, no plan for coping with his own and society's problems. He is likely to be either apathetic or aggressive, as were White and Lippitt's (1960) young subjects in the authoritarian group atmosphere.

There remain questions about the realistic possibility of solutions to these problems. In a day when even the Congress has difficulty in understanding the problems of the nuclear age and in proposing solutions, broad political participation may be impossible. But the nature of man as we can now see it in broad outline suggests that the search for a truly participatory form of democratic society will continue.

McCloskey (1964) sees hope in the increasing articulateness of the public. He has identified hopeful developments that are tending to increase the political awareness of the American electorate:

> . . . the extraordinary spread of education, rapid social mobility, urbanization, the proliferation of mass media that disseminate public information, the expansion of the middle class, the decline in the size and number of isolated rural groups, the reduction in the proportion of people with submarginal living standards, the incorporation of foreign and minority groups into the culture and their increasing entrance into the professions, and so on [pp. 103–4].

It remains to be seen how these developments will affect the balance of public versus private concerns in the average voter.

References

ADLER, A. *Social interest.* New York: Capricorn Books, 1964 (first English edition published 1938).

ADORNO, T. W., FRENKEL-BRUNSWIK, E., LEVINSON, D. J., AND SANFORD, R. N. *The authoritarian personality.* New York: Harper & Row, 1950.

ALLPORT, F. H. *Social psychology.* Boston: Houghton-Mifflin, 1924.

ALLPORT, G. W. A test for ascendance–submission. *Journal of Abnormal and Social Psychology,* 1928, *23,* 118–36.

ALLPORT, G. W. The historical background of modern social psychology. In G. Lindzey (Ed.), *Handbook of social psychology.* Vol. I. Reading, Mass: Addison-Wesley, 1954.

ALLPORT, G. W. The psychology of participation. In G. W. Allport, *Personality and social encounter.* Boston: Beacon, 1960.

ALLPORT, G. W., AND POSTMAN, L. *The psychology of rumor.* New York: Henry Holt, 1947.

ALMOND, G. A. A functional approach to comparative politics. In G. Almond and J. S. Coleman (Eds.), *The politics of developing areas.* Princeton: Princeton University Press, 1960.

ALMOND, G. A. AND VERBA, S. *The civic culture.* Boston: Little, Brown, 1965.

ARGYLE, M. The attitudes of religious people. In M. Jahoda and N. Warren (Eds.), *Attitudes.* Baltimore: Penguin, 1966.

ASCH, S. E. *Social psychology.* New York: Prentice-Hall, 1952.

ASSOCIATED PRESS. *Almanac,* 1973.

ATKINSON, J. W., AND FEATHER, N. T. (Eds.) *A theory of achievement motivation.* New York: Wiley, 1968.

AXELROD, R. The structure of public opinion on policy issues. *Public Opinion Quarterly,* 1967, *31,* 51–60.

BALES, R. F. Task roles and social roles in problem-solving groups. In E. E. Maccoby, T. M. Newcomb, and E. L. Hartley (Eds.), *Readings in social psychology.* (3rd ed.) New York: Holt, Rinehart, 1958.

BARBER, J. D. *The lawmakers.* New Haven: Yale University Press, 1965.

BARBER, J. D. *The presidential character.* Englewood Cliffs, N.J.: Prentice-Hall, 1972.

BARONE, M., UJIFUSA, G., AND MATTHEWS, D. *The almanac of American politics.* Boston: Gambit, Inc., 1972.

BASS, B. M. Authoritarianism or acquiescence? *Journal of Abnormal and Social Psychology,* 1955, *51,* 616–23.

BAVELAS, A. Communication patterns in task-oriented groups. *Journal of the Acoustical Society of America,* 1950, *22,* 725–30.

BELL, D. *The end of ideology.* New York: Free Press, 1960.

BERELSON, B., LAZARSFELD, P. F., AND McPHEE, W. N. *Voting.* Chicago: University of Chicago Press, 1954.

BIDERMAN, A. D. *March to calumy: The story of American POW's in the Korean war.* New York: Macmillan, 1963.

BIRD, C. *Social psychology.* New York: Appleton-Century, 1940.

BLANCHARD, E. B., AND SCARBORO, M. E. Locus of control and prediction of voting behavior in college students. *Journal of Social Psychology,* 1973, *89,* 123–29.

BODERMAN, A. Feelings of powerlessness and political and religious extremism. (Doctoral dissertation, University of Minnesota) Ann Arbor Mich.: University Microfilms, 1964, No. 65–15, 307.

BOGART, L. *Silent politics: Polls and the awareness of public opinion.* New York: Wiley, 1972.

BROWN, J. F. *Psychology and the social order.* New York: McGraw-Hill, 1936.

BROWN, R. *Social psychology.* New York: Free Press, 1965.

BROWNING, R. P. The interaction of personality and political system in decisions to run for office: Some data and a simulation technique. *Journal of Social Issues,* 1968, *24* (3), 93–109.

BROWNING, R. P., AND JACOB, H. Power motivation and the political personality. *Public Opinion Quarterly,* 1964, *28,* 75–90.

BYRNE, D. Interpersonal attraction and attitude similarity. *Journal of Abnormal and Social Psychology,* 1961, *62,* 713–15.

BYRNE, D., BOND, M. H., AND DIAMOND, M. J. Response to political candidates as a function of attitude similarity–dissimilarity. *Human Relations,* 1969, *22,* 251–61.

CAMPBELL, A. The passive citizen. *Acta Sociologica,* 1962, *6,* 9–21.

CAMPBELL, A., CONVERSE, P. E., MILLER, W. E., AND STOKES, D. E. *The American voter: An abridgement.* New York: Wiley, 1964.

CAMPBELL, A., GURIN, G., AND MILLER, W. E. *The voter decides.* New York: Harper & Row, 1954.

CARDEN, M. L. *Oneida: utopian community to modern corporation.* Baltimore: The Johns Hopkins Press, 1969.

CHRISTIE, R. Review of The Psychology of Politics, by H. J. Eysenck. *American Journal of Psychology,* 1955, *68,* 402–704.

CHRISTIE, R. Eysenck's treatment of the personality of Communists. *Psychological Bulletin,* 1956, *53,* 411–30. (a)

CHRISTIE, R. Some abuses of psychology. *Psychological Bulletin,* 1956, *53,* 439–51. (b)

CHRISTIE, R. AND GEIS, F. L. *Studies in Machiavellianism.* New York: Academic Press, 1970.

CHRISTIE, R., AND JAHODA, M. (Eds.) *Studies in the scope and method of the authoritarian personality.* Glencoe, Ill.: Free Press, 1954.

CONNELL, R. W. Political socialization in the American family: The evidence re-examined. *Public Opinion Quarterly,* 1972, *36,* 323–33.

CONVERSE, P. E. Information flow and the stability of partisan attitudes. *Public Opinion Quarterly,* 1962, *26,* 578–99.

CONVERSE, P. E. The nature of belief systems in mass publics. In D. E. Apter (Ed.), *Ideology and discontent.* New York: Free Press, 1964.

COOLEY, C. H. *Human nature and the social order.* New York: Scribner, 1902.

DAWSON, K. E., AND PREWITT, K. *Political socialization: An analytical study.* Boston: Little, Brown, 1969.

DEFRONZO, J. Religion and humanitarianism in Eysenck's T dimension and left–right political orientation. *Journal of Personality and Social Psychology,* 1972, *21,* 265–69.

DESOTO, C. B., LONDON, M., AND HANDEL, S. Social reasoning and spatial paralogic. *Journal of Personality and Social Psychology,* 1965, *2,* 513–21.

DEWEY, J. *The public and its problems.* New York: Henry Holt, 1927.

DEWEY, J. *Freedom and culture.* New York: G. P. Putnam, 1939.

DIRENZO, G. J. *Personality, power, and politics.* Notre Dame, Ind.: University of Notre Dame Press, 1967.

DONLEY, R. E., AND WINTER, D. G. Measuring the motives of public officials at a distance: An exploratory study of American presidents. *Behavioral Science,* 1970, *15,* 227–236.

DREYER, E. C., AND ROSENBAUM, W. A. *Political opinion and behavior: Essays and studies.* (2nd ed.) Belmont, Cal.: Wadsworth, 1970.

ELMS, A. C., AND MILGRAM, S. Personality characteristics associated with obedience and defiance toward authoritative command. *Journal of Experimental Research in Personality,* 1966, *2,* 282–89.

ERIKSON, E. H. *Childhood and society.* (2nd ed.) New York: W. W. Norton, 1963.

EXLINE, R. V., THIBAUT, J., HICKEY, C. B., AND GUMPERT, P. Visual interaction in relation to Machiavellianism and an unethical act. Pp. 53–75 in Christie and Geis, 1970.

EYSENCK, H. J. General social attitudes. *Journal of Social Psychology,* 1944, *19,* 207–27.

EYSENCK, H. J. *The psychology of politics.* London: Routledge & Kegan Paul Ltd., 1954.

EYSENCK, H. J. The psychology of politics and the personality similarities between fascists and communists. *Psychological Bulletin,* 1956, *53,* 431–38.

EYSENCK, H. J. *The structure of human personality.* (3rd ed.) London: Methuen, 1970.

EYSENCK, H. J., AND COULTER, T. T. The personality and attitudes of working-class British Communists and Fascists. *Journal of Social Psychology,* 1972, *87,* 59–73.

FESTINGER, L. *A theory of cognitive dissonance.* Evanston, Ill.: Row, Peterson, 1957.

FESTINGER, L. *Conflict, decision and dissonance.* Stanford, Cal.: Stanford University Press, 1964.

FESTINGER, L., AND CARLSMITH, J. M. Cognitive consequences of forced compliance. *Journal of Abnormal and Social Psychology,* 1959, *58,* 203–11.

FOLLETT, M. P. *Creative experience.* New York: Longmans, Green, 1924.

FREEDMAN, J. L., CARLSMITH, J. M., AND SEARS, D. O. *Social psychology.* Englewood Cliffs, N.J.: Prentice-Hall, 1970.

FRENCH, J. R. P., JR., AND RAVEN, B. The bases of social power. In D. Cartwright (Ed.), *Studies in social power.* Ann Arbor, Mich.: Institute for Social Research, 1959.

FREUD, S. *Group psychology and the analysis of the ego.* New York: Liveright Publishing Corp., 1951 (first published 1922).

FREUD, S. *Civilization and its discontents.* New York: W. W. Norton, 1961 (first published 1930).

FREUD, S. *Totem and taboo.* In J. Strachey (Ed.), *Standard edition of the complete psychological works of Sigmund Freud.* Vol. 13. London, 1953–1966. (Originally published in 1913).

FRIED, A. (Ed.) *Socialism in America.* New York: Doubleday, 1970.

FROMM, E. *Escape from freedom.* New York: Holt, Rinehart & Winston, 1941. (Page references to 1965 Avon Books Edition).

GEIS, F., WEINHEIMER, S. AND BERGER, D. Playing legislature: Cool heads and hot issues. Pp. 190–209 in Christie and Geis, 1970.

GEORGE, A. L., Power as a compensatory value for political leaders. *Journal of Social Issues,* 1968, *24,* 29–49.

GEORGE, A. L., AND GEORGE, J. L. *Woodrow Wilson and Colonel House: a personality study.* New York: John Day, 1956.

GERGEN, K. J. Social psychology as history. *Journal of Personality and Social Psychology,* 1973, *26,* 309–20.

GORE, P. M., AND ROTTER, J. B. A personality correlate of social action. *Journal of Personality,* 1963, *31,* 58–64.

GOTTESFELD, H., AND DOZIER, G. Changes in feelings of powerlessness in a community action program. *Psychological Reports,* 1966, *19,* 978.

GREENE, D. L., AND WINTER, D. G. Motives, involvements, and leadership among black college students. *Journal of Personality,* 1971, *39,* 319–32.

GREENSTEIN, F. I. *The American party system and the American people.* Englewood Cliffs, N.J.: Prentice-Hall, 1963.

GROSS, N., McEACHERN, A. W., AND MASON, W. S. *Explorations in role analysis.* New York: Wiley, 1958.

GUMP, P. V. Anti-democratic trends and student reaction to President Truman's dismissal of General MacArthur. *Journal of Social Psychology,* 1953, *38,* 131–35.

HALL, C. S. Temperament: A survey of animal studies. *Psychological Bulletin,* 1941, *38,* 909–43.

HALL, C. S. *A primer of Freudian psychology.* New York: Mentor Books, 1954.

HALL, C. S., AND LINDZEY, G., Psychoanalytic theory and its application in the social sciences. In G. Lindzey (Ed.), *Handbook of social psychology.* Vol. I. Reading, Mass.: Addison-Wesley, 1954.

HANDLON, B., AND SQUIER, L. H. Attitudes toward special loyalty oaths at the University of California. *American Psychologist,* 1955, *10,* 121–27.

HANLEY, C., AND ROKEACH, M. Care and carelessness in psychology. *Psychological Bulletin,* 1956, *53,* 183–86.

HARRIS, L. Public opinion survey on political philosophy, reported in *The Bangor Daily News,* Bangor, Maine, April 20, 1972, p. 25.

HARVEY, O. J., HUNT, D. E., AND SCHROEDER, H.M. *Conceptual systems and personality organization.* New York: Wiley, 1961.

HAYTHORNE, W. The composition of groups: A review of the literature. *Acta Psychologica,* 1968, *28,* 97–128.

HAYTHORNE, W., COUCH, A., HAEFNER, D., LANGHAM, P., AND CARTER, L. F. The effects of varying combinations of authoritarian and equalitarian leaders and followers. *Journal of Abnormal and Social Psychology,* 1956, *53,* 210–19.

HEALY, W., BRONNNER, A. F., AND BOWERS, A. M. *The structure and meaning of psychoanalysis.* New York: Knopf, 1930.

HEIDER, F. *The psychology of interpersonal relations.* New York: Wiley, 1958.

HEILBRONER, R. L. Socialism and the future. *Commentary,* 1969, *48,* (6), 35–45.

HERO, A. Public reaction to government policy. In J. P. ROBINSON *et al., Measures of Political Attitudes.* Ann Arbor, Michigan: Institute for Social Research, 1968.

HESS, R. D., AND TORNEY, J. V. *The development of political attitudes in children.* Chicago: Aldine, 1967.

HINCKLEY, E. D. The influence of individual opinion on construction of an attitude scale. *Journal of Social Psychology,* 1932, *3,* 283–296.

HOBBES, T. *Leviathan.* Reprint of 1st (1651) Ed., Cambridge, Eng.: University Press, 1904.

HOLLANDER, E. P., AND WILLIS, R. H. Some current issues in the psychology of conformity and nonconformity. *Psychological Bulletin,* 1967, *68,* 62–76.

270
References

HORKHEIMER, M. (Ed.) *Studien über autorität und familie.* Paris: Felix Alcan, 1936.

HOVLAND, C. I., JANIS, I. L., AND KELLEY, H. H. *Communication and persuasion.* New Haven: Yale University Press, 1953.

HOVLAND, C. I., AND WEISS, W. The influence of source credibility on communication effectiveness. *Public Opinion Quarterly,* 1951, *15,* 635–50.

HOWE, I. (Ed.) Special issue: The world of the blue collar worker. *Dissent,* Winter, 1972.

HULL, C. L. *Principles of behavior.* New York: D. Appleton Century, 1943.

HYMAN, H. H., AND SHEATSLEY, P. B. The Authoritarian Personality—A methodological critique. Pp. 50–122 in Christie & Jahoda, 1954.

HYMOFF, I. H. An experimental investigation of the relationship of Machiavellianism to guilt and compliance. Unpublished doctoral dissertation, University of Maine, 1970.

INKELES, A. *Public opinion in Soviet Russia.* Cambridge, Mass.: Harvard University Press, 1958.

IRISH, M. D., AND PROTHRO, J. W. *The politics of American democracy,* (5th ed.) Englewood Cliffs, N.J.: Prentice-Hall, 1971.

JAMES, W. *Psychology: The briefer course.* New York: Harper Torchbooks, 1961 (first published, 1892).

JAMES, W. *Pragmatism.* New York: Longmans, Green, 1907.

JANOWITZ, M., AND MARVICK, D. Authoritarianism and political behavior. *Public Opinion Quarterly,* 1953, *17,* 185–201.

JENNINGS, M. K., AND NIEMI, R. G. The transmission of political values from parent to child. *American Political Science Review,* 1968, *62,* 169–84.

JOURARD, S. M. *The transparent self.* (Rev. ed.) Princeton: Van Nostrand, 1971.

KAGAN, D. *The great dialogue: History of Greek political thought from Homer to Polybius.* New York: Free Press, 1965.

KAHN, R. L. The work module—A tonic for lunchpail lassitude. *Psychology Today,* February 1973, p. 35.

KASSARJIAN, W. M. A study of Riesman's theory of social character. *Sociometry,* 1962, *25,* 213–30.

KATZ, D. The functional approach to the study of attitudes. *Public Opinion Quarterly,* 1960, *24,* 163–204.

KATZ, D., SARNOFF, I., AND McCLINTOCK, C. Ego-defense and attitude change. *Human Relations,* 1956, *9,* 27–46.

KELMAN, H. C., AND BARCLAY, J. The F scale as a measure of breadth of perspective. *Journal of Abnormal and Social Psychology,* 1963, *67,* 608–15.

KELMAN, H. C., AND HOVLAND, C. I. "Reinstatement" of the communicator in delayed measurement of opinion change. *Journal of Abnormal and Social Psychology,* 1953, *48,* 327–35.

KENISTON, K. The sources of student dissent. *Journal of Social Issues*, 1967, *23* (3), 108–37.

KEUTHE, J. L. Social schemas. *Journal of Abnormal and Social Psychology*, 1964, *64*, 31–36.

KEY, V. O., JR. *Public opinion and American democracy.* New York: Knopf, 1961.

KEY, V. O., JR. *The responsible electorate.* Cambridge, Mass.: Harvard University Press, 1966.

KIMBLE, G. A. (Revisor). *Hilgard and Marquis' conditioning and learning.* 2nd Ed. New York: Appleton-Century-Crofts, 1961.

KINKAIDE, K. *A Walden Two experiment: The first five years of Twin Oaks community.* William Morrow, 1972.

KINKEAD, E. *In every war but one.* New York: W. W. Norton, 1959.

KNUTSON, J. N. *The human basis of the polity.* Chicago: Aldine, 1972.

KRAUS, S. (Ed.) *The great debates.* Bloomington: Indiana University Press, 1962.

KRECH, D., CRUTCHFIELD, R. S., AND BALLACHEY, E. L. *Individual in society.* New York: McGraw-Hill, 1962.

KUHN, M. H., AND McPARTLAND T. S. An empirical study of self-attitudes. *American Sociological Review*, 1954, *19*, 68–76.

LANE, R. E. Political character and political analysis. *Psychiatry*, 1953, *16*, 387–98.

LANE, R. E. *Political life.* New York: Free Press, 1959.

LANE, R. E. *Political ideology.* New York: Free Press, 1962.

LANE, R. E. *Political thinking and consciousness.* Chicago: Markham, 1969.

LANE, R. E. *Political man.* New York: Free Press, 1972.

LANGTON, K. P., AND JENNINGS, M. K. Political socialization and the high school civics curriculum in the United States. *American Political Science Review*, 1968, *62*, 852–67.

LANZETTA, J. T., AND DRISCOLL, J. M. Effects of uncertainty and importance on information search in decision making. *Journal of Personality and Social Psychology*, 1968, *10*, 479–86.

LASSWELL, H. D. *Psychopathology and politics.* Chicago: University of Chicago Press, 1930.

LASSWELL, H. D. *Power and personality.* New York: W. W. Norton, 1948.

LAZARSFELD, P. F., BERELSON, B., AND GAUDET, H. *The people's choice.* (2nd ed.) New York: Columbia University Press, 1948.

LEBON, G. *Psychologie des foules.* Paris: F. Olean, 1895. (Transl., *The crowd.* London: T. Fisher Unwin, 1896.)

LEVENS, H. Organizational affiliation and powerlessness: A case study of the welfare poor. *Social Problems*, 1968, *16*, 18–32.

Leventhal, H., Jacobs, R. L., and Kudirka, M. Z. Authoritarian ideology and political candidate choice. *Journal of Abnormal and Social Psychology,* 1964, *69,* 539–49.

Lewin, K. *A dynamic theory of personality: Selected papers.* New York: McGraw-Hill, 1935.

Lewin, K. *Field theory in social science.* New York: Harper, 1951.

Lippman, T., Jr., and Hansen, D. C. *Muskie.* New York: W. W. Norton, 1971.

Lipset, S. M. Democracy and working-class authoritarianism. *American Sociological Review,* 1959, *24,* 482–501.

Litt, E. Civic education, community norms, and political indoctrination. *American Sociological Review,* 1963, *28,* 69–75.

Locke, J. *Second treatise on government.* In *Works,* Book II. London: Churchill, Manship, 1714.

McClelland, D. C. (Ed.) *Studies in motivation.* New York: Appleton-Century 1955.

McClelland, D. C. *The achieving society.* Princeton: Van Nostrand, 1961.

McClelland, D. C. Toward a theory of motive acquisition. *American Psychologist,* 1965, *20,* 321–33.

McClelland, D. C., and Winter D. G. *Motivating economic achievement.* New York: Free Press, 1969.

McCloskey, H. Conservatism and personality. *American Political Science Review,* 1958, *52,* 27–45.

McCloskey, H. Consensus and ideology in American politics. *American Political Science Review,* 1964, *58,* 361–82.

McGinnis, J. *The selling of the president 1968.* New York: Pocket Books, 1970.

McGuire, W. J. Inducing resistance to persuasion. In L. Berkowitz (Ed.), *Advances in experimental social psychology.* Vol. I. New York: Academic Press, 1964.

MacKendrick, P., and Howe, H. M. (Eds.) *Classics in translation.* Vol. I. *Greek literature.* Madison, Wis.: University of Wisconsin Press, 1952.

McLuhan, M. *Understanding media.* New York: McGraw-Hill paperback edition, 1965.

Machiavelli, N. *The prince.* Chicago: The Great Books Foundation, 1955.

Mahler, I. Attitudes toward socialized medicine. *Journal of Social Psychology,* 1953, *38,* 273–82.

Marcuse, H. *Eros and civilization.* Boston: Beacon, 1955.

Maslow, A. H. The role of dominance in the social and sexual behavior of infra-human primates. *Journal of Genetic Psychology,* 1936, *48,* 261–77.

Maslow, A. H. *Motivation and personality.* New York: Harper & Row, 1954.

Merriam, C. E. *Political power.* New York: Collier paperback edition, 1964.

Merton, R. Bureaucratic structure and personality. *Social Forces.* 1940, *17,* 560–68.

Milbrath, L., and Klein, W. Personality correlates of political participation. *Acta Sociologica*, 1962, 6, 53–66.

Milgram, S. Behavioral study of obedience. *Journal of Abnormal and Social Psychology*, 1963, 67, 371–78.

Milgram, S. The small world problem. In *Readings in social psychology today*. Del Mar, California: CRM Books, 1970, pp. 29–35.

Miller, N. E., and Dollard, J. *Social learning and imitation*. New Haven: Yale University Press, 1941.

Miller, W. E., and Stokes, D. E. Constituency influence in Congress. In A. Campbell, P. E. Converse, W. E. Miller, and D. E. Stokes, *Elections and the political order*. New York: Wiley, 1966.

Mirels, H. Dimensions of internal versus external control. *Journal of Consulting and Clinical Psychology*, 1970, 34, 226–28.

Mowrer, O. H. *Learning theory and personality dynamics*. New York: Ronald Press, 1950.

Murphy, G. Social motivation. In G. Lindzey (Ed.), *Handbook of social psychology*. Cambridge, Mass.: Addison-Wesley, 1954.

Murphy, G., Murphy, L. B., and Newcomb, T. M. *Experimental social psychology*. (2nd ed.) New York: Harper & Row, 1937.

Murray, H. A. *Thematic Apperception Test manual*. Cambridge, Mass.: Harvard University Press, 1943.

Mussen, P. H., and Wyszynski, A. B. Personality and political participation. *Human Relations*, 1952, 5, 65–82.

Nadler, E. B. Yielding, authoritarianism and authoritarian ideology regarding groups. *Journal of Abnormal and Social Psychology*, 1959, 58, 408–10.

Newcomb, T. M. *Personality and social change*. New York: Dryden, 1943.

Nikelly, A. G. Social interest: A paradigm for mental health education. *Journal of Individual Psychology*, 1962, 18, 147–50.

Noyes, J. H. *History of American socialisms*. Philadelphia: J. B. Lippincott, 1870.

Osgood, C. E. Cognitive dynamics in human affairs. *Public Opinion Quarterly*, 1960, 24, 341–65.

Osgood, C. E., Suci, G. J., and Tannenbaum, P. H. *The measurement of meaning*. Urbana, Ill.: University of Illinois Press, 1957.

Osgood, C. E., and Tannenbaum, P. H. The principle of congruity in the prediction of attitude change. *Psychological Review*, 1955, 62, 42–55.

Perlman, D., and Oskamp, S. The effects of picture content and exposure frequency on evaluations of Negroes and whites. *Journal of Experimental Social Psychology*, 1971, 7, 503–14.

President's Commission on Registration and Voting Participation. *Report*. Washington, D.C.: U.S. Government Printing Office, 1963.

Ransford, H. E. Isolation, powerlessness, and violence: A study of attitudes and participation in the Watts riot. *American Journal of Sociology*, 1968, *73*, 581–91.

REICH, W. *The mass psychology of fascism.* New York: Farrar, Strauss, 1970.

RESTLE, F. *Psychology of judgment and choice.* New York: Wiley, 1961.

RHINE, R. J. The 1964 presidential election and curves of information seeking and avoiding. *Journal of Personality and Social Psychology*, 1967, *5*, 416–23.

RIESMAN, D. *The lonely crowd.* New Haven: Yale University Press, 1950.

ROAZEN, P. *Freud: Political and social thought.* New York: Knopf, 1968.

ROBERTS, R. E. *The new communes.* Englewood Cliffs, N.J.: Prentice-Hall, 1971.

ROBINSON, J. P. Perceived media bias and the 1968 election. *Journalism Quarterly*, 1972, *49*, 239–46.

ROBINSON, J. P., RUSK, J. G., AND HEAD, K. B. *Measures of political attitudes.* Ann Arbor, Mich.: Institute for Social Research, 1968.

ROKEACH, M. *The open and closed mind.* New York: Basic Books, 1960.

ROKEACH, M. *Beliefs, attitudes and values.* San Francisco: Jossey-Bass, 1968.

ROKEACH, M. *The nature of human values.* New York: Free Press, 1973.

ROKEACH, M., AND HANLEY, C. Eysenck's tendermindedness dimension: A critique. *Psychological Bulletin*, 1956, *53*, 169–76.

ROKKAN, S. Cross-national studies in political participation. *International Social Science Journal*, 1960, *12*, 7–14.

ROKKAN, S., AND CAMPBELL, A. Citizen participation in political life: Norway and the United States of America. *International Social Science Journal*, 1960, *12*, 69–99.

ROSE, M. *The power structure.* New York: Oxford University Press, 1967.

ROSEN, B., AND SALLING, R. Political participation as a function of internal–external locus of control. *Psychological Reports*, 1971, *29*, 880–82.

ROSENBERG, M. J. An analysis of affective–cognitive consistency. In C. I. Hovland and M. J. Rosenberg (Eds.), *Attitude organization and change.* New Haven: Yale University Press, 1960.

ROSENBERG, M. J. Self-esteem and concern with political affairs. *Public Opinion Quarterly*, 1962, *26*, 201–11.

ROSSI, P. H. Trends in voting behavior research: 1933–1963. In E. C. Dreyer and W. A. Rosenbaum (Eds.), *Political opinion and electoral behavior.* Belmont, Cal.: Wadsworth, 1966.

ROTTER, J. B. Generalized expectancies for internal vs. external control of reinforcement. *Psychological Monographs*, 1966, *80*, 1–28.

ROTTER, J. B. Generalized expectancies for interpersonal trust. *American Psychologist*, 1971, *26*, 443–452.

ROUSSEAU, J. J. *The social contract.* New York: Dutton, 1930.

RUSSELL, B. *Power: a new social analysis.* London: Allen & Unwin, 1938.

SANFORD, F. H. *Authoritarianism and leadership*. Philadelphia: Stephenson Bros., 1950.

SCHACHTER, S. Eat, eat. *Psychology Today*, April 1971, p. 45.

SCHATZ, L. An evaluation of the Eysenck R and T scales and their relation to personality. *Dissertation Abstracts*, 1958, *19*, 589.

SCHEIN, E. H. The Chinese indoctrination program for prisoners of war: A study of attempted brainwashing. *Psychiatry*, 1956, *19*, 149–72.

SCHLESINGER, J. A. *Ambition and politics: political careers in the United States*. Chicago: Rand McNally, 1966.

SCHULMAN, J., SHAVER, P., COLMAN, R., EMRICH, B., AND CHRISTIE, R. Recipe for a jury. *Psychology Today*, May 1973, p. 37.

SCHUTZ, W. C. What makes groups productive? *Human Relations*, 1955, *8*, 429–65.

SCHUTZ W. C. *FIRO: A three-dimensional theory of interpersonal behavior*. New York: Rinehart & Co., 1958.

SEARS, D. O. Political behavior. In G. Lindzey and E. Aronson (Eds.), *Handbook of social psychology*. (Rev. ed.) Vol. 5. Reading, Mass.: Addison-Wesley, 1969.

SEARS, D. O., AND TOMLINSON, T. M. Riot ideology in Los Angeles: A study of Negro attitudes. *Social Science Quarterly*, 1968, *49*, 485–503.

SEEMAN, M. Alienation and social learning in a reformatory. *American Sociological Review*, 1963, *69*, 270–84.

SEEMAN, M. Alienation, membership and political knowledge: A comparative study. *Public Opinion Quarterly*, 1966, *30*, 359–67.

SEEMAN, M. Powerlessness and knowledge: A comparative study of alienation and learning. *Sociometry*, 1967, *30*, 105–23.

SEEMAN, M. The urban alienations: Some dubious theses from Marx to Marcuse. *Journal of Personality and Social Psychology*, 1971, *19*, 135–43.

SEEMAN, M., AND EVANS, J. W. Alienation and social learning in a hospital setting. *American Sociological Review*, 1962, *27*, 772–82.

SHAW, M. E. Acceptance of authority, group structure and the effectiveness of small groups. *Journal of Personality*, 1959, *27*, 196–210.

SHAW, M. E. AND WRIGHT, J. M. *Scales for the Measurement of Attitudes*. New York: McGraw-Hill, 1967.

SHERIF, C. W., SHERIF, M., AND NEBERGALL, R. E. *Attitude and attitude change: The social judgment–involvement approach*. Philadelphia: Saunders, 1965.

SHERIF, M., AND CANTRIL, H. *The psychology of ego-involvements*. New York: Wiley, 1947.

SHILS, E. A. Authoritarianism: 'Right' and 'Left.' Pp. 24–49 in Christie & Jahoda, 1954.

SILVERN, L. E., AND NAKAMURA, C. Y. Powerlessness, social–political action, and social–political views: Their interrelation among college students. *Journal of Social Issues*, 1971, 27, 137–57.

SKINNER, B. F. *Science and human behavior.* New York: Macmillan, 1953.

SLATER, P. E. *The pursuit of loneliness.* Boston: Beacon, 1970.

SMITH, B. L., LASSWELL, H. D., AND CASEY, R. D. *Propaganda, communication and public opinion.* Princeton: Princeton University Press, 1946.

SMITH, M. B. A map for the analysis of personality and politics. *Journal of Social Issues*, 1968, 24 (3), 15–27.

SMITH, M. B. A psychologist's perspective on public opinion theory. *Public Opinion Quarterly*, 1971, 35, 36–43.

SMITH, M. B., BRUNER, J. S., AND WHITE, R. W. *Opinions and personality.* New York: Wiley, 1956.

STOKES, D. E. Some dynamic elements of contests for the Presidency. *American Political Science Review*, 1966, 60, 19–28.

STONE, W. F. The Feminism Scale. Unpublished manuscript, Lafayette College, 1966.

STONE, W. F., AND ARTHUR, J. D. Judging presidential candidates: Evaluative dimensions employed before and after the 1968 election. Paper presented at the 63rd Annual Meeting of the Southern Society for Philosophy and Psychology, Athens, Georgia, 1971.

STRICKLAND, B. S. The prediction of social action from a dimension of internal–external control. *Journal of Social Psychology*, 1965, 66, 353–58.

STROUT, R. L. The 'stunning' drop in U.S. voters. *Christian Science Monitor*, 20 April 1973.

TERHUNE, K. P. From national character to national behavior: A reformulation. *Journal of Conflict Resolution*, 1970, 14, 201–63.

THOMPSON, R. C. AND MICHEL, J. B. Measuring authoritarianism: A comparison of the F & D scales. *Journal of Personality*, 1972, 40, 180–90.

THORNDIKE, E. L. *Selected writings from a connectionist's psychology.* New York: Appleton-Century, 1949.

THURSTONE, L. L., AND CHAVE, E. J. *The measurement of attitude.* Chicago: University of Chicago Press, 1929.

TOMKINS, S. Left and right: A basic dimension of ideology and personality. In R. W. White (Ed.), *The study of lives.* Chicago: Athenton, 1963.

VERBA, S. *Small groups and political behavior: A study of leadership.* Princeton: Princeton University Press, 1961.

VERBA, S. Comparative political culture. In L. W. Pye and S. Verba (Eds.), *Political culture and political development.* Princeton: Princeton University Press, 1965.

VEROFF, J. Development and validation of a projective measure of power motivation. *Journal of Abnormal and Social Psychology*, 1957, 54, 1–8.

VEROFF, J., ATKINSON, J. W., FELD, S. C., AND GURIN, G. The use of thematic apperception to assess motivation in a nationwide survey study. *Psychological Monographs*, 1960, *74*, 1–32.

VEROFF, J., AND VEROFF, J. B. Reconsideration of a measure of power motivation. *Psychological Bulletin*, 1972, *78*, 279–91.

WALLAS, G. *Human nature in politics.* (4th ed.) London: Constable and Company, Ltd., 1914. (Originally published 1908).

WATSON, J. B. *Behaviorism.* New York: W. W. Norton, 1925.

WEISS, W. Effects of the mass media of communication. In G. Lindzey and E. Aronson (Eds.), *The Handbook of social psychology* (rev. ed.) Vol. 5. Reading, Mass.: Addison-Wesley, 1969.

WEST, C. Shattered lives of despair and tragedy fate of most of 13 returning turncoats. *Florida Times–Union*, August 4, 1963, pp. 1–2.

WHITE, R. K., AND LIPPITT, R. *Autocracy and democracy: An experimental inquiry.* New York: Harper & Row, 1960.

WHITE, R. W. Motivation reconsidered: The concept of competence. *Psychological Review*, 1959, *66*, 297–334.

WHITE, R. W. *The abnormal personality.* (3rd ed) New York: Ronald Press, 1964.

WHITING, J. W. M., AND CHILD, I. L. *Child training and personality.* New Haven: Yale University Press, 1953.

WILLIAMS, C. D. Authoritarianism and student reaction to airplane hijacking. *Journal of Social Psychology*, 1963, *60*, 289–91.

WINTER, D. G. The need for power in college men: Action correlates and relationship to drinking. In D. C. McClelland, W. N. Davis, R. Kalin, and E. Wanner, *The drinking man.* New York: Free Press, 1972.

WINTER, D. G. *The power motive.* New York: Free Press, 1973.

WINTER, D. G., AND WIECKING, F. A. The new puritans: Achievement and power motives of New Left radicals. *Behavioral Science*, 1971, *16*, 523–30.

WITKIN, H. A., LEWIS, H. B., HERTZMAN, M., MACHOVER, K., MEISSNER, P. B., AND WAPNER, S. *Personality through perception.* New York: Harper & Row, 1954.

WOODWORTH, R. S., AND SCHLOSBERG, H. *Experimental psychology.* (rev. ed.) New York: Henry Holt, 1954.

WYLIE, R. C. *The self concept.* Lincoln, Neb.: University of Nebraska Press, 1961.

YINGER, J. M. *Toward a field theory of behavior.* New York: McGraw-Hill, 1965.

ZAJONC, R. B. Social facilitation. *Science*, 1965, *149*, 269–274.

ZAJONC, R. B. Attudinal effects of mere exposure. *Journal of Personality and Social Psychology, Monograph Supplement*, 1968, *9* (2, part 2), pp. 1–27.

ZAJONC, R. B. Brainwash: Familiarity breeds comfort. *Psychology Today*, 1970, *3* (9), 33ff.

ZILLER, R. C. *The social self: Schemas of the self and significant others.* Elmsford, N.Y.: Pergamon Press, 1973.

ZILLER, R. C., ALEXANDER, M., AND LONG, B. H. Self–social constructs and social desirability. Unpublished manuscript, University of Delaware, 1964.

ZILLER, R. C., CUNNINGHAM, J., GOLDING, L. H., AND KING, M. The political personality. Unpublished manuscript, University of Oregon, 1969.

ZILLER R. C., SMITH, M. D., AND THOMPSON, E. Complexity of the self concept and social acceptance. Unpublished manuscript, University of Oregon, 1970.

ZIMBARDO, P., AND EBBESON, E. B. *Influencing attitudes and changing behavior.* Reading, Mass.: Addison-Wesley, 1969.

Index